Reader's Digest Paperbacks

Informative.....Entertaining.....Essential.....

Berkley, one of America's leading paperback publishers, is proud to present this special series of the best-loved articles, stories and features from America's most trusted magazine. Each is a one-volume library on a popular and important subject. And each is selected, edited and endorsed by the Editors of Reader's Digest themselves!

Berkley/Reader's Digest books

THE AMERICAN SPIRIT
THE ART OF LIVING
CURIOUS CREATURES
DRAMA IN REAL LIFE®
"I AM JOE'S BODY"
KEEPING FIT
LAUGHTER, THE BEST MEDICINE®
THE LIVING WORLD OF NATURE
LOVE AND MARRIAGE
MEDICAL MIRACLES
MIND POWER
RAISING KIDS
SECRETS OF THE PAST
TESTS AND TEASERS
UNFORGETTABLE CHARACTERS
WORD POWER

CURIOUS CREATURES

THE EDITORS OF
READER'S DIGEST

A BERKLEY/READER'S DIGEST BOOK
published by
BERKLEY BOOKS, NEW YORK

CURIOUS CREATURES

A Berkley/Reader's Digest Book, published by arrangement with Reader's Digest Press

PRINTING HISTORY
Berkley/Reader's Digest edition/November 1981

ISBN: 0-425-05156-0

A BERKLEY BOOK ® TM 757,375
PRINTED IN THE UNITED STATES OF AMERICA

Grateful acknowledgment is made to the following organizations and individuals for permission to reprint material from the following sources:

"The Coyote Copes with Civilization" by George Laycock, reprinted from *Audubon*, the magazine of the National Audubon Society, copyright © 1974. The Bobbs-Merrill Company for "Encounters in a Winter Wilderness" from the book THE LIVING WILDERNESS by Earl W. Hunt, copyright © 1977 by Lerner Publications Company. Charles Scribner's Sons for "Year of the Whale" from the book THE YEAR OF THE WHALE by Victor B. Scheffer, copyright © 1969 by Victor B. Scheffer; reprinted with the permission of Charles Scribner's Sons. Jack Denton Scott for "Prince of Cats—The Lethal Leopard" by Jack Denton Scott, copyright © 1962. William Morris Agency for "Where Did the Animals Go?" by James A. Michener, copyright © 1976. Mr. H.R. Walrond for "The Elephant Baby-Sitter" from the book JUNGLE PICTURE by Norah Burke. Mrs. Leonard Dubkin for "The White Lady" from the book THE WHITE LADY by Leonard Dubkin, published by G.P. Putnam's Sons copyright © 1952. Random House Inc. for "The Bird and the Machine" from THE IMMENSE JOURNEY by Loren Eiseley, copyright © 1955 by Loren Eiseley.

Contents

FACTS AND FALLACIES

A NEED FOR HUMAN FRIENDSHIP

COPING WITH CIVILIZATION

THE WAY OF THE WILD

Brief Encounters of a Mystical Kind

"There Came a Cry of Joy"

by Loren Eiseley

WE ENTERED that southwestern valley through the trailing mists of a spring night. It was a place that looked as though it might never have known the foot of man, but in fact scouts for our expedition had been ahead of us and so we knew all about the abandoned cabin that lay far up on one hillside.

I arrived at the cabin first. From near its entrance I could see our cavalcade—mostly the reflection of truck lights on our collecting tins—winding in and out through the mist below. I stood on a rock a moment looking down and thinking what it cost in money and equipment to capture the past.

We had, in addition, instructions to lay hands on the present. The word had come through to get them alive—birds, reptiles, anything. A zoo somewhere needed restocking. My job was to help capture some birds and that was why I was there before the trucks.

The cabin had not been occupied for years. There were holes in the roof, and birds were roosting in the rafters. A cabin going back to nature in a wild place always draws birds. They find a hole, come inside; then suddenly the place is theirs and man is forgotten.

I got the door open softly, holding a spotlight with which to blind the birds so they couldn't see to get out through the roof. I had a short piece of ladder to put against the far wall, where there was a shelf on which I expected to make the biggest haul. As I pushed the door open, a bird or two stirred but nothing flew.

I padded across the floor and slithered up the ladder till my head and arms were over the shelf. Everything was dark as pitch except for starlight coming through a little hole back of the shelf near the eaves. I reached my arm carefully over in order to be ready to seize whatever was there, and I put the flash on the edge of the shelf, where it would stand by itself. That way I'd be able to use both hands.

I snapped on the flash and sure enough there was a great beating and feathers flying, but instead of my having the birds, they—or rather he—had me. I heard him give one short metallic cry when the light went on and my hand descended on the bird beside him; after that, he was busy digging his claws and beak into my thumb. In the struggle, I knocked the lamp over on the shelf, and his mate got her sight back and whisked neatly through the hole in the roof. It all happened in 15 seconds.

You might think I would have fallen down the ladder, but no, I had a professional assassin's reputation to keep up, and the bird, of course, made the mistake of thinking the hand was the enemy and not the eyes behind it. He chewed my thumb up pretty effectively and lacerated my hand with his claws. But in the end I got him.

He was a sparrow hawk—a fine young male in the prime of life. The little fellow had saved his mate by diverting me, but he made no outcry now, resting hopelessly in my hand, peering toward me in the shadows behind the lamp with a fierce, almost indifferent glance. He neither gave nor expected mercy, and something out of the high air passed from him to me, stirring a faint embarrassment.

I put the hawk in a box too small to allow him to injure himself by struggle, and walked out to welcome the arriving trucks. In the morning that bird would be just another episode. He would go back in the truck to a small cage in a city where he would spend the rest of his life. And a good thing, too. I sucked my aching thumb and spat out some blood.

IN THE MORNING, the mist was gone. The sky was a deep blue, and one could see for miles over the high outcroppings of stone. I was up early and brought the box in which the little hawk was imprisoned out onto the grass where I was building a cage. A wind as cool as a mountain spring ran over the grass. It was a fine day to be alive. I looked up and all around and at the hole in the cabin roof out of which the other little hawk had fled. There was no sign of her. "Probably in the next county by now," I thought. Before beginning work, I decided I'd have a look at my last night's capture.

I got him in my hand with his wings folded properly, careful not to startle him. He lay limp in my grasp. I could feel his heart pound under the feathers, but he only looked beyond me and up—one last look away into a sky so full of light that I could not follow his gaze.

I suppose I must have had an idea then of what I was going to do, but I never let it come up into consciousness. I just reached over and laid the hawk on the grass.

He lay there a long minute without hope, unmoving, his eyes still fixed on that blue vault above him. It must have been that he was already so far away in heart that he never felt the release. He just lay with his breast against the grass.

The second after that long minute he was gone. Like a flicker of light he vanished with my eyes full on him, gone straight up into that towering emptiness of light that my eyes could scarcely bear to penetrate. For another long moment there was silence. Then, from far up somewhere, a cry came ringing down.

I was young then and had seen little of the world, but when I heard that cry my heart turned over. It was not the cry of the hawk I had captured; for, by shifting my position against the sun, I was now seeing further up. Straight out of the sun's eye, where she must have been soaring restlessly above us for untold hours, hurtled his mate. And from far up, ringing from peak to peak of the summits over us, came a cry of such unutterable and ecstatic joy that it sounds down across the years and tingles among the cups on my quiet breakfast table.

I saw them both now. He was rising fast and they met in a great soaring gyre that turned to a whirling circle and a dance of wings. Once more, just once, their two voices joined in a harsh wild medley of questions and response, struck and echoed against the pinnacles of the valley. Then they were gone forever, into those upper regions beyond the eyes of men.

Deathwatch

by B. A. Clifton

THE OLD MAN sensed the animal's eyes on him as he tried to shift to a more comfortable position. Blackness rushed into his head and he held perfectly still, trying to beat back the waves of exhaustion that surged through him. A tingling sensation in his arm told him that he had blacked out for a while. "How long?" he asked himself frantically, aware of a shape that seemed closer than before.

"Damn you," he said in a low, controlled voice. "Keep your distance. I'm not done yet."

The wolf watched impassively.

The old man studied the animal. It had been there, staring at him, all last night for sure, and some of yesterday, but he couldn't remember when he'd first seen it. Damn thing was nearly as old as he was, from the look of its gray muzzle. When it yawned he could see the once formidable teeth, now dulled and chipped.

"Looking for an easy meal, huh?" he shouted suddenly. "I'll make you wait for it."

The old man's hip was broken. After his fall, he'd walked three impossible miles with the aid of an improvised crutch before the pain and fatigue halted him. Now he lay under a stand of pines, his thin, frail body cushioned by years of accumulated pine needles. The bitter wind sapped his remaining strength and, with little else to do, he wandered through his memories, seeking escape from the trap that 81 years, a rock slide and an early winter had made. At times a flicker of self-preservation burned through the fog of reverie, but these moments of clarity had come less and less frequently through the third night.

He found himself thinking of his folks' farm, and the way he and his dog Barney had run through the new-plowed fields, breaking up the rich, brown clods with their racing feet. *That's funny,* he thought, *I haven't recollected Barney in years.*

"A good mix," his pa had said when he brought the pup home. "Husky and shepherd. Be a good dog for the boy." Barney had turned out to be all the dog a boy could ask for. When he finally stopped growing he weighed over 100 pounds, with the powerful shoulders of a husky, the long limbs and markings of a shepherd, and a face that was a blend of the two. He had brains as well as strength, and the boy knew that the dog could feel what he was thinking before he said a word.

Barney lived to be 15 and, although the boy had become a man of 22, tears came when he buried his dog. In time, he pushed all thoughts of Barney deep inside where they couldn't hurt so much and now, in his tired loneliness, he brought back the cherished memories.

"A real good dog," he said softly. "Hey, there you are! Here, Barney, come here, pup."

He shook his head as if to recover from a blow and saw the wolf take a halting, lame step toward him.

"Get back there," he yelled, frightened. "Not yet, not yet." *A day or two more,* he thought desperately, *and they'll notice I haven't been to town. Just got to hold on.*

The wolf stopped and sat down again, a short distance closer.

Dusk was gathering when he felt the first feathery snowflakes landing on his forehead. He raised himself on one elbow, looking through the dark tree limbs at the granite sky. He shook his head wearily, pulled his coat tighter and tried to rest while keeping one eye on the wolf. Silence fell with the snow, and the woods became a quiet cathedral.

"Ma and Pa are going to be awful mad at us," he mumbled. "First getting lost in our own woodlot, and me hurting my leg, and you won't go home to let Pa know where I am. I'll get a switching and you'll get tied up." He shivered. "It sure is cold."

The fresh snowfall reflected the pale moonlight upon the two figures separated by ten feet of white ground.

"Come over here, Barn, so we can get warmer. Quit loafing around out there."

He opened his eyes and saw the big dark body standing over him.

"That's a good boy, good pup," he said, secure and happy at last as he reached up to smooth the soft fur of the massive head.

"Good old Barney . . ."

"GOD ALMIGHTY!" yelled Tom Hawkins, who was leading one of the search parties. "Over here!" As the group ran toward him, he shouted, "A wolf got him, but it looks like he had enough left to kill it, too."

The men approached the two cold shapes on the ground. Hawkins knelt and stared hard at the way the old man's arm encircled the wolf, the way his other hand rested lightly on the wolf's gray muzzle which was laid across his chest, and, finally, the gentle smile on the old man's lined face.

"Nope," he said, "I reckon that's not what happened at all." He touched the old man's face, then the ruffled fur on the wolf's neck. He blinked back the burning in his eyes and looked up at the faces of his friends.

"Not hardly," he murmured, and turned away.

Krag,
The Kootenay Ram

by Ernest Thompson Seton

KRAG was a joy to behold. As he bounded up the jagged cliffs of the Gunder Peak in the Kootenay Rockies of the far Northwest, barely touching each successive point with his clawed and padded hoofs and the sunbeams flashing from his back, he was more a spirit thing than a 300-pound ram with ten-year rings on his horns. And such horns, curling in one great sweep a circle and a quarter! Tucked away under their protective shadow were his beautiful eyes, large orbs of shining gold with dark misty depth in each.

For five years Krag had taught his band of mountain sheep to abjure the lowlands. The only land of safety was the open wind-swept peaks, where neither lions nor riflemen could approach unseen. But at length an old hunter, Scotty McDougall, arrived at a shanty on Tobacco Creek. The first time he saw Krag through his field glasses, he exclaimed, "What horns!" then added prophetically, "Them's mine!"

Then came a visitor to Scotty's shanty—a cattleman named Lee, with three Russian wolfhounds. Soon men and dogs were on the trail of the ram. One day they got a glimpse of him from afar, high above, and the men hurried along by the hollows toward the spot. They found his great hoofmark, but the hard rocks about refused further information. The dogs, nosing in all the near hollows and thickets of dwarf birch, broke out suddenly into a loud clamor, and up jumped the ram. Over the bushes, over the broken rocks, bounding, soaring, floating, supple, certain, splendid, he bore the curling wonders on his head as lightly as a lady might her earrings; and then, from various other coverts, sprang up his band and joined him. Up flew the rifles; but in a moment the three dogs, closing in, gave unwitting screen to the one victim on which every thought was fixed, and not a shot was heard.

Away they went, the ram forging quickly to the lead, and the others stringing along after, over the upland, flying, sailing, leaping and swerving. Krag, cut off from the peak, dashed southward. Now it was a straight race. One, two, three miles, and the chase was sweeping along a rocky ridge that ends in the sudden gash of Skinkler's Gulch. A minute more and the crowd of sheep were rounded up and cornered on the final rock. They huddled together in terror, 500 feet of dizzy canyon all around, three fierce dogs and two fiercer men behind.

Of the dogs Krag had no fear—them, he could fight; but the rifles were sure death. There was one chance left. The granite walls of the Yak-in-i-kak River could prove no harder than the human foe. The dogs were within 40 rods now. There was no time to hesitate; he, the leader, wheeled to the edge and *leaped*—down—down, not to the bottom, not blindly. Thirty feet downward, across the dizzy chasm, was a little jut of rock, no bigger than his nose—the only one in sight, all the rest smooth, sheer or overhanging. But Krag landed fairly, poised just a heartbeat. In a flash his blazing eyes took in another point, on the other side, hidden under the overhanging rocks he had leaped from. His supple loins and corded limbs bent, pulsed and floated him across; there he took fresh ricochet to another point, then back, to a mere roughness of the rock, on which his hoofs gripped for an instant. With a final drop of 20 feet, he reached a ledge of safety far below.

The other sheep followed fast in a long cascade. Just as the last had reached the second slender, speck-like foothold, three white-and-yellow creatures whirled past in the air to perish in the boiling Yak-in-i-kak below. The hounds, impetuous and brave, never hesitated to follow a foe.

Lee and Scotty stood blankly at the edge. Scotty uttered harsh, blasphemous words. Lee had a choking feeling in his throat.

"Bran! Rollo! Ida!" he called in lingering hope. But the

only response was from the western wind that whistled down Skinkler's Gulch.

During the years that followed, more than one hunter feasted his covetous eyes on the great ram's unparalleled horns. His fame even reached the cities. Dealers offered fabulous prices for the head that bore them. Even though winter was beginning, Scotty, fired by a large money offer, prepared for a long and obstinate hunt. His rifle, his blanket, his pipe, with matches, tobacco, a pot, a bundle of jerked venison, and three or four pounds of chocolate were all he carried. He followed the track of the ram in the snow, winding about, in and out, and obscured by the tracks of Krag's band, but always distinguishable by its size.

One day old Krag heard a *crack!* and a stinging something touched one horn and tore the hair from his shoulder. Dazed for a moment, Krag gave the signal which in our speech is, "Everyone for himself now"; and so the band scattered. But Scotty's one thought was old Krag: and when the ram made straightaway eastward down the hill, Scotty followed doggedly. The ram crossed the Flathead River on the ice, and keeping to the roughest ground he traveled all day northeastward, with Scotty steadily on the trail. On the fifth day a blinding snowstorm hid him from Scotty's view. The snow covered the great ram's tracks. The trail was lost.

Next day, as Scotty scanned the vast expanse between him and Kintla Lake, he saw a moving speck below. He quickly ran to intercept the traveler. But when he got to the spot he aimed at, there, 500 yards away, on the next ridge, stood the famous ram. Each was in plain view of the other. Scotty raised the rifle and fired; but the distance was too great.

The ram turned and made eastward. Sometimes the trail was easy to follow, sometimes blotted out by new-fallen snow. But day after day they went. The ram seemed to have learned that 500 yards was the farthest range of the rifle. Still it seemed as though he preferred to have the hunter within sight, for then he knew where he was. One time Scotty stole a march, and would have had a close shot had not the fateful west wind borne the taint. Krag was warned in time.

By the end of the first month the long pursuit began to tell on the ram. The man had his dried venison and chocolate, enough for many days; and when they were gone he could shoot a hare or a grouse and hastily cook it. But the ram required hours to seek the scanty grass that lay under the snow. His belly was pinching up, and weakening hunger was joining with his other foe.

Then came two weeks when they were daily in sight of each other. In the morning Scotty, rising wolflike from his frosty lair, would call out, "Come, Krag; time we wuz a-movin'." And the ram on the distant ridge would stamp defiantly, then, setting his nose to the wind, move on, now fast, now slow, keeping the safe 500 yards or more ahead. When Scotty sat down to rest, the ram would graze. Once when Scotty rose and scanned the northern distance for the ram, he heard the long snort far behind, and turning, saw old Krag impatiently waiting. The wind had changed, and Krag had changed his route to suit. Another day Scotty had a difficult two hours crossing a stream over which old Krag had leaped. When he reached the other side he heard a snort, and looked around to find that the ram had come back to see what was keeping him.

For 12 long weeks now the ram had led Scotty through the snow, over ten long mountain ranges—500 rugged miles. Both were growing hollow-eyed, gaunter every day. The man's hair had bleached since he set out on this insane pursuit, and the head and shoulders of the ram were grizzling.

One morning they sat at rest—Scotty on one ridge, the ram 600 yards away on the next. Then some evil spirit entered into Scotty and sketched a cunning plot. He cut some rods of the low-creeping birch and gathered some stones. Then, moving to the edge of the ridge, he made a dummy of himself, using what clothing he could spare. Keeping exactly behind it, he crawled backward over the ledge and disappeared. After an hour of crawling and stalking he came up on a ridge behind the ram.

There Krag stood, majestic as a bull, graceful as a deer, with horns that rolled around his brow like thunderclouds about a peak. He was gazing intently on the dummy, wondering why his follower was so long still. Scotty, less than 300 yards away, lay down and threw snow on his back till he was all whitened, then set out to crawl 200 yards, watching the great ram's head. Once old Krag looked about sharply. Nearer, nearer crawled the hunter. Then, safely reaching some sheltering rocks, he rested, a scant half-hundred yards away. For the first time he saw the famous horns quite close. He saw the great, broad shoulders, the curving neck, still massive, though the mark of famine was on all; he saw this splendid fellow creature blow the hot breath of life from his nostrils, vibrant in the sun; and he even got a glimpse of the life light in those glowing amber eyes. As he slowly raised the gun, the hand that had never trembled before now shook as though in fear.

But the hand grew steady; the hunter's face was calm and hard. The rifle sang. Scotty hid his head; he heard a rattling on the distant stones, then a long-drawn *snoof!* Two minutes later all was still, and he timidly raised his head.

There on the snow lay a great gray-brown form, and at one end, like a twin-necked hydra coiling, were the horns, the sculptured record of the splendid life of a splendid creature. Scotty walked slowly over and gazed in sullen silence, not at the dear-won horns, but at the calm yellow eyes, unclosed, and yet undimmed by death. He sat down 20 yards away, with his back to the horns. He did not know what he himself felt. Words played but little part in his life.

A long silence; then, "I'd give it back to him if I could."

FOUR YEARS went by. Scotty, now known as Old Man Scotty, had never hunted since. One day an old partner stopped at his shanty.

"Let's see him, Scotty."

"Suit yourself." The old man jerked his head toward the draped thing on the wall. The stranger pulled off the cloth, and the firelight reflected in the glassy eyes lent a red and angry glare.

"Kivver him up when you're through," said Scotty.

"Why don't ye sell him?"

"I'll nivver sell him—I'll nivver part with him. I stayed by him till I done him up, an' he'll stay by me till he gets even. He broke me down on that trip. He's made an old man o' me. He's sucking my life out now. But he ain't through with me yet. Thar's more o' him around than that head. I tell ye, when that old chinook comes a-blowin' up the Terbakker Crik, I've heard noises that the wind don't make. I've heard him just the same as I done that day when he blowed his life out through his nose, an' me a-layin' on my face afore him."

OLD SCOTTY is forgotten, but the ram's head hangs enshrined on a palace wall today, a treasure among kingly treasures; and men, when they gaze on those marvelous horns, still talk of the glorious Gunder ram who grew them far away on the heights of the Kootenay.

Nature's Utmosts

Africa's Speed King: The Cheetah

by Emily and Ola D'Aulaire

THE enormous sun was setting blood-red behind Kenya's rolling Ngong Hills as the big cat crouched low in the tall, dry grass. Every muscle aquiver, he watched a Thomson's gazelle in the distance. Then, with movements as smooth and deliberate as pouring honey, he began slinking forward.

Slowly, cautiously, the big cat approached unnoticed until the gazelle was just a hundred yards away. Suddenly, like a golden missile set loose on the darkening plain, he launched now into open attack, streaking toward the startled Tommy, which at once began a desperate pattern of run, weave, dodge. But even with its 45-mile-an-hour speed—plenty to escape from a lion or leopard attacking from any distance—the gazelle was no match for the cheetah. The drama ended quickly, in an explosive cloud of red dust.

The cheetah is the fastest wild animal on earth. From a crouching start, he can reach 45 m.p.h. in two seconds. A second or two more and he's hurtling along at more than a mile a minute, his long, thick tail acting as a counterbalance to let him corner like a jackrabbit. Zoologists have estimated that these cats can top a scorching 70 m.p.h.!

One hundred thirty pounds of rangy muscle (a relative lightweight compared to other big cats), the cheetah is clearly built for speed. Long-limbed and lean, he stretches more than seven feet from nose to tail-tip and stands two and a half feet high at the shoulder. His head is small and streamlined, with markings like tear-shaped ebony stains that run from the corners of his eyes to his mouth. His regal body is gracefully tapered from chest to waist, his coarse yellow fur punctuated with black dots.

There are many who confuse cheetahs with leopards—even some Africans, the Kikuyu, used to call both animals by the same name: *ngari*. But beyond their superficial similarity as tawny-furred, spotted cats, the two are as different as a *sumo* wrestler and a ballerina.

The thick-set leopard, heavier by 30 pounds, operates in the shadows of the night, relying on heavy cover, stealth and close-up ambush tactics. The trim cheetah is a creature of the day, particularly the cool hours just after dawn and before dusk, and he likes open spaces and long vistas. His eyesight, like that of all cats, is keen, enabling him to pick out well-camouflaged prey at great distances.

Though biologically a feline, the cheetah has some distinctly uncatlike features. His legs are long and thin-boned, like a dog's. His head looks too small for his body, and his jaws and teeth are undersized. Even such a feline basic as tree-climbing does not always come easily to him. In Nairobi National Park, we watched one playful young cheetah try to scramble up an acacia trunk. He made it about halfway to the lowest branches. There his claws lost their grip and, still clutching the tree, he slid indecorously to the ground. The trouble was that a cheetah's claws are not fully retractable and therefore become blunted.

For all his tremendous speed, the cheetah has one serious shortcoming: lack of endurance. He is strictly a sprinter; if an all-out chase lasts for more than about 300 yards, he runs out of steam. We once watched a cheetah stalk a young impala. Too soon the impatient cat broke into full pursuit, long tail streaming as he twisted and turned after his prey. Just before he got within striking distance, his gait faltered. He slowed to a walk, then sank to the ground, his sides heaving from exhaustion as he watched the impala trot to safety.

The cheetah seems almost painfully aware that he lacks the power, presence and savagery of other big cats. Except on rare occasions, he goes after only the smaller antelopes, killing quickly and cleanly. It is in keeping with his character that when he tries to roar, the sound that comes out is more like a "meow." In moments of contentment, he may even chirp like a bird.

The cheetah's family life is generally uneventful. When a female is in season, several males may court her at the same time with little or no rivalry between them. After mating, the female is left to herself and she must hunt for her own food right through the last stages of her 90-day pregnancy. The average litter size is five, with the newborn cubs looking as if their spots had got wet and the colors had run, turning the soft fur a neutral gray. After two or three weeks, the young are walking steadily on enormous-looking feet. In a month or two, they are ready to accompany their mother on hunts, learning as they go.

One evening in Kenya, we watched a mother trot along aimlessly as her four ten-month-old cubs explored behind her, sniffing each rock and termite mound. Soon the mother spotted a herd of Grant's gazelles and froze. In an instant, the cubs were at her side, sitting as erect as garden statues, ears perked, watching the grazing antelopes. As the mother went in for the kill, they followed slowly behind, not breaking into full speed themselves until the prey was down. Before their mother had released the gazelle's throat, the hungry cubs had begun to feed.

During the learning process, cheetahs, normally solitary animals, travel together in family groups (fathers not included). The young usually try to make their first kill at about 12 months. The mother helps them, but, when they are 16 months old and still learning, she departs for good.

The cheetah's domain is some 400,000 square miles of African countryside, ranging from dry, almost desert-like scrubland (where water is a problem, cheetahs can subsist on the body fluids of their prey) to open, rolling grasslands dotted with thorn bush and stately umbrella acacias. One afternoon, we spotted a cheetah resting on a hillock in just such a landscape. As we watched, he strolled over to a game warden's jeep, put his forepaws on the door and stretched. The warden rolled down his window and scratched the cheetah behind the ears. "I've known that fellow since he was a tiny cub," the warden explained later. "But you'd never catch me doing that with a leopard, no matter how familiar he was to me."

The cheetah's mild nature makes him one of the easiest of all wild animals to domesticate. There is no record of an unprovoked attack on man. In fact, once tamed, the cheetah seems to take an almost dog-like pleasure in pleasing. He is eager to learn, can be taught to retrieve sticks and balls, and becomes totally attached to his master. In place of his daily gazelle, he seems quite content with several cans of dog food, a fresh chicken, perhaps some frozen horsemeat.

History contains abundant examples of cheetahs kept as pets. Genghis Khan owned one. Charlemagne ruled much of medieval Europe with one dozing at his feet. In India, mogul emperors, princes and maharajas kept cheetahs by the thousands, even trained them to hunt.

Until quite recently, it was the cheetah that was hunted. But in 1972 the United States Department of the Interior placed the cheetah on the list of endangered species, banning all imports of cheetahs and cheetah skins. Before 1972, skins were used for coats.

The cheetah has already been wiped out in India, the land that gave him his name (*chita* means "spotted" in Hindi). There, where cheetahs once roamed in uncounted thousands, not one has been sighted since 1951. Eastern Africa is the regal beast's final stronghold—and no one knows just how long he can survive there. Though East African governments have proclaimed the cheetah a protected species and established stiff penalties, poaching is prevalent. In Ethiopia and Somalia, enforcement of protective laws is practically non-existent.

Moreover, the cheetah's domain is threatened as the open-bush and low-hill country of Africa increasingly comes under cultivation. This forces the cheetah to retreat into thicker bush, where he cannot use his speed so effectively. The problem is made more acute by the cheetah's notoriously slow breeding habits: each female produces only one litter about every two years. And infant mortality is high: of the average litter, only two or three survive to maturity.

Pessimistic conservationists continue to predict the cheetah's total eclipse. Others are more optimistic. In addition to the growing conservation-mindedness of people the world over, they point to Africa's many increasingly well-managed game reserves, which should give the cheetah more of a chance to carry on his kind in peace. Hopefully, it is not too late to turn the tide. In any case, it is a sad commentary on a speed-oriented age that the survival of nature's most magnificent entry in the field of speed should now be in question.

The Canniest Creature of the Countryside

by Jean George

A TRAPPER I know spent an entire October day setting five ingenious traps to take a large red fox he had seen. After brewing the traps in a mixture of wood chips and water to rid them of his telltale scent, he covered them with leaves. Pleased with his artful cunning, he turned to go home. There, not ten feet from him, sat the fox, as E. B. White says, "absorbed in apple-fall and mirth, and feeling very loud and nirsey." His ears were up, his nose licked wet, the better to "read" the subterfuge on the air. Not only had he followed the trapper to every site; he had doused each trap with his own musk to warn the next fox that danger lay under the leaves.

The more the American red fox is hunted, trapped and chased, the smarter he becomes. Today there are far more foxes—and far smarter ones—than our forefathers ever knew. In trying to outwit the fox, man has forced him to become the canniest animal in the countryside.

One thing early hunters learned about the American fox was that British hounds were no match for him. America's rough terrain had developed a smaller, more agile beast than had the tended, rolling fields of Great Britain. So hunters began to breed splendid lighter-boned hounds—dubbed such colorful names as Blue Tick, Red Bone, Billy Sunday—that take out after the red fox with a vigor and a voice dear to every hill-loving American who wanders in the fall.

But even these hounds are no match for the fox when he really wants to swing. Slender and long-legged under his dense fur, he is built like a race horse. Individual foxes have been known to run a pack of hounds for four days, wearing the pads off dogs' feet, leaving their bodies gaunt and skinny. Many dogs have been drowned during a chase—following the crafty and lighter fox over thin ice. Long chases do not faze a fox in good health. He will snack along the way on berries and mice, or spurt far ahead to doze under a bush until the hounds catch up.

A fox named White-Foot, who lived on the Potomac River near my childhood home, showed me why the fox usually wins. One day when the "field" went after White-Foot, he immediately lost hounds and horses by jumping to a rail fence and running it to the end of the meadow. The hounds worked this out after a slight delay and tongued on to a creek, where the trail disappeared again. But even the hounds knew that foxes run along shallow streams to throw dogs off their scent. The master of hounds sent half the field up the creek and half down to find where the fox stepped ashore. But they never picked up the scent again.

At twilight they gave up and went home. They were met by the wife of the keeper of the hounds, who said she had found the fox, round and full of chicken, sleeping in the henhouse.

Tracking back, the huntsman discovered that White-Foot had crouched in a patch of cattle manure below the stream bank, while momentum carried the hunt over his head and into the stream. Then he had trotted back past the hunt club, losing his own musty scent in the maze of odors on the smelly horse and dog trail, until he found the hennery.

Another intelligent fox kept springing a trapper's sets by yanking the chains with his teeth. But this trapper would not give up. In the mating season he baited a trap with "Persian Love Musk" (vixen scent). The fox, true to his routine, got up at 4 p.m. and trotted down his personal fox-road to the fields. On the way he caught the scent of vixen and swerved to find her. But he stopped short of the set, read the signs on the air and turned off. The trapper, beaten, was going home, when a yap arrested him.

Down the hill came his fox again, followed by another fox, an irate male on whose property he had no doubt trespassed. The first fox led the second right toward the trap. The love scent caught the defender by surprise and he swerved to sniff it clearly. As he did, the trap closed on his paw. No sound came from the captured beast; foxes are silent when hurt. They stoically await death. Immediately, the first fox circled back to the hill, where, the trapper was sure, the home-defender's vixen awaited the victor.

Foxes have flourished despite the American farmers' war against the species. Indeed, besides opening the land—which increases foxes—the farmer has helped with his plow. When digging dens in March in which to whelp their young, foxes refuse to claw anything harder than loose gravel. So the tilled land has helped increase their dens.

One fox in Michigan understood farm practices so well that he would wait at the edge of the woods until the farmer had not only plowed, but disked and harrowed. Each spring the farmer would see him lying on the horizontal trunk of a willow watching him work. When the harrow finally banged down the lane, the farmer would stop and look back. Sure enough, the fox was always in the field digging into the earth.

Over the years fox dens have become more devious. Usually there are three or more entrances, and several false tunnels wind downward toward the pantry. Nearby is the nursery where some five to seven kits are born in early April. A smart farmer will dig out the vixen and their kits at this time, for the female does not come out of the den for three days after the kits arrive.

A farmer in Wisconsin, eager to get rid of a den near his henhouse, waited until he did not see the female come or go. Then with dynamite he blew the den wide open—and found nothing there, not even a bone. The hole was merely a false front through which the foxes trotted to throw him off. The real den he discovered later on a nearby hill.

When the kits are a month old, the vixen brings them to the entrance of the den to begin their schooling. Training is rigid. I watched a vixen near my home drop a mouse before her kits and nearly take the hide off the little one that missed it. Kits at the den are warming to behold. Fearless, confident, the tannish-gray youngsters caper and run, fight and wrestle. They chase butterflies and moths and practice their arching pounce on leaves and flowers.

Mortality is high in foxdom during the early months. Diseases like distemper overtake the kits, and farmers and conservationists eliminate them while they can be caught in numbers. Their reasons are generally sound. Foxes kill not only ducks and chickens, but beneficial game—pheasants, rabbits and quail. Moreover, fox overpopulation the next fall will often result in a rabies outbreak. However, this weeding-out has only improved the fox. The sick and dull-witted are usually caught and killed, leaving the healthy and bright to breed more healthy and bright offspring.

The American red fox ranges in parts of every state except Hawaii. Actually, he comes in many tints and shades besides red. The silver fox, the black, the rust and the cross foxes are all the same animal, *Vulpes fulva*.

Foxes make excellent pets. They can be housebroken and are most affectionate. Two traits, however, keep them from becoming popular. They play vigorously all night; and, as a doctor friend of mine in Carlisle, Pa., discovered, you can't return them to the wild. He kept a kit one summer. It loped and played with his children, and followed them to nearby farms and yards and gardens. While everybody thought the fox was having fun, he was actually making tidy mental notes of all the local delicacies.

That autumn the doctor decided to set the fox free. A week later the countryside was up in arms. Thirty hand-raised pheasants had been purloined, a pond full of exotic ducks ravaged, and a Siamese cat and five kittens were missing! The doctor lured his fox home with beefsteak and penned him up. As far as I know, he is still living with them, demanding fresh hamburger and strawberries every day.

Every hunter I have talked with agrees that the fox enjoys the hunt. A fox in Seneca, Md., would call to the hounds from the hill, his weird yap encouraging them to come chase him. One afternoon I saw him run right up to a chained dog. There he flipped and sprawled on his forepaws like a playful terrier. The hound bayed and pulled at his chain. The fox spun into the woods and out again, speaking perfectly clearly in movement, "Come chase me!"

But the fox cunning I enjoy the most was thought up by a monarch of Whitford Woods, Ohio. This fox was old, and at last, one day, hunters cornered him against a cliff. The fatal bullet was in the chamber. Suddenly, as if the air had wafted to the fox the greatest weakness of man, he stood up, shook himself, trotted up to the gunman and looked him straight in the eye. Dogs howled and swirled in confusion, bedlam reigned—and the fox of Whitford lived on!

Meet the Mighty Mantis

by Scott Seegers

WHEN my wife and I swore off gardening with kill-everything pesticides, we substituted a helper right out of science fiction, the praying mantis. By tying mantis eggcases among our rose-bushes, we found that we could preserve from aphids and other rose-loving pests at least as many roses as we used to raise by spraying with indiscriminatingly lethal insecticides.

Come spring, a single mantis egg-case, a mere inch in diameter, produces from 100 to 300 hungry nymphs, which come boiling out of their winter quarters as a froth of tiny translucent beings and need only to hang upside down for a few minutes until exposure to the air hardens their legs and bodies. Then this ravenous horde gallops up and down the nearby plants and bushes, snatching and devouring destructive aphids or any other form of life small enough for them to kill.

The most voracious predator in the insect world, the praying mantis normally consumes its own weight in animal matter every day, and often a great deal more. An entomologist of Washington's Smithsonian Institution told me that he once watched a mantis devour 13 full-grown cockroaches at a single sitting. Another naturalist found that individuals of one species ate more than 700 insects over their life-span of a few months.

"The only thing a praying mantis really prays for," says Dr. Ashley Gurney, of the Smithsonian Institution, who has spent decades studying these weird, toothpick-legged creatures, "is a square meal."

The mantis's appetite for pests makes it the darling of

garden clubs and conservationists. Its fare includes grasshoppers, houseflies, wasps, caterpillars, moths, blister beetles and fruit flies. Unfortunately, mantises are also fond of some beneficial insects such as honeybees and ladybugs; but, on balance, they do away with harmful insects in far greater numbers.

Generally about four inches tall when full-grown, the praying mantis on the hunt personifies implacable doom. Alerted by any moving insect, it turns its head quickly to focus attention on the target. As the prey comes closer, the mantis almost imperceptibly raises its terrible forelegs into striking position, like a boxer. If necessary, it will remain completely motionless in this position for minutes at a time. When the quarry moves within range, the mantis's long, threadlike antennae wave slowly over it. Then the forelegs lash out too fast for the eye to follow—quickly enough to snatch a butterfly or moth in flight. The unlucky victim struggles in vain as the mantis brings it up to its mandibles and devours it.

The meal over, the mantis washes its face like a cat, using first one foreleg, then the other. This toilette can take as long as 15 minutes, after which the mantis settles down on a twig and waits for another course in its non-stop meal.

While nature ruthlessly wiped out the great dinosaur, the saber-toothed tiger and the mastodon because they could not adapt to changing environments, the mantis which patrols your garden looks little different from mantis fossils which date back 40 million years. Behind this durability lies a certain brute strength. A quarter-ounce mantis can hold aloft a 6-ounce object, or 24 times its own weight—equivalent to a 175-pound man hefting 4200 pounds. Fortunately, the mantis is harmless to man. A human finger, caught in the foreleg's thorny grip, might ooze a drop of blood if a spike hit a spot of tender skin, but that would be the extent of the damage.

There are 20 varieties of praying mantis in the United States, about 1500 throughout the world, ranging in size up to a 6½-inch African monster. All are fearless hunters. They seize with relish wasps, hornets and venomous scorpions. Naturalists report seeing the larger ones kill small birds, lizards, even the shrew, the most savage animal of its size on earth.

The same voracious savagery characterizes the mantis's sex life. Thus, understandably, a mantis courtship is one of the most tentative and cautious spectacles in the animal kingdom. The famous French naturalist Henri Fabre told of one lady mantis who mated with and promptly devoured no fewer than seven mates in succession.

Attracted by sight, and probably also by scent, the male approaches his intended bride with stealthy steps. If she looks his way, he freezes, and remains motionless until she turns away. Often his technique is in vain, and he gets embraced and eaten before achieving his objective. But if he manages to sneak to within two or three inches behind her, he leaps onto her back. About one in four husbands completes his duties and gets away intact; the other three serve as wedding breakfasts. Reaching over her head with an angular foreleg, the female drags the much smaller male off her back and devours him.

Shortly after mating, the female hangs upside down and deposits her egg-case on a nearby branch or stalk or stem. From her hind sections comes a constant flow of whitish foam, which is shaped into an almost spherical mass by three tiny, rapidly twirling, finger-like organs flanking the egg duct. Producing the egg-case takes two or three hours. Afterward, she hangs motionless for a long time, and her appetite declines until, finally, she stops eating.

A few days later, she dies. By this time the egg-case has hardened into a light but firm beige-colored lump from which the baby mantises will emerge the following spring. In the temperate zones, all adult mantises are killed by the first frost; in the tropics they live longer, but are generally dead before the next generation hatches.

To stock a garden with mantises, the easiest scheme is to buy egg-cases (sold mainly by mail order through ads in newspapers and gardening magazines) and tie them to bushes or low trees during late fall, winter or early spring. The firm egg-case provides insulation against even the severest cold, and the nymphs have a built-in timer which brings them out right after the insect world starts humming.

People who prefer to hunt their own egg-cases should search weedgrown fields or vine-covered fences, preferably those with weeds and small trees alongside. I have found them on honeysuckle and catbrier vines, or goldenrod and milk-weed—in fact, on almost any stalk strong enough to stand through the winter. The egg-cases are usually located from one foot to eight feet above the ground.

Throughout history mankind has been fascinated by the mighty mantis, often attributing to it superhuman powers. The

Greeks thought it had the gift of prophecy and named it *mantis*—meaning "seer" or "diviner." An ancient Chinese carving of a mantis bears the admonition, "Be as brave as the mantis—fear not your enemy." In various regions of the United States, the insect still goes by names such as prophet, soothsayer, devil's rear horse, mule killer. Many people still consider it good luck to see a mantis.

Not so a golfing friend of mine. One stroke ahead in a club tournament, he was preparing to tap a two-foot putt into the 17th hole when a mantis rose from the cup and waved at him. He missed the putt and, thoroughly rattled, blew the match.

Nature's Lofty Lord: The Giraffe

by Edward Hughes

ON A RIDGE in Tanzania, below Mount Kilimanjaro, I watched a scattering of giraffes browsing on acacia trees. Suddenly, two brown blurs flashed through the bush toward a lone giraffe calf. Hyenas! I reached for the horn of my Land Rover to sound a warning, but need not have bothered, for already the young giraffe was heading briskly for its mother and safety. Within seconds the other giraffes had spotted the high bobbing head—one of nature's most effective early-warning systems—and were on the move themselves.

Ungainly as the giraffe might seem, the world's loftiest animal—the tallest ever measured reached 19 feet, 3 inches—is in fact one of its most alert and agile. Atop the craning neck are eyes that come out on stalks, giving a giraffe almost 360-degree vision. And those long, spindly legs can propel a one-ton animal into a 35-mile-per-hour gallop.

African legend has it that God created the giraffe last of all the animals, using leftovers from the others: skin of the leopard, speed of the antelope, neck and legs of the camel. The ancient Greeks, certain that the giraffe was the result of the mating of a camel and a leopard, called it *camelopardalis*. Later the Arabs dubbed it *zarafa*, "swift creature." With a few changes, the Arab word stuck. Although nine varieties exist, all kinds will breed with one another, which makes them by definition a single species.

Along with grace, the giraffe has a certain elusive charm, with its big eyes behind long lashes, tears that owe their abundance to oversize lacrimal glands, and now and then a pathetic fragility. A vet's tranquilizer can send it into a fatal swoon. And if it slips and falls spread-eagled, the immobilized animal almost always dies.

Yet the giraffe, which began its evolutionary career as a kind of deer roaming much of Europe, Asia and Africa, has managed to survive for 25 million years. A century ago, giraffes roamed a vast belt across Africa just south of the Sahara. Today, man and his towns have squeezed them into a series of "islands" mostly scattered through East Africa. In all, they number perhaps 450,000.

Despite the shrinking rangeland, the giraffe has a brighter future than the rhino, elephant, leopard and lion. While rhinos smash farm equipment, elephants trample cornfields and rip up trees, leopards kill farmers' cattle, and lions sometimes chew up farmers themselves, giraffes seldom molest anyone. And they won't bend over for the grass that sheep and cattle eat. Instead, they feed high in the trees or tall bushes, gobbling as much as 100 pounds of greenery each day.

The giraffe's favorite meal is on the acacia tree, from which it bites off clusters of leaves and tender thorn tips. It treats a tall, leafy bush the way a hungry child deals with corn on the cob. First, the tip of its 1½-foot-long tongue curls around a succulent branch and draws it between lips as big as shoe soles and almost as tough. Then the animal closes its mouth and swings its head, neatly skinning off an appetizing mouthful of twigs, leaves, pods and ants. Saliva as thick as rubber cement and the chemicals in the giraffe's four-chambered stomach help soften the tougher morsels.

Some acacia seeds will not take root unless they have been through the giraffe's digestive system. Thus a part of Africa's afforestation follows the path of the meandering giraffe in its quarter-century of life. The animal's nibbling also manicures the acacia, trimming away the middle and creating an hour-glass effect. Or, working above a smaller tree, it can produce a flat top. "Browse lines" sometimes create surrealistic scenery for miles around.

The giraffe's neck, apart from its lofty uses as sentinel post and food collector, serves as a sort of cooling tower against the fierce temperatures of summer, its large surface helping to dissipate heat. It contains nature's longest trachea, a five-foot-long windpipe that expels stale air and brings in fresh wind with gale force, thanks to lungs that have seven times the capacity of human lungs.

The giraffe uses its neck to gain momentum when moving forward. As it walks, paces or gallops, the head is pushed forward to shift the animal's center of gravity, then jerked back again to prepare for the next forward thrust. And the neck is a mighty weapon. It has only seven vertebrae—like the neck of humans, whales and other mammals—but they are huge and buttressed by powerful muscles bigger than a man's arm. At the top is a formidable horned skull that grows thicker and heavier throughout the male giraffe's life, sometimes doubling its weight.

The director of West Germany's Frankfurt Zoo recalled with awe the result of a head-and-neck blow dealt by the zoo's bull giraffe Otto to its thousand-pound companion, an elk-like bull eland: The toppled eland's shoulder was broken, and the animal had to be destroyed.

Such aggressiveness is rare. More commonly, the giraffe engages in what scientists call "necking," a curious process once thought to be male-female courtship but which is in fact a ritual among males to establish rank in the local hierarchy. Often they do not even touch. The process can go on for hours until one or the other achieves subtle dominance. The winner then need only approach another male with his neck straight and chin up—typical threat behavior—for the other to step aside.

One day in Tanzania, I watched as two males curled and uncurled their necks around each other. After half an hour, they parted inconclusively. One resumed browsing; the other went to a nearby stream. "Shhh," whispered my companion, Game Warden Charles Mmari. "That's a rare sight." Below us, the giraffe had spread its front legs wide and, with knees bent grotesquely, thrust its long neck forward in an awkward reach for water. It knew that in this stance it was vulnerable to attack, so only seconds later it was lurching upright again, water dribbling from its jaw. Glancing around, the giraffe satisfied itself that the coast was clear, and bent over for another quick drink. Four times it rose and fell before its thirst was slaked.

As the giant head swooped to ground level and back, I marveled at the anatomical miracle that prevents it from blacking out as the blood rushes between heart and brain. A system of valves in the veins and arteries keeps blood flowing evenly in all postures. At the base of the brain, blood vessels expand to accommodate the increase of blood when the head is lowered, and contract to stop the flow when the head is suddenly raised. Cerebrospinal fluid around the blood vessels and the brain creates counter-pressure, much as the "g-suit" of a jet-fighter pilot helps ward off blackouts in steep dives. To aid the gigantic pumping job, the giraffe's blood pressure is the highest of any animal's. A 25-pound oblong heart two feet long pumps the blood at 15 gallons a minute.

Life for the male giraffe is almost entirely one big heart throb, for romance is its main preoccupation. Mating is on its mind even when it is browsing for food. With its head in the trees, the bull is well-placed to spot passing cows. When a ready cow is found, the dominant bull on the scene will do the mating.

Fifteen months after mating, the cow gives birth. The calf arrives with a bang, for the mother remains standing throughout, dropping it five or six feet to the ground. Until recently, giraffe mothers were thought to be indifferent to their newborn. Not so, says Robin Pellew, a biologist from Britain's Cambridge University, who with his wife, Pam, tracked herds of giraffe day and night for four years by Piper Cub and Land-Rover, and who has seen females savagely kicking out at predators to defend their young. Nonetheless, fewer than half the giraffe calves survive their first year of life; the others are victims of disease, drought and the lion.

Pellew's research also shows that the typical giraffe does not wander widely. It seldom lies down—and then usually only in the company of other giraffes. Actual sleep—with eyes closed—rarely lasts longer than five minutes at a time. Some scientists think the giraffe can sleep with its eyes open, and perhaps even while standing.

The giraffe is said to be the most intelligent of the ungulates (cloven-hoofed animals). This is not high praise, since the ungulates are considered to be among the most stupid of animals. To giraffe lovers, this is unimportant. What counts is what Karen Blixen recorded in her book *Out of Africa:* "their queer, inimitable, vegetative gracefulness, as if it were not a herd of animals but a family of rare, long-stemmed speckled gigantic flowers."

What future has this magnificent oddity? The encroachment of civilization makes its survival outside the big game parks of East Africa increasingly unlikely. Yet, in those huge preserves, such as Tanzania's Serengeti and Kenya's Amboseli, the giraffes thrive. If we are lucky and use common sense, they will be with us for quite a while.

Possums Play for Keeps

by Jack Denton Scott

EVOLUTIONARY WONDER? The least understood of our wild creatures? North America's most successful animal?

Consider: *Didelphis marsupialis virginiana* (or Virginia opossum, so named by English settlers in Virginia), was around when 20-foot-long triceratops roamed North America. That was 70 million years ago.

Few of us today regard this ancient, grayish-white mammal with much respect, and fewer still with understanding. Although we see it often enough—it remains widespread throughout North America—how many of us realize that this slow-moving creature is not only America's oldest wild animal, but our only marsupial? Actually the possum is a living fossil that should be admired for what it has accomplished merely by staying alive.

How did this physically preposterous little animal, not graceful or fast, apparently without cunning or charm, looking like an ugly cross between a house cat and a muskrat, manage to survive evolutionary holocausts that wiped out entire species? The answer is as many-faceted as the animal itself.

Our grizzled-gray possum's muzzle is long and sharp. Its clawed feet, at the end of short legs, are hairless. One of the five digits on each hind foot is a clawless big toe, opposable like a thumb so that the foot can be used somewhat like a human hand. Adult weight averages nine pounds. Length is 2½ to 3 feet, including a naked, 12-inch-long, half-black, half-pink tail.

The Virginia opossum can climb very well—not as skillfully as racoons, but expertly enough to use a tall tree for refuge during emergencies, or to obtain fruit. Its black eyes are keen and well adapted for night vision; sensitive, antennae-like face and body hairs (vibrissae) also aid in night travels. The claws help not only in climbing but in digging into rotting tree stumps and other areas for food.

Home is where the possum finds it—old burrows, or abandoned dens of other animals, hollow trees, caves, cavities in fallen logs. But it has a talent for making any place it lives in cozy. Using its prehensile tail, it draws a load of leaves into the nest and lines its den with them. Although not a true hibernator, it will hole up when the weather is extremely cold and completely cover itself with leaves.

Another attribute: It is tough. Although its naked ears and tail may become frostbitten, this doesn't seem to deter the possum. Many possums have been found with parts of tails and ears missing, sloughed off after having been nipped by subfreezing temperatures.

Some biologists believe that the possum has a determination to survive that is unequaled by any other mammal. Naturalist Victor H. Cahalane reported in *Mammals of North America* that of 95 possum skeletons examined near Lawrence, Kan., 39 had badly broken bones that had healed. One had recovered from two broken shoulders, 11 broken ribs, and a severely damaged spine. Many of these injuries would have killed other animals.

The possum seems able to evade most predators. Although generally slow-moving, it has been seen running rapidly for short distances, and is a fast and skillful swimmer. It is also adept at hiding in the dark, standing patiently motionless and then silently disappearing into a handy hole. Great horned owls and foxes do successfully prey upon the possum, but the plucky little animal often manages to bluff such predators by hissing, growling, and baring its conspicuous and formidable teeth.

It has 50 of those teeth—more teeth than any other American land mammal has—and this is surely a key to its astounding survival. It is said that the possum can tear meat, crack bones, even gnaw timber. It can eat anything, anywhere, from ants and insects in a rotting log, to fruit on a tree, berries on a bush, dead birds, or animals on the highway. Given this appetite range, it is doubtful that possums ever go for long periods without food.

The consensus among naturalists and biologists is that the possum isn't very bright. Yet, after extensive tests, William T. James, psychology professor at the University of Georgia, concluded that possums *can* learn complicated lessons. Where they have difficulty is in separating different body reflexes. For example, a possum couldn't be taught to avoid electric shock by raising its leg at the sound of a bell. But it quickly learned to scoot completely out of its box when the warning bell sounded.

There are other apparent misconceptions. Wildlife experts say the possum is positively a night creature and a coward. Yet a possum that lived under our house last winter would amble out into the sunshine promptly at ten o'clock each morning, reminding us very much of a portly old gentleman in a fur coat out for his daily constitutional. And I find it impossible not to call that same possum brave after its performance in a contest over food with two raccoons under a cold February moon. The coons were larger, fiercer, faster, with cunning fighting techniques that have bested coon hounds several times their size. It was astounding to us that they didn't quickly rout the much smaller, meeker possum merely with their angry sounds and menacing gestures.

Hissing, the possum kept edging toward the coons. And the coons, still screaming, moved backward. What the uproar was all about was a long strip of fat from a sirloin steak. The possum finally picked it up, then ambled off, the coons quiet, staring, doing nothing to take the prize from that "coward" of a possum.

Most of us are aware that the wily possum will sometimes "play dead" when danger threatens, and then shuffle off when the danger has passed. Indeed, "playing possum" has become part of our language. Although some naturalists believe this is a bona fide "act," opossum expert Carl Gottfried Hartman believed that the creature actually faints. Hartman theorized that the stimulus of a sudden touch may set off a charge of paralyzing substances that cause muscles to contract and limbs to stiffen. In short, the possum isn't playing.

Of all its many survival techniques, the one most responsible for keeping the possum on the scene for so long is almost certainly its prodigious birthrate. Breeding takes place twice a year, and each litter may include as many as 20 offspring. The young are born anytime from December to February in the South, later in other sections, with the second litter arriving in late spring or early summer.

The possum's gestation period—just 13 days—is the shortest among mammals. Thus its young are born smaller than honey bees, looking more like embryos than tiny replicas of the mother, with no eyes or ears and only fleshy buds for hind legs and clawed stubs for front legs. After the mother has licked the fetal fluid from them, the newborn must, unaided, crawl through a forest of coarse hair to get to her warm, furry pouch and to life. That pouch usually has 13 teats, and only the first 13 to reach them survive.

At ten weeks the young are able to leave the pouch and the mother, but they almost always scamper up on her back when she leaves the den. One of the weirdest sights in nature is a female possum with 13 offspring atop her back. This backpacking continues until the young are rat-size, at about 14 weeks, and weaned.

From this point, the young are on their own. Although the possum is phenomenally long-lived as a species, individuals have a relatively short life-span, probably topping at five years, with most not making it much beyond two.

One thing is certain: This living fossil is as much a survival wonder as those architectural relics that mankind holds in such awe—the Acropolis in Greece, the Colosseum in Italy, Egypt's pyramids.

The possum also is older. And in much better shape.

Struggle for Survival

Grizzly on the Nature Trail!

by John and Frankie O'Rear

Autumn in Alberta's picture-book Jasper National Park, high in the Canadian Rockies, is a special time of year. Although the summer visitors have gone home, the matchless wilderness continues to lure hikers and nature lovers. But, for the young Auseklis family of Kalispell, Mont., what began on September 14, 1972, as a beauty-filled hike on a well-traveled park trail turned into a morning of terror.

OUTDOOR enthusiasts Al and Nancy Auseklis had worked out a pretty good life for themselves. Former competitors on the national ski-racing circuit, they both had coaching jobs with the Kalispell junior racers, and this helped augment the income from their small-engine sales business. Last September, after several weeks of hard training to get in shape for the coming ski season, they decided to take a break. With their two children, Alex and Anna, ages 3½ and 2½, they headed up to Jasper National Park for a hiking holiday.

On arrival in Jasper, Al and Nancy consulted a park map and chose a short, not-too-steep nature trail well-suited for the children. Alex immediately forged ahead, with his sister skipping along behind, her blond ponytail flying. After about an hour of hiking, the children tired and asked to ride in their parents' backpacks. This may have saved their lives, for no sooner were they happily under way again, Alex in Al's pack and Anna in Nancy's, than a paralyzing roar knifed through the silence of the dark pines around them.

Nancy saw the grizzly bear first. Her heart all but stopped as she instantly recognized the dark, silver-tipped coat, the unmistakable hump between the shoulder blades, the sheer bulk of the awesome beast. Al and Alex were just ahead, out of Nancy's sight over a slight rise, and the grizzly was charging in their direction. From the corner of her eye, Nancy also saw a bear cub, running away in the opposite direction.

One horror-filled moment after the grizzly disappeared from sight, Nancy heard what she later described as a "shattering roar and then what sounded like a pack of angry dogs fighting, only much worse." But "above that terrifying clatter"—and worst of all, she remembers—"came the ear-piercing screams of my son, Alex."

Shocked into action, and recalling that grizzlies are unable to climb trees, Nancy sought safety in a nearby pine. But, with 30-pound Anna in her backpack, she was unable to get off the ground.

"It was then that an instinctive rage coursed through me," she says now. "I had to do *something*. I had to try to save all that was dear to me in life." Fighting off feelings of helplessness, she hunted for weapons—a tree branch, rocks, anything.

Warned by the grizzly's roars, Al had wheeled about just in time to see the bear "charging at us like a freight train." He tried frantically to pull up a young lodgepole pine, but the roots refused to let go, and there was no time to struggle with it. At the last instant, he jumped to one side, and the grizzly charged past. It turned immediately, however, and charged again—this time from behind Al, making straight for his back, where Alex was strapped in the pack. Al pivoted fast, to protect the screaming child. This time the bear plowed headlong into Al, knocking him to the ground and pinning Alex beneath him.

Snarling with rage, the grizzly pounced on the fallen father and son. Al could feel his flesh tearing as the bear shook his left leg in its jaws. In desperation, Al kicked the bear on its sensitive nose with his free foot. The grizzly suddenly let go and headed toward Nancy. But when Al managed to struggle up onto his good leg, the grizzly charged back at him. Knocking Al to the ground again, it started chewing and tearing his right leg. Cursing the pain, Al kicked the bear's face with his injured leg. Once more the mother grizzly let go and charged toward Nancy.

Meanwhile, Nancy had scavenged a long pine pole and

anchored it under her arm. Now she came running down the trail toward Al. When she caught sight of the onrushing bear, she ducked into a clump of pine saplings and, with Al shouting orders to poke and jab at the grizzly, backed up to a tree to protect Anna. Then, like a knight of old, she jousted with the panting grizzly—driving the pole into its shoulder each time it lunged at them. All this time, not a sound came from little Anna: the child was frozen in shock.

Suddenly, unaccountably, the frenzied mother grizzly turned away and lumbered off down the trail that the Auseklis family had been following so happily only minutes earlier. In the eerie silence after the bear's departure, Nancy felt a new flood of terror gripping her. Not daring to think about what she would find, she ran toward Al. He was struggling to get up, she remembers, and "swearing in anger that this could have happened. Somehow his cursing was a tremendous relief to me." Alex was trembling and crying in Al's backpack but, miraculously, was unharmed.

Both of Al's legs were brutally mangled, with gaping holes where chunks of flesh had been torn away. As Nancy ripped up her windbreaker to make pressure bandages, questions raced through her mind: *Should I leave Al and go for help? Could I find him again? Will he bleed to death? What if the bear comes back?* A whimper from Alex interrupted her jumbled thoughts. "Are we going to die, Mama?" he asked. "Is Daddy going to die?"

That was enough for Al. "Let's get out of here!" he said, struggling up with Nancy's help. In terrible pain, fighting shock, getting weaker every minute, Al dragged himself along on crutches that they jury-rigged from tree branches. Nancy carried Alex in her backpack and cradled Anna in her arms—65 pounds in all.

"It was essential, at this point," says Nancy, "to appear lighthearted and unafraid, for there is nothing more terrifying for a child than to realize that his parents are hurt and unsure of what to do. Anna still had not said one word, and I was really beginning to worry about her."

Since the grizzly had headed down the trail in the direction they had been following, Al and Nancy bushwhacked through the thick brush in another direction that they hoped would lead them out. They finally came upon, and followed, what they thought was another hiking trail—but after about an hour it gave out. Arguing over which direction to take, Al and Nancy came to a clearing. From there they could see, at the base of a long slope, the Athabasca River. They felt they had no choice but to head toward the river and trust it to lead them back to civilization.

A steep cliff blocked their way, but they found a game trail zigzagging down through a wooded ravine—the only passable route. Nancy remembers that she was "near collapse from the weight of the children and my constant fear that Al would pass out." She persuaded Alex to get out of her pack and hike on his own.

To this day she's not sure how Al made it down the ravine, "unless it was his hard training for the ski season that pulled him through." Al says simply that he knew he had to have medical attention, fast, and so he literally crawled down on his belly, using the stick crutches when he could and sliding his legs behind him.

At the bottom they came upon railroad tracks and, with overwhelming relief, heard the throb of machinery from a nearby oil-pumping station. Knowing that help was near, Al gave in to a state of semiconsciousness. The children stayed with him while Nancy ran to the station and flung open the door. She shouted for help above the noise of the pumps. No answer. She finally found and pushed open a door marked EMPLOYES ONLY. Five men were seated inside, eating lunch. "Thank God!" she said to herself, and then, "Please help! My husband has been attacked by a grizzly!"

While one man telephoned the park warden and Seton General Hospital in Jasper, others grabbed up a big first-aid box and headed for Al. He was fully conscious when they reached him, though his face was white with shock. They were treating his wounds as best they could when another of the men drove his car up. After Al had been stretched across the back seat, the rest of the Auseklis family climbed in and the car sped off to the hospital.

It took about two hours for a waiting team of doctors to sew up Al's wounds. He had been lucky on three counts: although both legs were horribly torn, all the vital tendons were intact; nerves and muscles were damaged, but not irreparably; most important, no main artery had been severed.

Leaving Al at the hospital, Nancy described the incident to the park warden, who immediately closed all trails in the attack area while a search—unsuccessful—was made for the grizzly. When the warden dropped Nancy off at the Auseklis' car, she "felt uneasy just walking from the warden's truck to our car—one of those ridiculous reactions that you laugh at later."

After two months of slow, painful convalescence, Al was up on his feet, eager to get back into training. By midwinter he was skiing as usual, with nothing to show for his ordeal but some scars and a bit of numbness in one leg. The children, too, have bounced back. "They still ask questions about the attack," says Nancy. "But we have tried to make them understand that the grizzly wasn't simply vicious. We had walked into her house, and got too close to her baby, and in that sense the attack was our fault."

Speaking of the ordeal, Nancy says, "In our family we love animals, and we want to keep it that way. Even now, we feel no real malice toward that grizzly. It was a mother's instinct that provoked her attack and a mother's instinct that drove me to courage I never knew I had. She was protecting her cubs; I was protecting mine."

Adds Al, quietly, "I will never forget Nancy's courage. And I'll challenge anyone who maintains that 'the family is dead.' Or God, either, for that matter."

Locked in the Lion's Jaws

by Arnold Shapiro

THE 18-MONTH-OLD LION CUB, already bigger than a Great Dane, leaped out of the thick underbrush, put his furry front paws up on Tony Fitzjohn's broad shoulders and rubbed heads joyously with his friend. It was Thursday, June 12, 1975, and in lion fashion Freddie was welcoming Tony back to Kora Camp from a two-day supply trip.

Kora is an isolated huddle of tents protected by a high wire fence in northern Kenya, where 75-year-old naturalist George Adamson rehabilitates lions in a unique conservation project. Orphaned cubs or young zoo lions—lions that would otherwise remain in captivity—grow up, reproduce and live free in an area the Kenya government has designated a national game reserve.

Conditions at the camp are rugged: intense heat and biting tse-tse flies, no electricity or plumbing, and a six-hour drive to the nearest settlement. But 31-year-old, English-born Fitzjohn had read the *Born Free* books as a teen-ager and been captivated by the story of Joy and George Adamson raising the orphaned lioness, Elsa. Living in Africa and working with Adamson for the last three years was a dream come true for Tony.

One of his regular jobs was a monthly trip by Land Rover to buy supplies at the tiny outpost of Garissa. This morning, before his return, he had stopped to see the district game warden and thank him for evicting a gang of armed poachers who had been leaving poison traps for rhinos inside the reserve.

The warden had asked about Freddie, the abandoned lion cub he had found in the bush some 17 months earlier and turned over to Tony. "That was the first cub I'd known," Tony recalls. He had taken the frail, fluffy animal in his arms, driven him home to Kora and given him the name Freddie.

Later, three more cubs were brought from zoos. But Freddie always held a special place with Tony. Freddie was not only good-natured, but he was the bravest of the cubs, scrappier and more inclined to take liberties with the fully grown wild lions that prowl around the fence. He and Tony had slept in the same bed until Freddie outgrew it. Tony's girl friend, Lindsay Bell, who lives in Nairobi, has said that he is completely relaxed only when he is with his lions.

AFTER TWO DAYS of rough driving, Tony was exhausted and glad to be back at Kora. He was dressed only in shorts and sandals, his tan skin glistening with perspiration in the 97-degree heat. It was time to gather the cubs—the other three had joined Freddie now in welcoming Tony—and take them inside the fence for the night. To gentle the frisky Freddie, Tony sat down, his arms clasped around his knees, his back to the underbrush a few yards away, and began talking quietly. One rule in the bush is *never* to sit on the ground outside camp, because of the possibility of unexpected contact with animals. But Tony felt safe within shouting distance of the tents.

It was 5:10 p.m. The camp, 50 yards away, was quiet. Then, without warning, Tony felt a giant creature pounce on him from behind. He crashed forward to the ground and momentarily lost consciousness. When he came to, it was to the terrifying awareness that his head was locked between the jaws of an enormous lion.

The attacker clamped down hard, then released the headlock and began a barrage of biting and clawing—sharp bites to the neck and head, deep bites to both shoulders, slashing claws to back and legs.

To Tony this horror was a "series of jerky slides separated by periods of blackout." His glasses were smashed and he saw flashes of the camp he had thought close; it seemed to be moving farther and farther away, getting smaller and smaller. Which lion was attacking him? One of George's? He only knew that the beast was fully grown and powerful—400 pounds and eight feet long.

Tony didn't have a chance. He covered his genitals and closed his eyes. More blows from mighty paws struck his head; more deep gashes from razor-sharp claws opened his face.

Because of shock and concussion, he felt no pain and heard no sounds. Paralyzed by injuries and bewilderment, he was experiencing his own death as a silent movie.

Now the lion grabbed Tony's neck and bit down. Tony couldn't breathe through his nose and couldn't open his mouth. He remembered that lions often kill by strangulation, holding their vise-like grip until the prey stops breathing. It takes no more than a minute.

During this minute, Tony suddenly realized that there were two lions in the battle. As he forced his bloody eyelids open, he saw Freddie charging toward him. *Oh, no, not Freddie, too!* he thought.

But little Freddie wasn't attacking Tony; he was after the mighty lion, four times as big as he. Proper juvenile behavior is to submit to adult lions; to attack an enraged adult was suicide.

Freddie kept charging, however—snapping and snarling and biting at the flanks of the lion who stood astride Tony's torso. And for an instant it worked. The lion released his grip on Tony's neck and charged after Freddie, who ran for his life. Tony lay in a pool of blood, gasping for air. The attacker could have caught Freddie and torn him apart on the spot. But he stopped his pursuit and ran back to the victim. Again, he clamped down on Tony's neck in the fatal strangulation hold. *God, I'm dying! I can feel it,* Tony thought. In seconds, he lost consciousness again.

But Freddie returned to the fray and bit the surprised beast's rear, then circled with snarls and yelps, bold charges and nips. Freddie withdrew only when the bigger animal swiped at him with his powerful paw. But he could not stop the foe.

Throughout the attack, Tony was a silent victim and the lion a silent killer. The only sounds were Freddie's unrelenting growls and piercing yelps that Tony could not hear.

BUT FREDDIE'S shrill cries *were* heard by Erigumsa, the compound's cook. At first, he thought two cubs were fighting, but Freddie's distant voice sounded too desperate. The cook ran to the gate—and saw Tony being mauled to death. Erigumsa raced to the dining tent, 75 feet away, where Adamson was having tea.

"Simba ame kamata Tony inje! Anataka kuua yeye!" he cried in Swahili. ("The lion has caught Tony outside! He's trying to kill him!")

George believed the cubs' playfulness had unintentionally got too rough. So he took only a walking stick, by-passing a loaded rifle, when he ran from the tent.

Outside the gate, George saw Tony's neck locked between the jaws of a full-grown lion. There was no time to return for the rifle—he had to act instantly. Without a second thought, he charged the lion, frantically yelling and waving the walking stick.

Now George was vulnerable to attack. But the beast released Tony and retreated to stare at George. The lion prepared to spring, but George kept moving forward, shouting and brandishing the stick. It worked! The lion hesitated, then slunk off into the bush, splotched with Tony's blood.

THE NEXT THING Tony realized, he was stumbling back to camp, supported by George. "George, I think I'm dying. Whatever you do," Tony pleaded, "don't shoot the lion. My fault. . . . Caught unaware. . . . Shouldn't have happened."

The minute he got Tony into his tent, George rushed to the shortwave radio to call the Flying Doctor Service in Nairobi. It was too late—the 135-mile flight would take an hour and a quarter, and regulations firmly prohibit landing on a bush strip after dark, even for a critical emergency.

The nurse assured George that the plane would come first thing in the morning and advised him on first-aid treatment for Tony's myriad, deep wounds. George signed off, staring at the setting sun. Could Tony make it through the long night ahead without a surgeon and blood transfusions?

Drifting in and out of consciousness, Tony fought for breath—and life. "I've got to live—for Lindsay, George and the lions. I know if I just think about living, I'll make it."

At dawn, outside camp, George and Erigumsa managed smiles; 13 hours after his mauling, Tony was still alive.

Lindsay was the first one out of the Flying Doctor aircraft when it touched down—George had radioed her the night before about Tony's condition. "I was expecting bad wounds, but not all over his head," she recalls. "He could hardly breathe. The right side of his neck was completely open and his wounds were oozing. It was horrible." During the flight back to Nairobi with Tony, Lindsay broke down and wept. "I knew how much he loved his work," she says. "If he lived, would he ever want to return to the lions?"

Tony spent two hours in surgery when they got him to the hospital. There were three dozen wounds—some so deep and dangerous they couldn't be stitched at that time. His trachea had been squeezed but not broken. Miraculously, the lion's teeth had not severed any nerve, artery or vein. Tony would be one of the few people ever to survive a lion-mauling.

THE DAY after the attack, a large lion appeared outside Kora with dried blood on his chest and muzzle. It was a 2½-year-old wild lion George had known since infancy, a creature so placid that he'd been named Shyman.

Now the cubs wouldn't go near Shyman, and he, uncharacteristically, began growling menacingly at them. George drove outside the compound and positioned the Land Rover between Shyman and the frightened cubs. Then he observed Shyman carefully. His movements were erratic and unusual. The once-gentle lion had probably eaten from a poisoned carcass left by the rhino poachers. Since he had attacked once, he could do it again. The lives of humans and other lions were in jeopardy. After an hour of watching Shyman's behavior, George sadly raised his rifle and put a bullet into the lion's brain.

Such a mauling as Tony had received would make even the bravest soul re-evaluate the risks of work in the bush. He had been literally eaten by a lion, who had chewed the flesh off his face and neck—the scars will be with him always. But Tony remembered how a lion cub whom he loved had tried to save him.

Two months after the accident, Tony returned to Kora, wondering what kind of greeting, if any, he'd receive after his absence. As he reached camp, he saw the cubs atop a large rock. And when they saw him, they rushed toward him, Freddie in the lead, making woofing sounds all the way. Typical lion greetings last less than a minute; this one lasted close to ten—the excited cubs leaping all over Tony.

"I never had any thoughts about not going back," Tony told me when I visited him. "We're creating an animal reserve. People from all over the world can eventually come and see our lions, and the lions can live free and unmolested in nature. I belong here."

The Elephant Baby-Sitter

by Norah Burke

TO HIS KEEPER, KARIM, Gajpati was the biggest, best and most intelligent elephant in all Asia. He belonged to India's Forest Department and was employed in the Himalayan foothills as a *shikar* (hunting) elephant; he could penetrate the jungle like no other animal.

Gajpati stood ten feet tall and weighed more than four tons. His legs were like trees—his tracks 20 inches across—and he had more than once stamped a bear to a pulp. Yet Gajpati was a gentle animal. He was especially so with Karim, whom Gajpati loved with unselfish devotion, and with Karim's infant son. If the elephant was doing nothing when Karim's wife had water to fetch, or dinner to cook, either she or Karim would draw a circle in the dust in front of the tethered animal, and put the baby into it.

"Keep him inside there, O Lord of Elephants," they would order the big tusker, who gently restrained the child if he tried to crawl away.

One afternoon when they were camped near the Rapti River, Karim's wife took a big earthen jar and went off toward the river to fill it. After a while, when she failed to return, Karim shouted in the direction she had taken. But there was no reply. At his yell, every jungle sound had stopped except the roar of the river.

Quite suddenly Karim, with his heel, marked a circle in front of the elephant and put the baby into it.

"Look after him, Gajpati!"

He ran full speed to see what had happened to his wife.

Under Gajpati's trunk, next to his immense toenails, the baby lay and laughed up at the elephant. The infant could do as he liked, but each time he tried to crawl out of the circle he was picked up and put back in again. Gajpati scooped up some dust with his trunk and blew it over himself. Sometimes he flicked a little dirt over the baby, to discourage flies. And sometimes drops of green spit fell from Gajpati's pointed underlip onto the baby's tummy and tickled him. They were perfectly content together, these two. Here, inside the cool shade of the huge wild-mango tree to which Gajpati was tethered, time meant nothing.

Suddenly the sun was gone, drawing over it a sky of velvet and diamonds. Immediately, the air was colder, and the baby began to cry. Jackals howled in the dusk, and there came the whoop of an eagle owl.

Not far away, in the rough grassland, a male hyena emerged from his burrow and stood silently sniffing the night air for news of food. He was a scavenger of carrion and an eater of skeletons. He would pick up any small, helpless creature he might find. In India, hyenas take human children every year.

His mate and an almost full-grown young hyena came out of the den, too. When they heard the baby crying, these bold and loathsome beasts, with their powerful crushing teeth, trotted off in that direction.

In camp, Gajpati was beginning to be agitated about the child. He realized that something was the matter, but what? He offered the baby a mouthful of leaves, and fanned him. It was no good. He put up his trunk and trumpeted for the owners of this baby to come back and do something.

They did not appear.

Gajpati scented the hyenas. He froze, and felt the breeze with his trunk to find out more.

There were three of them, out of sight, but quite close. Gajpati gathered the baby closer to his feet and squealed a threat.

An elephant's sense of smell is acute, but his vision poor. It was not till the hyenas were in the camp that Gajpati saw them. The sight made him range angrily, straining the chain that bound him. The elephant grumbled and blew.

The hyenas were nonplused. One sat down out of reach

and fixed its nocturnal eyes on the child. The others began to circle around behind.

In sudden exasperation, the elephant put his forehead against the mango tree, and braced the whole of his giant strength against it to break it down. He did not succeed, but the tree groaned at the roots.

Gajpati swung back and made for the sitting hyena, which sprang smartly away.

The hyenas behind him darted at the baby, so he wheeled toward them instead. They jumped out of reach.

He attacked the tree again. It shrieked as he strove against it. Now the baby was yelling at the top of his lungs, and blindly trying to crawl away; so Gajpati gave up. He backed up, shook his head, and gathered the baby to him.

Changing his tactics, he stood perfectly still, close to the now leaning tree, and watched.

The hyenas were hungry, bold, and began to close in.

They were watching the elephant with respect, but they did not allow for the slack of the chain.

Gajpati struck like lightning and in a moment got one hyena under his forefeet. Almost at once the struggle was over, the body stamped to a pulp. With a squeal of triumph and rage, Gajpati threw the carcass aside.

It scattered the others, who made off, leaving elephant and baby in peace for an hour or two.

Pillowed in dust, and exhausted by hunger, the baby lay half-sleeping, half-sobbing, and sucked at the stub of sugar cane that Gajpati offered him. Then, warmed by the elephant's sweet breath, he slept. A little after midnight, Gajpati dozed, too.

Presently, the baby stirred, sat up, and began to crawl away.

He was already out of reach when the elephant woke.

In the gray of early morning, Gajpati saw the hyenas coming back, and the baby several yards away.

He forged out to the full length of his range. Iron links bit into his flesh. Blood poured down.

The hyenas saw their chance and darted in.

At the same moment, the great tree gave and smashed down upon elephant and baby together. Breaking branches and rushing leaves covered them both.

The violence sent the hyenas off in a flash, and they did not return.

When Karim and his wife ran gasping into camp, they saw only the fallen tree and Gajpati under it.

Their baby?

They tore their way into the leaves and branches. Beneath it all, the child lay sleeping in the curl of the elephant's trunk. His mother, in tears, snatched him up. He was very dirty and scratched, but whole.

And Gajpati?

He lay with closed eyes beneath the tree.

"Fool! Traitor!" raged Karim. "So! Was the baby nothing to thee, that thou wouldst break loose and leave him?"

He took his ax and began to free the elephant, watched by his wife, who stood with her son in her arms and trembled still after her night's adventures.

To have dropped her water jar into the deep rapids had been bad enough. Then, as she tried to recover it, to be swept downstream had been a nightmare. Karim had raced off down river to look for her, but was overtaken by night and lost in the jungle. At dawn they had found each other as both rushed home to the child.

Now, panting and grunting, Karim cleared away the branches and undid Gajpati's chain.

"He will die of his injuries," choked the woman.

But the elephant got his front feet onto the ground and heaved free of the last branches. He was up, bruised, bleeding and shaking.

"Thou worthless traitor!" Karin told the animal bitterly.

The big elephant stood and sucked his trunk in shame and remorse for wrongdoing.

"Look!" gasped the woman.

Where Gajpati had heaved himself free of branches, these had parted to disclose the body of the hyena, and hyena tracks were everywhere. Karim and his wife read the story: Gajpati was no traitor. There followed such words of praise that made Gajpati lift his head and blink.

Terror of the Deep

by Carsten Stroud

ALONG THE WINDWARD SHORE of the popular resort island of Cozumel off Mexico's Yucatan Peninsula, my wife Linda and I discovered a small, reef-bound lagoon. It was isolated, reachable only by Jeep on a spine-cracking road through jungle palms, but it was ideal for scuba diving. A rocky spur ran down the beach at the northern edge, curving out into the sea for almost 300 yards. It stopped at a deep-water trench that had been cut away by a rapid tidal flow, leaving a sea gate about ten yards wide. The circle was completed by a ragged chain of limestone rocks. The area contained by this natural breakwater was close to 400 yards across, and reached a depth of 50 feet. Beyond the reef, the waves boomed and crashed, but within, all was calm.

At least on the surface; underneath, the lagoon was filled with the bizarre flora and fauna of tropical oceans. Most of the larger predators—the barracuda and sharks—were kept out by the sea walls. This pool was teeming with life. In it, we became completely involved in the visual and spiritual delight of tropical diving.

At three o'clock on the afternoon of March 18, we were finning along in 30 feet of water just inside the mouth of the lagoon. A few minutes before, I had been pulled through the sea gate by the tide. Linda, always a cool head in a crisis, had braced herself in a seam and dragged me back in. The whole action hadn't taken 30 seconds, but I had blown a fair amount of air in my fright, and my lungs were still laboring.

People are less alert after such an incident, so neither Linda nor I realized what was happening when a large, dark shape hurtled by us, putting out a pressure wave strong enough to send us spinning. Linda's mask came off. My mind screamed *Shark!* as I fumbled for the shark billy I always carry. Then I spotted Linda swimming toward me, mask back in place. At that moment a smaller form rocketed through the sea gate.

Instinctively, Linda and I lined up back to back, scanning the waters above, behind and beneath for whatever it was that had buzzed us. Forty yards away, swimming in a tight, agitated circle, were a bottle-nosed dolphin and her pup. We could hear their high-pitched, chattering squeals through the water and, when the pup turned, we saw a cut which was trailing a dark mist just back of the blowhole.

I wondered why the pair had strayed so far from their school, and then a slow chill gathered around the back of my neck. Linda and I moved closer to each other, and I pulled her to the bottom of the lagoon. Somewhere nearby, and closing fast, there must be a shark.

In the taut seconds that followed, local marine life slowed into a profound silence. Just beyond the sea gate, something was moving up the incline of the sea floor—a dark flicker of sinuous motion. My breath stopped, and a vein began to pound in my right temple. Suddenly, a 12-foot-long tiger shark weighing perhaps 500 pounds cruised through the gate, head moving from side to side as he sensed the waters. A school of pilot fish clustered around his flanks, and we could make out his markings, dirty brown on top, with faint shadowy stripes, a notched dorsal and a gray-white belly. As he passed by, no more than 20 feet away, one black eye tracked us. His jaws were open slightly, his gills were distended and his tail fin was stroking; his nostrils stirred with the blood scent of the wounded dolphin pup.

If the shark ran true to form, concentrating on his bleeding prey, we might be able to bottom-crawl to the shallows and—with luck—get out of the water safely.

I hooked into Linda's weight belt (she would guide us while I watched the rear), and we began moving slowly along the bottom. We covered 100 yards without seeing either the shark or the dolphins. Another 20 . . . no sign, no movement, no sound anywhere. Where was he? What was he doing?

Something moved to our right. I snapped my head around

and saw a thick, black shadow rippling over the sandy bottom. Flipping over on my back, I got my shark billy up barely in time to plant the spikes in the shark's gills. He was on top of us, massive jaws pushed open, jagged rows of triangular teeth inches from my face. With a hideous snaking twist he drove us down into a small trench.

I heard a muffled snap as his jaws closed down on the water in front of my faceplate. They sprang open, and he snapped again and again at my chest, shredding my gear, held off by the flexing shaft of the shark billy, his sheer brute force driving it into the rocks at the base of the trench. Linda twisted underneath me, and sank her blade into the shark's throat. Blood began to darken the water. I heard a splitting crack, and the handle of the shark billy gave way. The tiger turned above me, jaws opening, and then something struck him heavily in the side, knocking him away from us.

Blood and sand swirled around us as we lay in the trench. Linda, her eyes wild behind her faceplate, put her hand out and ran it tentatively over my chest, unable to believe that I hadn't been bitten. My wet suit was in tatters, my flotation vest had been chewed away, but I was all right.

The tiger was within ten yards, circling without rhythm, shudders rippling down his flanks as he jerked his head and bit at the water. Whatever had delivered that ferocious blow, knocking him away from the trench, had saved our lives—for the moment.

Then he turned to come in again—one obscene killing machine, jaws gaping between cold eyes. He got to within 15 feet of us when, with blurring speed, the female dolphin shot in from the right. She struck him with terrible force near his pectoral fin. A huge black bubble burst out of the shark's mouth, and he swerved to strike at his assailant. He was certainly hurting, but how badly it was impossible to guess.

The shark was now less than six feet away in the murk, rolling on his side to pursue the dolphin. We seized the moment to try to get into clear water again. While we were kicking out of the blood and wrack, expecting the tiger's bull-like snout to explode out of the mist in front of us, I ran out of air. I pulled the reserve rod and gave Linda the throat-cutting sign to let her know that I was now on emergency air. It might last three minutes.

Suddenly, the dolphin pup skimmed over us, taking this

chance to run for the open sea. It flew past with eyes wide and beak shut tight, and was gone. With the pup safe, the mother might run for it. That would leave us roughly 70 yards from the beach, with the wounded tiger shark about 50 feet away. As we knelt in the sand, he turned and headed for us again, passing overhead, looking like some lighter-than-air craft and trailing a steady stream of blood from his gills.

Out of the corner of my eye I saw the dolphin, swimming some distance to our right, moving roughly parallel and making a clicking with her blowhole. The shark was at the edge of the shallows, between us and land. He stopped his erratic turns, and began to swim quickly along the shoreline; then he gave a violent twist of his muscular torso and hurled himself away from the beach, right at us. I kicked up and away from Linda, holding out the splintered shaft of the shark billy. I think I had some idea of wedging it into his jaws. When he was within six feet of me, I struck out—and hit nothing. In less than a second the tiger had covered the distance separating us, dipped underneath me and cut straight out for the gap in the sea wall. Within seconds he was out of sight. The dolphin circled us and flashed out to sea in the wake of the tiger shark.

For some seconds, Linda and I hung suspended in the water, minds blank. Then we blew out hard and kicked for the surface. When our heads broke into the air, we were ten yards from shore. Wordlessly, we swam to the shallows, staggered up the beach and collapsed on a rock facing the ocean. I was vaguely aware that the vein pounding in my temple was slowing its beat. Linda burst out in a short laugh, and showed me her watch. It was 3:10 p.m. The entire episode had lasted less than ten minutes.

That evening, we went down to the beach in front of our hotel room and tried to make some sense out of what had happened. Why the shark decided to attack us instead of his chosen prey, we can't imagine. I wouldn't care to speculate on why a shark does anything; I doubt they know themselves. I think that the mother dolphin took advantage of the shark's interest in us to try to eliminate the danger to herself and her pup. Linda sees it differently. She thinks the dolphin fought for us—that in the midst of all the cruelties of nature, there is room for kindness as well.

Facts and Fallacies

The Gorilla Is a Paper Tiger

by Allen Rankin

HE'S THE hulking monster of horror tales and nightmares, a beetlebrowed killer who's supposed to get his kicks from making off with luscious young women or rending jungle explorers limb from limb. Such is the lurid legend of the gorilla, mightiest of the great apes, our closest relatives in the animal kingdom. It is all a far cry from reality, say today's zoologists, who in the last dozen years have finally learned the truth. Beneath those gargantuan chests, glowering scowls and bared fangs lies a tender and loving nature. When left alone in their native habitat—the rain forests of equatorial Africa—gorillas are among the gentlest and most peaceable of souls. In carefree tribes of up to 30 individuals, they spend their days stuffing themselves with tender plants and roots, taking long naps and otherwise harmlessly enjoying life. Even when their home ground is invaded, they're inclined to take a live-and-let-live attitude.

In 1970, Dian Fossey, a plucky investigator for the National Geographic Society, emerged unscathed after living for three years among wild gorillas in central Africa. She reported that in 2000 hours of direct observation of her hairy hosts—often within grabbing distance—they showed "less than five minutes of what might be called aggressive behavior." Once five awesome, full-grown male gorillas *did* charge the lone lady simultaneously. With the leader towering within three feet of her, she spread her arms wide and shouted, "Whoa!" The startled assault force stopped—and all five resumed their company manners.

This confirmed the findings of George B. Schaller, of the New York Zoological Society, who in 1959 undertook the first thorough scientific study ever made of these mystery-shrouded animals.

Six feet tall and weighing between 400 and 500 pounds, a grown male gorilla is 10 to 14 times as powerful as the strongest man. Standing erect, massive arms flung skyward, he seems much like King Kong, the 50-foot-high apparition of fiction. But Schaller learned that gorillas prefer to use their power and menacing display not to seek trouble but to *avoid* it. Many times, when he approached, the tribe would retreat in orderly fashion, while the ape-king stood fast. Facing the "enemy," he ripped up and hurled masses of underbrush, slapped his chest with the resonance of bongo drums, gave a cavernous show of teeth and horrific roars that scared even the elephants in the area. Occasionally, he would charge—always stopping just short of the mark.

"It's all a masterful bluffing act," concluded Schaller. "The big fellows seem to be torn between their duty to defend their tribes and their desire to flee from danger. So, to blow off tension and frighten their enemies, they pound their chests and throw things around."

As the animals gradually became accustomed to the naturalist's presence, their threats subsided to grunts of annoyance or curiosity. In his 20 months of research, Schaller had 314 encounters with gorillas, some of whom ventured within five feet of him. One curious female even came to sit beside him on the same tree branch.

Since man and the gorilla began branching away from common ancestors some 26 million years ago, the gorilla, in certain simple respects, has done better than we have. Food? Gorillas can get all the succulent greenery they want without moving far out of their tracks. And in satisfying their gourmet appetites they have become masterly botanists, able to locate a great variety of plant foods, which they dissect with surgical skill. (The soft hearts of banana trees are especially irresistible—causing many a plantation owner to swear a vendetta against the culprits.) Shelter? To make their crude bed-nests they simple rake in the nearest mass of foliage and tuck it under and around them.

Peace and tranquillity? They have it—or did before man invaded their Eden. No other animal preys on them. (Of course, if they are taxed beyond their patience, they can and will demolish a man, or even a powerful leopard, with a single squeeze or lion-size bite.) They don't have to fight each other for *any* need and don't war among themselves. Frequently, several groups will share the same territory, meet on friendly terms and even interchange members.

Their government is a dictatorship so benign that it's almost democratic. The male boss of a tribe is always less a Hitler than an easygoing politician. He does sometimes assert his right to the choicest food, the most receptive female or the driest spot when it's raining. But, in general, he's tolerant and doesn't object much even if another male abducts one of his concubines right before his eyes. Intelligence and a knack for getting along seem to count as much as brawn in determining who emerges—and remains—as chief.

As long as the old king holds his job, his subjects look to him for every decision—when to go foraging, where to camp. Communication is by voice signals—low grumbles and grunts when contented, sharp grunts and barks when scattered in dense vegetation, harsh barks when annoyed, and screams and roars when angry or alarmed. Schaller counted about 20 distinct such vocalizations.

Indulgent fathers and uncles, the males spoil the "children." Even the leader allows them to pull his hair, tweak his nose and mock his chest-beating. Child care and discipline are left strictly up to mama, and she's superb at the job. She lets the youngsters go ape at their favorite games—follow-the-leader, swinging and stunting on vines, and sliding down the mountainous backs and bellies of the grownups. But with only a sharp glance, she can abruptly send the kids scurrying obediently to bed. Since every infant is almost totally dependent on her for about three years, she practices admirable birth control and produces a new offspring only about every third or fourth year. (The male gorilla is no rampant sex maniac; indeed, judged by human standards, he seems almost indifferent to sex.)

Once it was thought that gorillas aren't as bright as chimpanzees. But a top authority, Switzerland's Dr. Ernst Lang, a former director of the Basel Zoo, says, "It's not that gorillas can't do the things that chimps do, but just that they're smart enough to do only what *they* want to do. They're all individualists—independent and superior personalities."

The gorilla's world is far from all bliss, however. They're plagued with the same diseases as people are—especially the common cold and other respiratory ailments; their average life-span in the wild is only 20 years. Though gorilla hunting is now illegal in most sections, poaching persists, and some African tribes still hunt them for food, assailing them with nets and spears.

Much worse, proliferating farms and roads are fast encroaching on the gorillas' habitat, threatening them with gradual extinction. "If their forests continue to be destroyed at the present rate," says Schaller, "they'll soon find themselves at an evolutionary dead end."

Wildlife sanctuaries like the Congo's vast Albert National Park offer the best hope of saving the great apes. But zoos are playing an increasingly important role in perpetuating the species. For decades all captive gorillas died before reaching maturity. The situation has gradually improved, thanks in part to antibiotics and high-protein diets. Today, 470 of the finicky animals thrive in 119 different zoo collections, some living much longer than could be expected in the wild (the Philadelphia Zoo's Massa, world's oldest captive gorilla, is still hale at 50).

For obvious reasons, gorillas are handled with utmost caution at zoos. But leading zoo keepers have also come to agree with Dr. Lang, who says, "The big secret of keeping gorillas alive and happy is to treat them like people—pampered people." The pampering has paid off. In 1956, at Ohio's Columbus Zoo, Baron and Christina finally did what caged gorilla couples had not done in the past: they produced an offspring. In the years since, there have been over 190 more gorilla births in zoos. The most successful has been the Basel Zoo, the first to possess a large family of gorillas living together and reproducing almost as naturally as in the wild.

All signs now point toward a happy future for city-dwelling ape royalty. At model zoos they live in spacious, indoor-outdoor complexes closely resembling their natural habitat. The gorillas are treated like stars—and rightly so. For, like other top stars at zoos, they render a vital service to the cause of conservation. Bill Conway, general director of the New York Zoological Society, explains: "By fascinating city people, zoo animals do more than anything else to interest these people in the fate of wildlife and awake them to the urgent need of saving at least a token number of our wild creatures before it is too late—for them, and for us."

In Praise of Porcupines

by Bil Gilbert

CERTAIN CREATURES possess an obvious characteristic that strikes people as being so improbable, entertaining or spooky that they seldom get beyond this single attribute in considering the beast. A classic example is the porcupine. On meeting it, we noted that it had a formidable covering of sharp spines. And since then our attention has remained largely fixed on this prickliness, almost as if the porcupine were a kind of zoological vacuum—part moron, part nasty imp—enclosed in a bundle of quills.

Which is a pity, for both porcupine and man. In fact, this animal has evolved an integrated complex of interesting adaptations and habits, making it one of our most successful native species.

Porcupines exist in numerous and varied shapes around the globe. However, only one species, *Erethizon dorsatum* (meaning "irritable back"), is found in the United States, where it ranges from the North Atlantic coastal states westward to the Sierras and northward to Alaska. Only the southeastern states are free of porcupines.

Perhaps the best way to approach the inner porcupine (and the only way it can be approached in practice) is by first considering its hair. Porcupines grow a dense layer of wool next to the skin, excellent insulation for an animal that remains abroad (though not especially active) in the worst of winter weather. Above the undercoat, a layer of much longer, coarser guard hair protects the soft inner fur from dirt and moisture.

The guard hairs and facial whiskers are sensitive tactile devices; the primarily nocturnal porcupine navigates largely from information received through them.

Underneath the stout tail is another type of hair, a set of rigid bristles. In climbing, a porcupine braces its tail and, using these bristles, can hold itself firmly against a trunk or on a limb. The tail itself—about 11 inches long—is strong and mobile, and is used as a balancing pole in climbing and as a stool for sitting.

The porcupine can manipulate its outer hairs at will. One afternoon, with the snow three feet deep in the forest, I met a porcupine moving slowly but steadily *over* the snow—astonishing for such a short-legged, heavy-bodied animal. When it approached close enough, however, I could see how. With all outer hairs rigidly extended, the porcupine had converted itself into a kind of snowshoe; in effect, it was floating on the surface, progressing by paddling its feet. Also extended were the famous quills, which are yet another kind of specialized hair.

Myth to the contrary, a porcupine's quills are not venomous, nor can they be "shot." Their principal function is protective, and in this they are most efficient.

Porcupines are born fully quilled. At birth, the quills are soft and pliable but harden after exposure to the air. New quills, fed by tiny blood vessels, grow about half a millimeter a day, reaching lengths of around three inches. Mature quills are dead matter and have bases that shrink so that they can slip out of the porcupine's hide and into that of other things easily. A mature porcupine bears some 30,000 quills on its head, back, flanks and tail; the belly is the only large area without armor. The quills are replaced year-round, new ones emerging as old ones drop.

The quill tips are sharp enough to penetrate flesh easily, and have a series of barbs pointed toward the base. Because of this reverse barb arrangement, and the inevitable muscular contractions of the victim, once a quill enters a body it is difficult to remove and tends to "travel" inward. (A porcupine researcher whose leg was impaled with a quill in a laboratory accident noted that it took exactly 30.5 hours for the tip of the quill to emerge on the far side of his leg.)

When approached by a real or imagined enemy, a porcupine lowers its head, hunches over, raises its quills, and pivots so as always to present the attacker with its heavily armored back and thrashing tail. Thus confronted, prudent animals will quickly abandon the attack, for a full charge of quills can be excruciatingly painful, or even fatal. Infection may occur and, more serious, the quills, working their way inward, may strike a vital organ.

Porcupines are relatively solitary animals, but obviously they have to get together during mating (a fact which has given rise to a whole genre of north-woods jokes). According to porcupine expert Albert Shadle, who observed their mating in his University of Buffalo laboratory, they do so with considerable courtship, nuzzling, even some fairly musical vocalizing. When the female is thoroughly receptive, she arches her tail over her back and carefully holds this position while the male approaches—slowly and cautiously.

The gestation period is about seven months; a single "porcupette" (though twinning may occasionally occur) is born to the female in spring or early summer, in hollow logs, tree trunks or rocky caves. Porcupettes begin to feed on vegetable matter within two weeks after birth, and supplement their foraging by suckling from their mothers until they are about a month old. For several more months, mother and cub forage together, communicating by scent and vocal signs.

Porcupines have a keen sense of smell and average hearing. Their vision is exceptionally weak—not surprising since they usually operate in dark, shady places and have no reason to spot distant food sources or even potential enemies. In Victor Cahalane's *Mammals of North America,* zoologist Hartley H. T. Jackson reported a strange meeting with a porcupine. Standing still, he watched as the animal waddled up, sniffed at his leather leggings—and began to gnaw on them!

From spring through mid-fall porcupines are ground feeders. There is almost nothing herbaceous, from trees to cactus to water lilies, which they cannot chop up and grind with their beaver-like teeth. In consequence, they come close to being starvation-proof. And they are rarely scrawny, growing steadily throughout a life-span of approximately ten years to an average weight of about 15 pounds (although 40-pounders have been known).

In the winter, when terrestrial succulents have disappeared or been covered by snow and ice, porcupines take to the trees, feeding largely on the tender bark of upper limbs.

They may move to hollows or caves to escape the worst weather or predators, but usually they are far aboveground, often sleeping and feeding in the same tree for days.

Porcupines also have a strong inclination to gnaw away on human possessions, especially those permeated with perspiration. One night in Vermont, my wife and I were entertained by a herd of porcupines (at peak visitation there were eight) who lumbered and grunted about the camp looking for anything saline. They dismantled the rock-lined fire pit, shredded a loose pack strap and ate the handle off a plastic cup. The next day, we came upon an aluminum canoe hidden in the brush. Porcupines had made sawdust out of the sweat-impregnated paddle handles and, incredibly, had even gnawed some holes in the metal thwarts and gunwales.

Easily tamed, porcupines make affectionate, playful pets with a variety of moods and responses. While it is never possible to cuddle porcupines, they can be fed by hand or even carried about by their forepaws—after their suspicions are allayed. Also, once having developed a good relationship they are remarkably faithful to it. Acquaintances of mine, who had a summer cabin in Pennsylvania, tamed a young porcupine so that it would come to the front steps to eat from a food pan and then mingle easily with the family. The same porcupine showed up the next three summers and easily settled back into a pattern of intimate association.

Despite an essentially lovable nature, porcupines arouse irrational hostility in some people, who, because of ignorance and superstition, have tended to regard them as a kind of mammalian slug, and thus beneath contempt. Nothing could be further from the truth, as I hope this report has suggested. For beneath the hard, sharp, peculiar exterior of the porcupine lies a creature of varied talent, considerable wit and no little charm. An ecological and esthetic adornment to our land, *Erethizon dorsatum* may be an occasional nuisance—but which of us is not, now and then?

Misunderstood "Monster": The Octopus

by Betty Pratt-Johnson

OCTOPUSES LIKE TO BE ALONE. Indeed, they are territorial to the point of being cannibalistic, and will devour intruders that dare to crowd their space. Yet most of their reported contacts with people—even in the wild—are either friendly or tinged with fear on the part of the octopus.

Larry Hewitt, a diver who has wrestled giant Puget Sound octopuses, reported: "When faced with a fight-or-run situation, they run." Tales of attacks on people come about because when an octopus is molested it will latch on to the closest hard object. If you are trying to catch him, that object will be you. An experienced diver will place the octopus against his chest, and in most cases the animal will ride contentedly to the surface in this friendly hug. When you want to be rid of it, just pat, massage or tickle it.

Jock McLean, a retired British Columbia diver, says that it is hard indeed to make an octopus bite. If frightened, it will usually do other things to save itself. Protected by one of the speediest color-changing systems in the animal kingdom, it can turn white with fright, or red with rage to alarm its enemy. It may also turn greeny-white, brown, reddish-brown or speckled for camouflage. Sometimes it will squirt ink to distract a predator and numb its sense of smell. And the octopus will always try to escape to its den or a nearby crevice.

Octopuses are found in nearly all coastal seas of the world from the Tropics to the Arctic and Antarctic. There are at least 100 known species, ranging from the giants of the

North Pacific (a mature specimen of this *Octopus dofleini* may touch the sides of a circle with a diameter of 32 feet) to the midgets (only a few centimeters long) in the South China Sea. Most octopuses, however, are middle-sized and grow to three or four feet across. Some sun themselves in shallow offshore waters; others may live as much as a mile deep on the ocean floor.

Their natural food is shellfish—crabs, clams, lobsters or abalones. Occasionally they catch fish. Some species, such as Hawaii's "day octopus," hunt by daylight, but most octopuses are shy and wait for random prey or hunt nocturnally.

An octopus grabs its food with the circular suckers on one or more of its eight strong arms. According to the species, there may be as many as 240 suckers running the length of each arm in double rows, varying in size from a pinpoint to two and a half inches in diameter. A quarter-inch sucker requires a pull of six ounces to break its hold, which, multiplied by the 2000 or so suckers found on most common octopuses, equals considerable pulling force. With these suckers the octopus carries prey to its mouth and bites it with its beak (an 18-inch octopus has a beak like a parakeet's). Then it injects poison from its salivary glands to stun or kill the prey.

Though octopuses prefer solitude in the wilds, in captivity they become tame and affectionate. According to Gil Hewlett, Vancouver Public Aquarium curator, "They like to be stroked. They are quite intelligent, and may play jokes, too. Once we had an octopus that had a habit of squirting passers-by. Sometimes their curiosity and intelligence work against them. One octopus pulled the plug in its tank and died when the water drained out.

"One morning we discovered a more mysterious casualty: We found that half of a foot-long skilfish had been eaten, and there was nothing else in the tank with it. The next day we caught an octopus red-handed, climbing into the skilfish tank to eat the rest of its meal. You must keep octopus tanks tightly sealed with fine screening because a 60-pound specimen can creep through a two-inch hole. You must weigh down the cover, too, or an octopus will push it up and escape."

"Octopuses may live five or six years," said Cecil Brosseau, retired director of Point Defiance Aquarium in Tacoma, Wash. Their growth rate depends partially upon temperament. If an octopus is very shy and seldom ventures out of its den to eat, it will grow slowly. If food is plentiful and it is aggressive, it will grow enormously. Brosseau once had a 69-pound octopus that increased to 109 pounds in nine months.

Brosseau has devoted a great deal of time to helping man and octopus overcome their fear of each other. At Point Defiance, Brosseau used to let kindergarten children feed herring to the octopuses. Now, there are octopuses in two waist-high open-topped tanks (the tanks have burlap-wrapped rims, over which an octopus won't venture). "It takes a good week to get an octopus to lose its fear of you," Brosseau says. "But people can overcome their fears immediately. You talk them into touching the animal. Then they play with it. Then they don't want to leave."

Embryologist and cytologist John Arnold, of Hawaii's Kewalo Marine Laboratory, claims that octopuses have individual personalities and are quite intelligent. He tells about an octopus from the Bahamas to which he started feeding small snails. Given six shells each day, it carried them around under its web, eating them one at a time when hungry. Then it learned to pry open Arnold's fingers in search of snails. To avoid overfeeding, he sometimes gave it an empty shell. But the octopus soon learned to insert an arm tip into each shell to see if it held anything before it would take it.

If the animal is clever, it is also diligent. The female common octopus, said F. G. Wood, a former curator at Marineland of Florida, near St. Augustine, is one of the most faithful mothers in the sea. Her eggs are about half the size of a grain of rice. As the eggs emerge, she weaves and cements their stems together to form strands up to six inches long that hang under a ledge or in a cave. There may be 1000 eggs in a strand. And one octopus may lay as many as 325,000 eggs in two weeks.

During the four to six weeks it takes the eggs to hatch, the mother octopus cares for them without pause. From the moment she starts nesting, she refuses food and repels intruders. By blowing water on the egg strands and running her arms through them, she keeps the eggs well-oxygenated. When they hatch, her job is done. She dies.

Octopuses may have acquired their bad name by being mistaken for their close relative, the quick-to-bite squid. But the octopus's beak and venom are for its natural prey. Only the small (average size: four inches) blue-ringed octopus of

Australia is very poisonous to man. In the last 25 years, it has caused three deaths and six injuries.

Photographer-writer Valerie Taylor was once taking stills in Port Hacking near Sydney "when I saw a common octopus in the entrance to a small cave. It tried to blow my camera away with jets of water, then tried pushing with its arms. All its efforts were concentrated on the camera. It seemed to ignore the huge creature attached." Taylor has even gently handled the blue-ringed octopus many times. She finds that it does its utmost to avoid contact with people, just as other species do.

Taylor, like everyone else who becomes familiar with the octopus, has found it to be not a gruesome monster, but an intelligent creature with a distinct, even lovable, character.

What Rattlesnakes Are Really Like

by Colin Fletcher

WE HUMANS have always tended to see other creatures through a smoke screen of folklore and legend, but our misconceptions have rarely persisted as stubbornly as in the case of the rattlesnake. As usual, our ignorance has bred deep and unreasoning fear. Every summer countless hikes and picnics are ruined for people who regard the rattlesnake as a vicious and cunning brute with a deep hatred of man. Actually, the rattler is timid and retiring; it does not have the brain capacity for cunning. And although it reacts to man as to any big and threatening creature, it could hardly have built up a hatred: the first man it sees is often the last.

The only "facts" of rattlesnake life that most people know are that it grows an extra rattle every year, revels in blistering heat, is fast and unfailingly deadly. Not one of these "facts" is true. The number of rattles is almost no indication of age. A rattler soon dies if the temperature around it rises much over 100°, and it crawls so slowly that the only dangerous rattler is the one you don't see. Nor does it attack with great speed—a rattler's strike is slower than a man's punching fist. Although bites are serious, especially for children, few prove fatal.

Rattlesnake folklore, however, thrives wherever the snakes are found—virtually all over the United States and as far south as Argentina. One bit is the Boot Story, which I first heard beside the Colorado River. "This rancher," the oldtimer told me, "put on some boots that belonged to his father, ten years dead. Next day the rancher's leg began to swell. He went to a doctor—just in time to avoid amputation from rattlesnake poisoning. Then he remembered that ten years ago his father had been struck by a rattlesnake while wearing the boots. One of the snake's fangs had broken off and lodged in an eyehole. After all this time it had scratched the son."

This story runs to many versions. As read before the Royal Society of London by a New World traveler in 1714, the boot killed three successive husbands of a Virginia woman. Today the boot is sometimes modernized into a struck and punctured tire that proves fatal to successive garagemen who repair it. In solid fact, the minute amount of venom remaining on a fang under such circumstances could not possibly do any harm.

Some superstitions are harmless. Many a cowpuncher has circled his bed with horsehair rope as "protection" against the almost negligible risk of rattler-in-the-blankets. (Rattlers will pass over a hair rope readily.) But misconceptions can be dangerous, too—such as the popular one that rattlesnakes strike only when coiled, and never upward. In fact, they'll strike from any position and in any direction.

Rattlers are astonishingly tenacious of life, and one old saying which approaches truth warns that they are dangerous even after they're dead. Dr. Laurence M. Klauber, author of a masterly two-volume work on rattlesnakes, proved in laboratory tests that severed heads could bite a stick and discharge venom for almost an hour. He even found some basis for the old idea that "rattlers never die until sundown." When pinched, decapitated bodies squirmed for an average of six hours, and the hearts went on beating for a day, often for two.

Many people believe that injured rattlers "commit suicide" by biting themselves. A desperate snake will certainly thrash about and strike at anything, even its own body; but rattlers are virtually immune to rattlesnake venom.

Another misconception is that rattlesnakes seek out the very hottest resting places. True, they avoid cold. Like all reptiles, they lack an efficient mechanism such as we have for keeping body temperature constant; they rarely choose to prowl in temperatures below 65°, and at 45° they can scarcely move (in cold climates they hibernate until the weather warms). But the temperature range they like best is 80° to 90°. At 100° they're in danger; at 110° they die. When desert temperatures go high, the rattlers rest in deep holes. By moving up or down in them, they adjust their body temperature almost as efficiently as we mammals do.

Unlike many snakes, which lay eggs, female rattlers retain the eggs inside their bodies until they hatch, and bear their young alive, anywhere from 5 to 18 months after mating (temperature greatly affects the gestation process, and females can store live sperm for long periods). A litter numbers from 1 to 50, averages about 9. The young possess venom from birth, and soon begin feeding on lizards or other suitable prey. Later, small mammals form their main diet. Rattlers eat their meals whole, although they cannot, like some snakes, unhinge their jaws for swallowing. If two rattlers seize the same prey, one is likely to carry the meal to its logical conclusion and consume the other.

Rattlers sulking in captivity have fasted up to two years, but in the wild they probably feed once every week or ten days. A single meal averages 40 percent of their own weight—equivalent to a 200-pound man putting away 80 pounds at a sitting. Rattlers definitely drink water, but some of them seem to go through life with no moisture except that found in prey. Outsize eastern diamondbacks may grow to weigh over 20 pounds and measure almost eight feet in length, but most of the 30 different species grow to no more than two to six feet. They may live for as long as 20 years.

Although rattlesnakes have good eyesight only at short range, they are highly sensitive to ground vibration. Consequently, they hunt largely by ambush. They have no hearing at all, but their two small facial pits contain nerves so sensitive to heat that they can strike accurately at warm-blooded prey in complete darkness. Many species hunt mostly at night.

Nostrils just above the mouth furnish a sense of smell very like ours. A rattler can also smell by flicking its forked tongue—the tongue's moist surface picking up tiny particles in the air and, at each flicker, transferring them to two small cavities in the roof of the mouth. These cavities interpret the particles to the brain in terms of smell just as do the moist membranes inside our noses.

Harmless in itself, the rattlesnake's rattle warns and intimidates, like the growl of a dog. It is a chain of hollow, interlocking segments made of the same hardened, transparent keratin as human fingernails. A new segment is not formed each year, but is left each time the snake sheds its skin—which occurs, in adults, from one to four times a year. The rattles are fragile and rarely remain complete for long.

A rattlesnake's enemies include other snakes, many birds, mammals and even fish (not long ago a California fisherman caught a big rainbow trout with a nine-inch rattler in its stomach). When a rattlesnake meets a large potential enemy, such as man, it rarely attacks. Its first reaction will most likely be to lie still and escape attention. Then it may crawl slowly toward safety. Detected or alarmed, it will probably rattle and rise into a menacing defensive coil. When a big specimen rattles, it sounds off with a strident hiss that rises to a spine-chilling crescendo—"like a pressure cooker with the safety valve open," says one observer. Finally, it may strike. Usually, though not always, it will rattle before striking.

Defense is not the main purpose of a rattler's fangs and venom. Primarily, they're for securing food. The two fangs, regularly replaced, are hollow precision instruments, sometimes as long as three quarters of an inch, each connected to a venom sac beneath the eye. When the fangs stab into a prey, the snake injects a controlled dose of venom from an aperture just above the fang's point. In the small mammals on which rattlers feed, the venom causes almost instant paralysis, rapid death. Quantity and strength of the venom vary widely. But, in general, the bigger the snake the greater the danger.

First-aid treatment recommended by many experts is cut-and-suck. Have the victim lie completely still, to slow the blood circulation and the spread of venom. If the bite is in an extremity, tie a bootlace an inch above the bite (between it and the heart) only tight enough to make surface veins stand out. Then, using a razor blade or knife, sterilize the blade in a match flame and open the fang marks with shallow cuts. Make the cuts in an X running lengthwise on arm, leg or hand, about ¼-inch long and ⅛-inch deep—just enough to cut through the skin without severing a nerve or artery. Then suck out the poison-filled blood with your mouth or a suction cup—the vital time for sucking is the first few seconds or minutes. Get the victim to a doctor as soon as possible.

Snakebite's greatest danger is probably hysteria. People bitten by harmless snakes have come close to dying from fright, and it is probably true that what a snakebite patient needs most is rest and reassurance.

Fortunately, rattlesnake bite is rare. Possibly 1100

Americans will be bitten this year, and 4 or 5 of these may die. But this figure includes people who have been badly frightened, some with weak hearts, and small children whose bodies cannot absorb the venom. A healthy, properly treated adult rarely succumbs. Even without treatment, odds on survival are long. Treat the rattlesnake with respect and he is likely to respond in kind.

Who Needs the Mole?

by George Heinold

EARLY one summer morning I received a telephone call from a neighbor. "Your dog's tearing up my lawn!" he howled.

I hustled over. There, barking as excitedly as if he had treed a panther, Bruno, my huge German shepherd, was ripping trenches in the immaculately groomed lawn. Turf flew in all directions as he frantically pursued a creature which was tunneling so close to the surface that I could see the ground rising. Bruno soon captured it—a common ground mole, a mere six inches of luxuriant gray fur. Then I saw, scattered about this disaster area, the bodies of three more moles which my mighty hunter had already unearthed and slain.

I knew moles as mouse-like little animals that live underground and disfigure lawns and gardens by raising unsightly mounds as they tunnel along. Some I caught rumpling my own lawn I'd swatted with the flat side of a spade—the simplest, most humane way for getting rid of them when you don't have the time to flatten their tunnels with a ground roller until they become discouraged enough to vacate. But it wasn't until Bruno's indiscretion cost me a week's pay that I began to take a serious interest in moles.

I learned that these creatures, belonging to the order *Insectivora,* are among the most valuable control agents of destructive insects nature ever designed. The common or Eastern ground mole appeases an appetite so voracious that he must consume close to his own weight in food every 24 hours, or perish. Not only does he devour astonishing quantities of Japanese beetles (and the underground larvae from which they develop), this burrowing trencherman also consumes cut-worms, wireworms, grubs and other garden enemies.

Householders are perturbed, however, by the ridges a mole creates, and the hills formed when a mole pushes excess soil through the roof of his tunnels. It is the mice which invade his tunnels that destroy vegetables and bulbs growing beneath the ground. Still, most of us blame the mole. And so we wage warfare againt our benefactor, with such mole-exterminating devices as harpoon, choker or scissor-jaw traps, or powerful poisons. One man I know attaches a hose to the exhaust pipe of his car, sticks the other end of the hose in tunnels, and destroys moles with carbon-monoxide asphyxiation.

Our unappreciated friend is scarcely a thing of beauty. Cylindrical in shape, he has no visible neck; nearly blind, his slits of eyes are just strong enough to distinguish between night and day. His awl-shaped snout is unattractive, his inch-long tail is naked, and most of us would rather shake hands with a lobster than grasp one of his rough, oversized forepaws.

But the fur of this tiny underground projectile is another matter. Called "moleskin," it looks well no matter how brushed, for it sets forward as well as backward. It is a prized fur for evening wear in Europe and has often been the garb of royalty. Because each skin is so small, a full-length coat requires about 300 moleskins. A similar coat could be made from about 50 mink pelts.

The young are born during March or April. The common mole has one yearly litter of three to six offspring—whereupon the father deserts home and family. The infants, completely blind, hairless and about the size of a black-eyed pea at birth, are nearly fully grown by the end of two months. With the coming of another spring, they themselves are ready to breed. The mole's life is short, a maximum of three years.

Unless evicted from his tunnels by such enemies as man, dogs, foxes or skunks, a mole emerges aboveground only in the early spring, to gather dry leaves and dead grasses for the nest. He does so at great risk. Poor eyesight and a weak sense of smell put him completely at the mercy of his enemies. Once while watching a mole search for nest grass. I caught sight of a shadow and, before I could look up, a diving hawk pounced on the mole, and airlifted him swiftly away. Another time, a large black snake caught a mole I was studying. On another occasion the executioner, to my amazement, was a crow.

But the battles a mole wages within his underground domain are another matter. With his sharp, sickle-shaped teeth, he can readily slay field mice, not much smaller than he is, and overcome even more impressive trespassers. While walking in a pasture one spring afternoon, I suddenly heard hisses, faint angry squeals and scuffling sounds. Then I saw the forward end of a two-foot-long black snake emerge writhing from a molehill. A mole was clinging to its stomach and slashing viciously. The badly wounded reptile soon expired, and the mole feasted until he was scarcely able to waddle back into his tunnel.

Moles wage war against one another, as well—particularly the males during the courtship season. Often, while visiting mole homesites in early spring, I have heard them fighting in their tunnels. And such fights are in deadly earnest.

Several years ago, in order to learn more about their dietary habits, I captured a pair of ground moles and placed them in separate cages in our garage. Then one day my young son rushed into my study. "Dad, I've pulled an awful goof!" he cried. "I thought those moles were lonesome, so I put them in the same cage. Now they're fighting—real hard!"

I ran into the garage but I was too late. One mole, his throat torn open, was already kicking his last. Ignoring the supply of insects and earthworms I'd placed in his cage less than an hour before, the winner was already dining on mole cutlet. In this case he ate his own weight—his opponent—in just 11 hours.

Whatever his personality defects, no one can deny that a mole is a leading mining engineer. His powerful, five-toed forepaws, much larger than his hind ones, are an efficient pair of shovels, ideal for excavating. In loose sandy soil, mole tunnels have been measured at over a mile in length. One mole that I captured and released took only 11 seconds to dig himself out of sight; in three minutes he had tunneled 14 inches. Naturalist Dr. Robert W. Hegner reported one mole that dug 68 feet in 25 hours, and another that dug 100 yards in a single night. He said, "To do a proportionate amount, a man would have to dig a tunnel 50 miles long, large enough for him to crawl through."

The industrious mole maintains two kinds of tunnels: the shallow type, which we see and from which he obtains most of his food during the warm months; and deeper excavations, some of them more than two feet belowground. These he uses in cold weather as well as in periods of drought. His dome-shaped dens are also deep, often built underneath protective boulders and stumps.

Of the seven species of moles distributed across our country, the eight-inch Western or Oregon Townsend mole is the largest. No true moles live in the far north because the ground freezes to too great a depth for them. There is an aquatic mole, the star-nosed species of our northerly and middle states, that lives in marshlands and around brooks and ponds and can swim and dive. But the common ground mole, which ranges from southern Canada southward to the lowlands of Florida, is non-aquatic—though he virtually "swims" through the earth with his powerful breaststroke.

As they burrow along in their constant pursuit of food, moles bring subsurface soil to the top, where it mixes with decaying vegetation and other organic material to create good, loamy topsoil. Moreover, mole tunnels act as irrigation systems in dry pasturelands, and as drainage conduits in our rich bottomlands. Thus, moles enrich our priceless soil and help to keep it fertile. All this, plus insect control—truly these miniature bulldozers in fur are more friend than pest.

A Mole's Prayer

I dig and dig,
looking
for life itself.

You have chosen darkness
for me, Lord,
and my tunnel
lengthens
in cavernous night.

A hidden life,
Lord,
but not a poor one—
my velvet coat shows that.

In shadowy gloom
one can walk without presumption
and be perfectly safe—
but the sun
can turn one's head.

Lord, keep me from
the vanities of the world,
and guide the strivings
of my little paws
so that they reach
some secret Paradise.

—Carmen Bernos de Gasztold

A Need for Human Friendship

The Divided Life of a Canada Goose

by Charles T. Drummond

JANE WAS a Canada goose. Her full name, Calamity Jane, arose from her strange and inauspicious birth: she came into this world on the back seat of an automobile, born prematurely as the result of a collision between that vehicle and a roadside pine.

I had fallen asleep at the wheel while returning from an expedition on which, under government permits, we had gathered flooded-out goose eggs. A maelstrom of flying glass, snow and dirt was followed by sudden silence; then came a tiny, insistent "peep, peep" from the rear seat. I looked to see a broken egg and a newly hatched gosling, still wet. To shelter it from the freezing temperature, I thrust the downy mite under my shirt, next to my skin. The peepings gradually quieted, and the uncomfortably clammy object turned warm and dry and almost unnoticeable.

The car would still run, and we limped home. The baby goose was put in a cardboard box and introduced to a diet of mash and chopped greens.

Jane flourished, and soon graduated to an outdoor playpen of wire mesh. When she wanted attention, she would peep raucously. But once satisfied—usually with either warmth or food—her protestations turned to the young Canada goose's fluty *chirr*, certainly one of nature's most charming sounds. With fierce loyalty she attached herself to my wife and me. Released from her pen, she would follow us wherever we went, a ball of olive-and-yellow fuzz toddling along on jet-black legs and feet.

When she was half-grown we began taking her with us about the ranch in the pick-up truck, letting her graze on grass while we inspected cattle or fences or tended to irrigation. Periodically my wife took Jane for a dip in the stream which ran past the fenced enclosure protecting 20 or 30 crippled geese of different species (our place has always been run as a private wildlife refuge). But the fledgling who lived with humans paid them no attention, considering herself a thing apart.

The day came when Jane was too large to fit into the truck cab with us. We placed plenty of feed in front of her and started off without her.

Suddenly my wife exclaimed, "She's coming!" I glanced in the mirror to see Jane running wildly after us, her not yet fully grown wings spread. In her frenzy she actually began to fly a little, and this was such a surprising experience that it threw her off and we were able to draw out of sight, behind some trees. In a moment we glimpsed Jane coming cross-lots, half-running, half-flying, and gabbling in near-hysteria. We took her in, moved almost to tears by the neck weavings with which she greeted us.

The next time we tried to sneak away, Jane took to the air. Flying unsteadily, she pulled ahead of us and landed in the road. We were forced to stop and take her aboard.

Within a few days Jane was flying alongside the truck wherever we went, honking and gabbling companionably. About 15 miles an hour seemed to suit her best.

We let her fly freely through the summer, but as the shooting season drew near we decided Jane would be safer in the enclosure with the other birds. So we clipped her right wing and, one evening feeding period, walked her down to the duck-and-goose pond. Seeing the others, she clung close to us like a child being taken to school for the first time. When I picked her up and threw her over the wire mesh fence, she paced back and forth, trying to get back to her human friends.

Ultimately she settled down contentedly with the other Canada geese, and spent the winter with them. But she was always the first to greet us at feeding time, and she never gave up honking disconsolately as we climbed the hill toward her former home.

The next spring an especially large wild Canada gander began to light daily in the marsh, clearly interested in something within the fenced area. A lordly chap, he was at first content to stalk the marsh and honk in stentorian tones. Then one day we spotted him inside the three-acre enclosure, sitting with another goose. His companion was Jane! Although she was really too young, by Canada goose standards, for the honor and responsibility, her human parents raised a toast that evening to her somewhat premature marriage.

We spied on the connubial pair shamefully, first with a pair of binoculars, later moving in for a closeup. Jane, on the nest, would lower her head and neck at our approach, but not to the same extent as a wild bird. The gander would withdraw to a far corner, fixing us with outstretched neck and beady eye.

Then one afternoon we came upon both birds sitting together at a distance from the nest. We had a premonition of disaster. Sure enough, at the nest-site we discovered scattered and mangled eggshells, torn feathers and general dishevelment. No bird could have done it; the gander was more than a match for any of the feathered tribe. Some predator must have leapt the fence to break up the nest. "Poor Jane!" we exclaimed, but she eyed us calmly, sitting on one leg in philosophical content.

Jane and "the wild one" remained together—the Canada goose usually mates for life—and when Jane's clipped wing feathers were shed and replaced, the gander lured her to far corners of the ranch. We saw them frequently, and invariably Jane would gabble and honk in recognition and waddle toward us. But the gander would sound warnings and make off in the opposite direction. Rather than cause domestic difficulties, we went our human way.

With the coming of spring we noticed that Jane was acting strangely. After eating grain at the back door, with the gander looking on disapprovingly from a distance, she would circle the house on foot, gazing at it speculatively. Then one morning at daylight my wife and I were awakened by the sound of measured footsteps on the roof.

"What in the world?" my wife gasped. She jumped from bed and ran outside.

"It's Jane!" she called.

That evening, seated in the living room, we were astonished to see Jane's head and neck appear suddenly over the edge of the roof. Her dark eyes were directed not at us but at the space under the eaves.

Of course! Her previous nest, fashioned in the duck-and-goose enclosure, had proved too vulnerable. Now she was looking for the securest possible spot, and what could be more secure than the top of the house in which her people lived? The idea apparently was not entirely agreeable to "the wild one"; during this house-hunting period he stood at a distance and honked reprovingly, but his wife merely talked back with great cheer and confidence.

"If she wants to nest on the roof, why don't we fix her a place?" my wife said. I found a wooden box, stuffed it with marsh grasses and fastened it at a spot where two roof lines converged—a site which would offer maximum protection from wind and sun. Next morning we were awakened by honks and gabbles and by the sound of Jane landing on the roof. She walked here and there, gabbling to herself. Suddenly sound and motion ceased. "She's found the box!" we exclaimed to each other.

After some seconds of silence Jane flew down to join her mate and gabbled earnestly with him. This time he rubbed necks with her, and the pair flew to the stream for a dip.

Early each day now both geese landed on the hillside near the house, and the gander assumed a watchful stance while Jane flew to the roof, entered her box and stayed an hour or so. After each visit I climbed a ladder, found that an egg had been laid. When there were four, Jane came for her "confinement." For four weeks all we could see of her was head and part of neck projecting above the nest-box. The gander spent this period half a mile upstream.

There was one daily interruption of this routine. About mid-morning Jane would start honking, and immediately, from half a mile away, would come the gander's answer. We learned from observation that at the same instant he would start flying. Jane would leave the nest and fly to the marsh where the two birds arrived almost simultaneously. Their meeting was transparently joyful: they honked and gabbled, rubbed necks and "billed" each other in true lover fashion. Jane then dipped and flapped in the water. A few minutes of sitting together while she preened and prinked concluded the morning's reunion.

We, meantime, were marking each day on the calendar.

The eggs should hatch 28 to 30 days from the beginning of incubation. Jane had to get her babies from the roof to the ground, a distance of some 12 feet, and we didn't want to miss the event. It is not unusual for Canada geese to nest in trees, but few human beings have witnessed the descent of the fledglings.

At dawn on the morning of the 29th day we heard Jane honk softly. This was a break in the usual pattern. Surely it signified something. I ran out to look, and there, standing on Jane's back, was a mite of a gosling! While I stood watch, my wife prepared breakfast and we ate by separate windows. Another baby appeared, and then another. Presently four goslings were scrambling about in the nest.

Suddenly Jane stood up and honked, full voice. The gander answered from the meadow, and soon he landed only 50 feet from the house. Spying Jane and his offspring at the roof's edge, he broke into redoubled honkings. Jane answered back. The result was bedlam.

Now Jane flew to the ground, and both of them walked close to the house, looking up at the babies. These balls of fluff were running about in some distraction, but it was evident that one of them was a creature of decision. He simply walked to the roof's edge and jumped off. He hit the ground with no indication of shock. We realized that his weight was so slight and his down so thick that he probably hardly felt the impact. He scuttled under his mother's body, and that was that.

Three remained. One of them approached the edge, looked down, drew back. He did this again and again until he was inadvertently bumped by one of the others and he had to go, quite unprepared. He hit the ground headfirst, but quickly righted himself and hurried to mama. The third gosling stepped off purely by mistake. The fourth and last was a showman. Stepping well back and pausing dramatically, he made a run for the precipice and launched himself into space in a veritable swan dive—head well up, tiny wings working madly. He landed well, and walked sedately to join the family group.

It was done. Jane turned downhill and led for the water. The gander trailed by several feet. Between them trotted the four fuzzy moppets, single file. It was a touching tableau.

We saw Jane and the wild one and their four youngsters on the lakes fairly frequently through the summer. Toward fall, we spied them flying together several times. Then the wild geese came in from the north, and for several months there were too many birds about to distinguish our friends.

After the shooting season, Jane did not reappear. That winter the wild one came around alone. For a week or so he sat with head under wing or stood on some vantage point and honked. Then one day we discovered his dead body, unmarked by violence, not far from the site of Jane's original marshland nest.

His death is hard to explain; it is possible that it was an affair of the heart. But Jane, we feel sure, came to grief through her divided personality. She regarded humans as her friends and protectors, and may well have flown within murderous range of a hunter's gun.

Since Jane, I have never shot at a Canada goose.

The Day I Met Midnight

by Ulmont Healy

IT WAS my first day on the ranch in California's San Fernando Valley. I was 20, and I was going to learn to be a cowboy. In my brand-new outfit—blue jeans, boots, bandanna and cheap Stetson—I felt self-conscious and a bit nervous. Sitting on the top rail of the corral, I watched the loops snake out among the milling horses, as one by one the men roped their mounts and led them outside to saddle up.

A white mustang in the bunch caught my eye. He was a beauty—lovely head and neck, trim legs, deep chest and good quarters. Just my kind of horse, I thought—strong and speedy. I wondered whose he was.

The straw boss's voice interrupted my thoughts. "Can you ride, kid?"

George, a lanky six-footer in a high-crowned hat that made him seem even taller, had looked me over skeptically the day before when he hired me, on a trial basis, at $30 a month and found. Now he grinned at me reassuringly.

"Yes, some," I said.

I was careful not to make any claims. Back home on our farm in Wisconsin my father had taught us boys what he knew about handling horses. Dad made us break them to ride without a saddle—he said they became gentler that way. So I thought I knew horses a little. But these men were professional wranglers. Also, one of them had tipped me off the night before. "These fellows take you for a tenderfoot, kid," he said. "They'll put you on a horse that will try to throw you."

George's voice was casual. "Anything there you like, kid?"

I pointed to the white mustang. *"He's* a lot of horse," I said.

"Yeah." George's arm moved. The mustang whirled like a flash, but too late. The noose settled over his head, and he came in snorting. George tied a piece of quarter-inch rope around his neck and handed the other end to me.

"We call him Midnight," George said. "When you get the mud off him, take him down to the shed and I'll fix you up with saddle and bridle and a rope."

I led Midnight outside and tied him to the rail, then got a brush. I was doing pretty well at cleaning him when my brush touched his left hock. His kick was so quick that only reflex action saved me. I stepped away and looked at his head. He was looking me right in the eye, and I knew he was not afraid.

You can read a horse's character from his head. Midnight had small ears and the broad forehead and wide-spaced eyes that indicate intelligence. But more than anything else there was a quality of spirit that looked out at me. With a head like that I didn't think he could be vicious. But he was an outlaw; he was at war against men.

"That's good enough," George said. He was sitting his horse with his rope in hand, the noose open.

I walked to Midnight's head and untied him. It was then I noticed that not a single man was mounted except George; they were all busy about their gear. They were waiting to see whether I would lead or ride the horse to the shed.

I put a half-hitch on Midnight's nose, and before he realized it I was on his back. We went away from there in standing leaps, and suddenly the men were all in the saddle with George in the lead. Their yells were enough to scare any horse, but I managed to keep Midnight's head up, and the ride ended at the shed. I quickly slipped off his back. I wanted no more until I had a saddle on him.

I stepped to his head to remove the torturing half-hitch, and as I touched it he reared, struck me in the chest and left shoulder with his front hoofs and knocked me spinning in the dust. He came after me screaming, his teeth bared, but I kept rolling until I was under the shed loading platform.

Then I saw the reason for George's open loop. He had

that horse roped and drawn up to his saddle before I got my first full breath. He watched while I brushed off the dust.

"You all right?" he asked.

"Yeh," I said. "Nice roping."

"Would you rather have another horse today and top this one off sometime when you feel better?"

I was mad to my toes. "No. If I could ride that black-hearted so-and-so bareback, I can ride him all day. Show me a saddle and bridle. We're gonna get acquainted."

George turned to one of the cowboys. "Shorty, dig out some gear and we'll get Slim and Midnight on the way to getting acquainted."

Well! Now it was "Slim"—not just "Kid." Shorty stepped down from his horse and passed me with a grin. I tried to grin back. He returned with a good double-rigged saddle and bridle. Midnight objected throughout the proceedings but, with George holding his head and Shorty helping, we got it done.

"Want me to hold him while you get set?" George asked.

My left shoulder and arm felt nearly normal. I looked at Midnight. "I don't think so," I said. "Maybe I can make him think it isn't important if I just step into the saddle."

George gave me an honest grin and turned Midnight loose.

Quietly, with the reins in my left hand I took hold of the left cheek strap of his bridle, put my right hand on the saddle horn, pulled him toward me, and as he started to turn I went into the saddle. Strangely enough, Midnight didn't seem to think it was important.

Then the foreman gave us orders for the day. We were to comb a certain area and bring in everything, particularly every longhorn we found. The boss had an offer from a motion-picture firm for all the longhorns he could furnish. There weren't many, perhaps a carload, but he wanted them off the place.

So we went to work. Midnight fought his head continually, but he was sure-footed and quick. We had brought quite a few cattle down the coulees when suddenly I saw sticking up from the brush the longest pair of horns I had ever seen. As we closed in, the steer made a fast break up a knoll. Now, a longhorn can run like a deer, and my respect for Midnight went up several notches when he turned that steer and kept him going through the live oaks and the greasewood beyond.

But suddenly the steer raised up and leaped over something. We were going too fast to stop: either hit the obstacle or jump. I gave Midnight my heels and lifted the reins. That beautiful, obstinate son of Satan chose that moment to fight the bit and blundered straight into a patch of cactus that the steer had jumped over.

By the time I got Midnight stopped on an open sandy spot my right knee felt as though it was on fire from the cactus spines in it. I had a notion I had ruined my horse. Luckily, I was wearing buckskin gloves and could pick the spines out of my knee; they work deeper if you move around. Then I got out of the saddle. Midnight was a mess from his nose to his heels. I knew from the pain in my leg what he must be suffering, but he stood perfectly still, looking at me with a question in his eyes that brought a lump to my throat.

Just then Joe, the foreman, rode up. He looked Midnight over carefully. "We can't get them out without tying him down," he said. "And if we do that they'll just work into him deeper until they kill him. Better take your saddle off, Slim." He drew his revolver.

"No, Joe, wait," I said. "I got him into this. I want to get him out if I can. Just stand by and let me try."

The foreman hesitated. "Okay," he said, finally. "But stay out of line with his head, because the first mean move he makes I'm going to put a bullet in him."

I reached out to Midnight's nose and picked off two strong spines driven in just above and between his nostrils. He flinched and looked startled, but made no move to retaliate.

By the time I got his face and neck clean, his ears had come forward. On down I worked and he never moved a muscle, though his coat was turning gray with sweat. Joe sat his horse quietly, and now and then I heard a gentle cuss word.

Down to Midnight's front hoofs, back on his sides and belly, down his hind legs, and he stood like a statue. I even took a large piece of cactus out of his tail. As I finished each section, I took off my gloves and ran my hands over him to make sure that I had gotten all the spines. Finally I stepped around to Midnight's head and looked at Joe. He took a deep breath and put away his gun.

"I'm obliged to you," I said, and I meant it.

"It's the damnedest thing I ever saw," said Joe. He looked at his watch, then off to where the men were moving the cattle to the corrals. "It's time for dinner. Let's go in."

As we rode in he gave me something of Midnight's history. He had been a stallion in a herd of wild horses, and he had never stopped fighting. This morning, Joe said, was the first time he'd seen Midnight use his front hoofs and teeth on a man, though. "I expect it was that half-hitch you had on his nose that made him so mad."

"I reckon that was it," I replied. "He just doesn't like men."

"No, he don't like men, and if you'd had the same treatment that he's had since he first met men, you wouldn't like them either."

We watered our horses and led them under a covered tie-rack where they would be in the shade.

"No need to tie 'em," Joe said. "They'll stand."

Joe went in to dinner, while I went to the bunkhouse to get out a cactus spine that had broken off under my trousers.

When I entered the cook shack, I was greeted with a chorus of remarks about my riding and given instructions about the various parts of a saddle and bridle, with explicit directions as to the purpose of the reins. Nothing was said about cactus. But Krimpy, the ranch-house joker, remarked, "If you're gonna follow a steer that close in the brush, ride the steer and give your horse a rest."

They were kidding in a way that let me know I was accepted.

After dinner someone produced a bat, ball and gloves and we started up a game of ball. I was taking a lead off third base and was pleading with Krimpy, who was at bat, to bring me home, when everyone stopped and stared at me. Suspecting a trick, I clapped my foot back on third—and received a push in the back that knocked me off the base.

I turned, and there was Midnight, standing quietly looking at me. He had walked out from the cool shade of the horse rack, trailing his reins.

I said, very gently, "Midnight, what are you doing here?"

He came forward two steps and, putting his head against my chest, began to move it up and down slowly. My hands came up and found the soft velvety spots behind his ears. I was aware of the cowboys gathering around and soft oaths of wonderment. Midnight had taken out his spite on most of them, and they could not believe their eyes.

George's chuckle broke the quiet. "Well, Slim, it sure looks like you and Midnight got acquainted."

"Yeah," was all I could say. The lump was back in my throat again.

Joe broke it up with, "Let's go, men." Then, as they turned away, he dropped a final word. "I don't want to see any of you dabbing a rope on Midnight. He's Slim's horse from now on."

I reckon he's still my horse in whatever pasture of Paradise he roams, for he gave me the love of his wild heart as none of the many horses I've known ever could. Those days are far gone, but the memory of Midnight is still as bright as the day he put his head against my chest to thank me and to say that he was sorry and wanted to be friends.

The Tale of That Rabbit

by R. M. Lockley

MR. X was a tabby cat with a white bow tie. Lordly and lazy, he was a much-indulged neuter, with his own fireside basket and a cat door on the back porch of our country home. Occasionally he would bring in a field mouse to prove he had earned his breakfast bowl of milk.

One January morning, my young son Martin rushed in screaming that Mr. X had caught a baby rabbit and was about to kill it. The victim was a tiny, gray-brown ball of fur, too terrified to do more than stay hunched up as the cat boxed with his paw. Its left ear bled from two punctures made by Mr. X's fangs.

"Save it, Daddy!" Tears of despair were in Martin's eyes as he stamped his feet, scaring the cat enough for me to grab the little rabbit, which flopped sideways in my arms, apparently dead from shock.

That Rabbit (as she became known, or TR for short) was kept alive only by Martin's determination that she should not die. She was barely breathing, but he hugged her for more than an hour. When at last she woke from her coma, she stayed hunched up, eyes closed, refusing all food. In the evening, Martin and I force-fed her with milk laced with glucose and brandy, through the rubber tube from my fountain pen. Then Martin sat up all night, watching her uneasy breathing as she lay wrapped in a doll's blanket in Mr. X's basket. Mr. X was furious at this indignity, but Martin sensibly made him stay in the room, determined that he must be taught never again to harm That Rabbit.

At breakfast, Martin yawned hugely, satisfied. "TR's going to live. She actually preened her whiskers after the last milk and brandy." Later, I brought her a handful of dandelion and clover leaves from the garden. Just as Martin was saying gloomily, "That Rabbit is much too young for solid food," TR crept forward and ate a leaf slowly, thoughtfully. After she had eaten the whole bunch, she suddenly hopped out of the basket, jumped into the air, did a little pirouette, then walked back to the basket, where she sat hunched up—apparently with a bad attack of indigestion.

On our property I had built some large, wire-netting enclosures in which I was studying, under near-natural conditions, the social structure of the wild-rabbit community. Now Martin refused to allow me to solve the problem of looking after TR while he was away at school by placing her in the safety of my enclosures. Quite rightly, he argued that the big rabbits would bully little TR, but the real reason was that he wanted to keep her as a pet.

So, That Rabbit became a full member of our household, and to my amazement (since it is notoriously difficult to tame and train a wild rabbit) exhibited an extraordinary confidence and intelligence from the start. Of course we were prejudiced, but her swift responses and affectionate behavior won our love and esteem.

TR became excessively playful. After tea (she liked hers weak with sugar), she would start some game or other. Catch-if-you-can was a favorite, and developed into hide-and-seek. She would run under the furniture, but if you were too long in discovering her she would stamp her feet as a clue to her whereabouts, and presently her splendid whiskers would emerge triumphantly round the leg of a sofa or armchair.

She enjoyed the freedom of the whole house and would often run upstairs, peering from behind corners to make sure you were following. (She was absolutely clean indoors, having quickly learned to run outside through Mr. X's private cat door—another humiliation for him.)

Her method of communicating with us gradually developed into clearly recognized signals. A grunting "Uh-huh" was her pleased affirmative; a stamp of the foot, a polite negative; two or more stamps signified a resolute "No," or anger, or fear; a sideways twist of the head and one eye up at you meant she hoped for your attention; a sibilant wheeze was her way of imitating my often-uttered "Please!" This pleading noise always preceded her attempts to get me to play.

Relations with the cat were strained. Warned by us never to hurt her, Mr. X stalked from his basket when she approached, his tail lashing with anger made more furious by her attempts to play with that noble appendage. Suddenly, one evening, we were amazed to find them reclining side by side on the hearth rug. Mr. X was purring as he lovingly licked TR. Then I remembered that I had found TR digging a hole under the catnip that afternoon. She still smelled of the plant—irresistible to almost any cat. After that they were close friends, though TR dominated the basket.

Rambling in the garden was TR's delight, but it took me many hours to teach her not to nibble and scratch in the flower beds and vegetable garden. By using her own language of a double stamp of my foot and a loud "No!" I scared her into obeying; but it was essential to say "Uh-huh" and praise her when she behaved well.

I would confine her within a movable wire pen for exercise and grazing when no one was free to amuse her. This was a success for a few days, but one afternoon she had to be placed there forcibly, stamping her feet with resentment.

Her sudden hatred of the pen proved to be terror: that day the weasel which, unknown to us, had been trying to enter the pen, succeeded. Paralyzed with fear, TR cowered helplessly, finally uttering a long, quavering "scream." Fortunately, I was nearby and rescued her before the weasel seized her.

Hours later, when she had recovered from her glassy-eyed coma, I promised TR I would never shut her up again: "If a weasel ever chases you, just run straight through the cat door and into my study. The door will always be open."

She understood all too well, and thereafter took to following me around. On a wet day, when she did not care to be outside, she would sit at the edge of my desk while I tried to get on with my work.

Sometimes, when she had pulled at my shoelaces for attention, she would ignore my foot stamp and loud request to get lost, then suddenly leap into my lap, and onto my desk. She would end up sitting on the book I was reading or the letter I was writing. And then what else could I do but pick her up and solemnly kiss her soft, whiskered face, admire her bold, beautiful eyes, and tell her she was an intolerable nuisance?

Rabbits have a gland beneath the chin from which they exude droplets of scent to mark territory and possessions. When I fondled her, TR "chinned" me with her faint aromatic scent; and with this rabbit's kiss she claimed and reclaimed me as her personal property.

She seemed to get satisfaction out of observing me and liked to listen to me talking. At such times, she would remain perfectly still, with one ear flopped down as if my voice was loud enough half-heard. When I stopped talking, she would flip up both ears and move restlessly as if to say, "Well, go on. Let's hear the rest."

Her sociability was such that on our walks she would not stray far from me. At the first sign of danger, such as a cat, dog or hawk, she would come running and leap into my arms, cradled to receive her.

By autumn, TR had grown into a sleek, mature, less playful, more independent creature. No longer afraid of visitors' dogs, she would stand firm, say her "No" foot stamp and strike with her sharp claws. One November night, she was so late in returning from her evening grazing that I went to the porch and called her. She loped back to Mr. X's basket, where she preened a lot of earth from her fur. "She's digging a burrow," announced my knowledgeable son. "I saw her this afternoon, up in the woods. Just look at the size of her tummy."

Somehow TR had found a mate, though we never saw him. Her first litter appeared just before Christmas; four babies emerged from the burrow, which had been cunningly stopped with earth during the first days while they were blind and naked. In the following months, TR and her mysterious mate produced four more litters—and with each she became less attached to us. Finally, her house calls ceased. But she did allow me to visit her.

Aided by her mate, TR repopulated the empty woods and fields rapidly. The daughters of her first litter were breeding that same summer, making That Rabbit a grandmother, as undisputedly queen and matriarch of a flourishing dynasty as she had been of our house.

"Where There Is Love"

by Aletha Jane Lindstrom

WE GOT HIM with the other animals when we bought the farm. Not that we wanted the black, shaggy mongrel. We had our hearts set on a collie—a pup we could train for the farm and as a companion for five-year-old Tim. But when the former owners failed to return for their dog, we resigned ourselves to keeping him. Temporarily, we thought.

"If we ignore him, maybe he'll just take off," I said to Carl, my schoolteacher husband. He didn't. In fact, the big beast apparently considered the farm *his* responsibility. Each dawn, he inspected the animals and the farm buildings. Then he made a complete circuit of the entire 80 acres. That finished, he bounded across the sloping fields to slip beneath the fence for a visit with old Mr. Jolliff, who lived near a brook at the farm's edge.

The big dog—we learned from Mr. Jolliff that his name was Inky—was pensive and aloof those first weeks. Grieving for his former master, Inky asked no affection, and we offered none. Except Tim, who sat by the hour on the back steps, talking softly to the unresponsive animal. Then, one morning, Inky crept close and laid his head in the boy's lap. And before we knew it, he had become Tim's second shadow.

And that summer the boy and the dog romped through fields and roamed the woods, discovering fox dens and groundhog burrows. Each day, they brought back treasures to share. "Mom, we're home!" Tim would shout, holding the screen door wide for Inky. "Come see what we've got!" He'd dig deep in his jeans and spread the contents on the kitchen table: a pheasant's feather; wilted buttercups with petals like wet paint; stones from the brook that magically regained their colors when he licked them.

September arrived all too soon, bringing with it school for Carl and Tim, and lonely days for Inky and me. Previously, I'd paid little attention to the dog. Now he went with me to the mailbox, to the chicken coop, and down the lane when I visited Mr. Jolliff.

"Why didn't they come back for Inky?" I asked Mr. Jolliff one afternoon.

"And shut him up in a city apartment?" Mr. Jolliff replied. "Inky's a farm dog; he'd die in the city. Besides, you're lucky to have him."

Lucky? I thought ruefully of holes dug in the lawn, of freshly washed sheets ripped from the clothesline. I thought, too, of litter dumped on the back porch: old bones, discarded boots, long-dead rodents. And beer cans! Each morning, on his way home from Mr. Jolliff's, Inky retrieved one can from the roadside and placed it neatly on the doorstep. He was noisy, too, challenging each truck and tractor on the road with loud barks that brought me running.

Still, I had to admit that Inky was a good farm dog. We learned this in early spring when his insistent barking alerted us to a ewe, about to lamb, lying on her broad back in a furrow, unable to rise. Without Inky's warning she'd have died. And he had an uncanny way of knowing when roving dogs threatened the flock, or when a sheep went astray.

One morning, instead of a beer can, Inky placed a starving gray kitten on the doorstep. He hovered anxiously while the fluffy mite lapped her fill of warm milk. Then he carried her to his blanket in the barn, licked her thoroughly and settled down beside her while she slept. From that day on she shared his bed.

But Inky's deepest affection was reserved for Tim. Each afternoon when the school bus lumbered down the road, Inky ran joyously to meet it. For Inky—and for Tim—this was the high point of the day.

One mid-October day when I had been in town, Tim rode home with me after school. He was instantly alarmed when Inky wasn't waiting for us by the driveway.

"Don't worry, Tim," I said. "Inky always expects you on the bus, and we're early. Maybe he's back by the woods."

Tim ran down the lane, calling and calling. While I waited for him to return, I looked around the yard. Its emptiness was eerie.

Suddenly I, too, was alarmed. With Tim close behind me, I ran down to the barn. We pushed the heavy doors apart and searched the dim coolness. Nothing. Then, as we were about to leave, a faint whimper came from the far corner of a horse stall. There we found him, swaying slightly on three legs, his pain-dulled eyes pleading for help. Even in the half-light I could see that one back leg hung limp, the bone partially severed. With a little moan, Tim ran to Inky and buried his face in the dog's neck.

By the time the vet arrived, Carl was home. We placed the dog on his blanket and gently lifted him into the pet ambulance. Inky whimpered, and Tim started to cry.

"Don't worry, son," the vet said. "He's got a good chance." But his eyes told a different story.

It was Tim's bedtime, so I took him upstairs and heard his prayers. He finished and looked up. "Will Inky be home tomorrow?"

"Not tomorrow, Tim. He's hurt pretty bad."

"You tell me that doctors make people well. Doesn't that mean dogs, too?"

I looked out across the fields flooded with amber light. How do you tell a little boy that his dog must either die, or be a cripple? "Yes, Tim," I said at last. "I guess that means dogs, too." I tucked in his blanket and went downstairs.

Carl had finished chores and was getting ready for a meeting at school. I tossed a sweater over my shoulders. "I'm going down to Mr. Jolliff's," I said. "Maybe he'll know what happened."

I found the old man sitting at his kitchen table in the fading light. He drew up another chair and poured coffee. "Tim in bed?" he asked. "I miss him now he's in school. Thank goodness Inky still comes to see me. Though come to think of it, he didn't show up this morning. I sort of worried about him."

Somehow I couldn't talk about the dog. Instead, I asked, "Do you know if anyone was cutting weeds around here today?"

"Seems to me I heard a tractor down along the brook this morning," Mr. Jolliff replied. "Why?" He looked at me. "Did something happen to Inky?"

"Yes," I said, and the words were right in my throat. "His back leg's nearly cut off. The vet came for him. . . ." I wanted to say more, but couldn't. "It's growing dark," I finally murmured. "I'd better be getting home."

Mr. Jolliff followed me into the yard. "About Inky," he said hesitantly, "if he lives, I'd give him a chance. He'll still have you folks and Tim, the farm and the animals. Everything he loves. Life's pretty precious . . . especially where there's love."

"Yes," I said, "but if he loses a leg, will love make up for being a cripple?"

He said something I didn't catch. But when I turned to him, he'd removed his glasses and was rubbing the back of his stiff old hand across his eyes.

By the time I reached our yard the sun was gone, leaving the world to the magic of cool, thin silver and shadow. I walked down by the barn and stood with my arms on the top fence rail. Beyond the lane the horses were moving toward the woods, grazing as they went. I watched until they vanished like phantoms in the moonlit mist brimming the meadow. Then I dropped my head to my arms and let the tears come.

I cried because Inky had been so gentle with the animals, and because he loved Tim so much, and Tim loved him. But mostly I cried because I hadn't really wanted him; not until now, when this terrible thing had happened. Why do we so seldom know how much we love something until we are faced with its loss?

INKY'S PAW couldn't be saved. Too vividly, I recalled how Inky had raced across fields and meadows, swift and free as a cloud shadow. I listened skeptically as the vet tried to reassure us: "He's young and strong. He'll get along on three legs."

Tim took the news with surprising calmness. "It's all right," he said. "Just so Inky comes home."

"But those long jaunts the two of you take may tire him now," I cautioned.

"He's always waited for me. I'll wait for him. Besides, we're never in much of a hurry."

The vet called a few days later. "You'd better come for

your dog. He's homesick." I went immediately, and was shocked at the change in Inky. The light was gone from his eyes. His tail hung limp and tattered, and the stump of his leg was swathed in a stained bandage. He hobbled over and pressed wearily against my leg. A shudder went through the hot, thin body and he sighed—a long, deep sigh filled with all the misery and loneliness of the past few days.

At the farm, I helped Inky from the car. The gray kitten came tumbling through the leaves, but Inky seemed unaware of her. He looked first to the sheep, grazing in the pasture; then, beyond the fields of green winter wheat, to the autumn woods where the horses, dappled with sunlight, moved among the trees. My heart ached as I realized how great must have been his longing for this place. At last, he limped to the barn and slipped between the heavy doors.

While his wound healed, Inky stayed in the barn, coming out only in the evenings. When the low sun slanted across the fields and the horses came up for water, we'd see him standing by the trough. After the horses returned to pasture, he disappeared into the barn.

Throughout those days the sick feeling never left me. *You are a coward to let him live,* I told myself. *Afraid of hurting yourself, of hurting Tim.* But in my heart I wasn't sure. We so seldom know the real reasons for the things we do, or fail to do.

About a week after bringing Inky home, I was in the yard raking leaves. When I'd finished under the maple, I sat on the steps to rest. It was a perfect Indian summer day; our country road was a tunnel of gold, and sumac ran like a low flame along the south pasture. Reluctantly, I reached for the rake.

Then, with a flurry of leaves, Inky was beside me. I knelt and stroked the fur so smooth and shiny again. He moved, and I was achingly aware of the useless limb. "I'm so sorry, Inky," I said, putting my arms around his neck and pressing my head against his.

Sitting awkwardly, he placed his paw on my knee and looked up at me with soft, intelligent eyes. Then he pricked his ears and turned to listen. In an instant, he was off to meet the school bus. He ran with an ungainly, one-sided lope—but he ran with joy.

Tim jumped from the high step and caught the dog in

his arms. "Oh, Inky! Inky!" he cried. Inky licked Tim's face and twisted and squirmed with delight. They remained there for a time, oblivious to anything but the ecstasy of being together again.

Watching them, I knew we'd been right to let the dog live. Most of us, God's creatures, are maimed to some extent either physically or emotionally, yet few of us want to die. What was it Mr. Jolliff had said?

"Life's pretty precious . . . especially where there's love."

A Fish Named Ulysses

by Jacques-Yves Cousteau with James Dugan

OUR UNDERSEA exploration had taken us to the Indian Ocean, and one day we dropped *Calypso*'s anchor in crystal-clear water just off Assumption, a tiny scimitar-shaped atoll near the equator. I passed the word that we would stay three or four hours and have a look around.

Jean Delmas, a member of our research team, was the first to dive. He went head down through the looking glass into the most enormous vistas he had ever scanned in the underwater world. The sea was transparent for 200 feet in every direction. The corals were richer than anything he had ever seen; the fish were more plentiful and had no fear. They came in multitudes, wearing every color imaginable. He stumbled back on deck under his heavy gear and said to me, "Let's stay here for a while. This is the place to make friends with fish."

Before I could reply, Luis Marden returned with the second relay of divers, and he was just as enthusiastic. "It is incredible down there," he said. "When I tried to take close-up photographs of the fish, they came too near to stay in focus. When I backed off, they came with me."

Then two more divers went under water—veteran, objective men, Frédéric Dumas and Albert Falco—and came out babbling. I couldn't get a sober report from either of them. I hefted an Aqua-Lung onto my back.

Under water, while I still had a hand on the ladder, I was enslaved by Assumption Reef myself. I climbed back and announced that we would stay as long as our fresh water lasted.

The structure of the island was classic. A shallow fringing reef, sparkling with sunshine and dancing color, extended perhaps 300 feet from the white beach. It dropped off rather abruptly in a chaos of standing coral and grottoes to about 200 feet, where a gray sedimental plain faded away into the ocean. Every foot of the slope was laden with coral unsurpassed in richness and beauty. Along the bank, mixing in friendly anarchy, were most of the species of fish we had met in a thousand different places and a quantity of new ones we had never seen before—as well as some that no one had ever seen. One incredible little fish sported a body pattern of perfect red and white squares—literally a swimming checkerboard. Among the animals there prevailed a spirit of mutual interest and confidence. It was almost as though the struggle for life were suspended and the Peaceable Kingdom had been translated into the bosom of the water.

We stayed 40 days, and none of us lost our enthusiasm for Assumption Reef. One of the reasons was a remarkable fish Luis Marden encountered—a 60-pound grouper with a brownish coat and a pale, marbled pattern that changed from time to time. The huge fish strolled up to Marden, and he prepared to take its portrait. The grouper nudged the flashbulb bag with its nose. Luis backed away to get proper focus. The fish followed. By a series of retreats, Marden finally shot it in focus and swam away to find other fish. The grouper tagged along, nuzzling the photographer and his glittering gadgets. As Luis lined up another subject, the big fish interposed itself in the camera field. The diver dodged and made his shot.

When Marden told us about his new acquaintance, we went down into the grouper's territory with a canvas bag full of chopped meat. The big fish came to us without hesitation. When we released some food in the water, the grouper's cavernous mouth opened. Like a flock of birds entering a tunnel, the meat scraps vanished. When we experimented cautiously with hand feeding, the big fish plucked meat off our fingertips harmlessly. We named the clever beast Ulysses.

Ulysses became our inseparable friend. He followed us everywhere, sometimes brushing against our rubber fins. When, after deep dives, we decompressed 30 feet down on a weighted and measured cable, Ulysses relieved our boredom by horsing around with us until we went up the ladder. Afterward he would hang around just under the surface, like a boy sadly watching his playmates being called in to supper.

Ulysses quickly got on to our diving schedule and would be found early in the morning waiting under the ladder for the day's first sortie. He would go bounding down with us for a round of clumsy mischief and meals from the canvas bag.

In a good mood Ulysses would let any of us pat him and scratch his head. Once Dumas, partially concealing the meat bag in his hand, turned in a slow, three-step tempo. Following the bait around, Ulysses joined the dance. When Dumas spun the other way, the fish followed right on the beat. It was done so lightly and rhythmically that we were able to film it as a waltz.

But Ulysses had a temper, too. Sometimes he bungled into camera set-ups, and we would have to shove him away. Then he would flounce off, slamming the door behind him. His first tail stroke was so powerful that it made an audible boom. He also grew angry with us when we forgot to bring the meat bag. He would hang 30 feet off, keeping that distance whether we went toward him or away from him. But, invariably, the following morning he would be waiting under the diving ladder again, grievances forgotten.

One morning, as Delmas opened the canvas meat sack to feed Ulysses, the big grouper made a rapid dash, tore the sack from Delmas' hand and swallowed it whole. Then he marched brazenly away, well aware that there was no more food forthcoming.

The next morning there was no Ulysses under the ladder. In the afternoon we spread out to look for him. We found him lying on the sand in front of his den, a deep crevice in the coral hardly big enough to contain him, but with the security of two entrances. The lair was 30 feet down, opening on a terrace of white sand. The entries were polished by his comings and goings. The place might as well have had his nameplate on the door.

But Ulysses was not enjoying his terrace this day. His gills were pulsing at an unreasonable rate. He had no interest in us. The following morning he was still in bed. On the third day, we found the fish flat on his side, seemingly critically ill.

I consulted our ship's surgeon, Dr. Denis Martin-Laval, who said Ulysses was in danger of a fatal intestinal obstruction. Martin-Laval was confronted with his most unusual case. Since he could not bring the fish to his surgery, he prepared to operate in the patient's bedroom. He gathered anesthetics, knives, surgical clips, and catgut and needle to suture the opening after he had removed the bag from Ulysses' tortured interior. The surgeon briefed three divers to act as his assistants. It was sundown before the preparations were completed. We went to sleep hoping that Ulysses could last through the night.

At first light, a reconnaissance team plunged. Ulysses was gone from his veranda. Several divers roamed about, looking for him. One felt somebody pulling at his back harness. It was Ulysses, announcing that everything was okay. He was gay and hungry. He had managed to eliminate the meat sack.

We experimented with feeding other denizens of the reef, and they all responded heartily. Watching us feed them put Ulysses in a towering rage. He would crash into the sack, bite our fins, tug on our bathing trunks and whip his big tail to scatter the smaller fish.

We wanted to film a golden host of yellow snappers following a manfish across the reef, but Ulysses kept breaking it up. Finally we assembled our anti-shark cage and dropped it to the bottom. Ulysses supervised the placing of the cage and the opening of the door. Delmas waved his feeding arm toward the opening, and the grouper swam in. The door clanked shut and Ulysses was in protective custody.

Delmas decided that Ulysses should have a special treat while he was in jail. That day we had killed a 20-pound barracuda. We took it down to the cage, and poked its head through the bars.

Without hesitation Ulysses gulped in half the barracuda's body, which was as long as he was, leaving the tail end sticking out from his jaws. Ulysses seemed to regard this as nothing out of the ordinary and remained for hours with the barracuda protruding from his mouth. When we left for the night, about a third of the barracuda was still visible. In the morning it was gone. We were puzzled over how Ulysses managed it. Apparently he simply turned on his gastric juices to melt away the front end, bones and all, and ingested the rest when he had made room for it.

Ulysses was caged for three days while we filmed the feeding of the others. When we opened the jail door, he watched with interest but made no move to depart. Considering the abundant food we provided him in the cage, he preferred to stay there. When we pushed him through the door, Ulysses swam off in a sulk, at a much slower pace than usual. He was fat and out of shape.

After five weeks at the reef, we ran low on food. I asked Delmas to go down and spear a grouper. I accompanied him, and so did Ulysses. It was like hunting with a retriever dog. Delmas selected a black grouper and triggered his speargun. As though synchronized with the flight of the spear, Ulysses hit the fish at practically the same instant. The fish's tail and the four-foot harpoon protruded from Ulysses' mouth. Delmas placed his foot against our friend's head and heaved hard to extract the spear. This gave Ulysses more room to accommodate the catch, and he swallowed it all except the tip of the tail. We returned to *Calypso* and told the hungry mob that our pet had eaten their dinner.

The time had come to continue our cruise. "Let's take Ulysses with us," Delmas suggested. The idea was met with enthusiasm, but I had to oppose the notion. In France, Ulysses would face life imprisonment in an aquarium, or he would have to be liberated in the Mediterranean. He was probably not adapted for colder water. On top of that, he was so friendly that the first spearman he met would have an easy kill. We dived for the last time and waved good-by to our friend.

Later, after Ulysses had become a movie star in our film, *The Silent World,* a boat sailing around the world made a special call at Assumption Bay and sent divers down to look for the tame grouper. They reported, "Ulysses is doing fine. He was easy to recognize. He swam up immediately to the divers." Perhaps we will go back someday and find Ulysses again. He is a fish worth going halfway around the world to see.

That Quail, Robert

by Margaret A. Stanger

ON THAT morning of July 15, 1962, my close friends and neighbors, Dr. and Mrs. Thomas Kienzle, took me into the kitchen of their house in Orleans on Cape Cod—and invited me to look into a carton. At first I saw nothing but a small lamp, a lamb's-wool duster and receptacles containing chick feed and water. Then Mildred Kienzle gently lifted the duster. Snuggled beneath was an exquisite, puffball-size baby quail with bright little eyes.

"Tom and I found the egg in an abandoned nest four days ago," Mildred explained. They took the egg home, and for two days nothing happened. Then on the third day the egg moved slightly. Holding it to their ears, the Kienzles could hear a faint ticking inside, like that of a miniature time bomb.

Transfixed, they watched tiny holes appear around the pointed end of the egg. When the circle of holes was complete, there was a silent convulsive shudder and the egg parted. Slowly there emerged something resembling a wet bumblebee. But within half an hour, the little quail's appearance began to change. When I saw him on the second day of his life, he was brown instead of black and growing fluffier and downier by the minute.

Neighbors were outspokenly gloomy about his chances for survival. "He'll never live," they prophesied. But the little quail snuggled under the lamb's-wool duster as he would have under the soft underfeathers of his quail mother. Tommy and

Mildred started calling him Bobby White, but I suggested a more dignified name. Robert he became.

Robert grew swiftly, and soon soft breast feathers appeared over the down in a tiny chain-mail pattern. The top of his head darkened, with gold lines down the sides that set off his dark-brown eyes startlingly. But the most incredible feature of his development was his emerging personality. Quail are among the shyest of birds, but Robert was a total extrovert. He filled the house with song—greeting Mildred and Tommy with distinctive chirps of pleasure and anticipation, cooing mournfully whenever he wanted companionship, and trilling ever more softly as he fell asleep.

On a warm, sunny August day, when Robert was two weeks old, Mildred and Tommy sadly decided it was time to free him. When they carried him to the lawn, Robert looked about in bewilderment for a minute or two, then spied a tiny bug which he ran after and ate. After a while, satisfied that Robert knew instinctively how to find food, Mildred and Tommy walked back to the house.

Tommy was just putting his hand on the door latch when a sharp, shrill call went up behind them. As the door opened, Robert, running as fast as his legs could carry him, darted into the house ahead of them. After this performance was repeated several days, the answer was plain: Robert had come to stay.

From then on, he was outdoors a great deal. Tommy, a retired doctor, has made their grounds a haven for birds and Robert remained nearby as Tom worked around the yard. Several times Robert's quail family, still in the vicinity, passed near—his mother and 11 chicks. There was never the slightest sign of recognition, much less desire for reunion, on either side. Who snubbed whom was not clear.

Robert made the Kienzles' house his own, stalking around investigating everything with outstretched neck. If Mildred was in the sewing room, Robert was there, investigating patterns, running off with bits of cloth. If Tommy was reading the paper, Robert was in his lap begging for attention. Highly sociable, Robert greeted guests with cries of delight. He would get up on the coffee table and preen himself, daintily help himself to any cookies that might appear, even drink tea when it cooled.

Mildred and Tommy, concerned about returning Robert to the wild, visited the Audubon Society's bird sanctuary on

Cape Cod. The sanctuary's director, Wallace Bailey, told them that quail will not accept any bird who has been in contact with humans. "Since he has done so well under your care," Bailey went on, "it might be better just to let things continue as they are. However, he should be banded. Then, if he leaves you, we would have the identification record."

The next day a light metal band was slipped on Robert's leg. In this age of zip codes and 11-digit telephone numbers, it was only fitting that Robert, having chosen to live with humans, should have his own number: 633-87201 Quail, U.S. Wildlife Service, Washington, D.C.

He chose as his sleeping place a red-velvet pillbox hat of Mildred's on the dressing-room shelf. "Up with the birds" did not apply to him; he often did not make an appearance until ten or eleven in the morning. He would fly down from the shelf and dash pell-mell into the bathroom, where he made two large deposits on a piece of Kleenex placed on the floor for that purpose. (Lest eyebrows rise at the thought of a quail loose in the house, Robert was beautifully housebroken.)

Physical changes in his surroundings upset him. Let a davenport be moved, a bottle of nail polish left where it did not belong, the corner of a rug inadvertently turned back, and Robert would stalk and call until someone came to straighten things out. When the telephone rang, he knew it should be answered, and would hop up on the shoulder of the person talking, to chirrup into the mouthpiece.

One day the telephone repairman came. He had read about Robert in the local paper, but was not prepared to find a quail standing on tiptoe looking into his toolbox. When the repairman called the operator, Robert hopped up on his shoulder and began to chirp. We heard the repairman say, "Sure it's in the house. You don't think I'm calling from out in the woods, do you? It's that quail, Robert."

As autumn set in, Robert's plumage grew heavier and richer in color, and the characteristic light and dark markings appeared on his topknot. When the first light snow fell, Robert made a few cautious steps in it, then rushed back into the house. His favorite spot on snowy days was a lamp by the kitchen window—he perched on the lampshade, warming his derriére, and smugly watched other birds braving the snow. After all, he was an indoor bird, accustomed to his creature comforts.

That Christmas I contributed an ornament to the Kienzles' tree—a fallen bird's nest I had sprayed with gilt and filled with three Christmas balls for eggs. On Christmas Eve the Kienzles fastened it near the top of the tree. Next morning Robert came in yawning as usual, had his orange juice and toast—and spied the tree. He flew toward it, giving his loud cries that sounded like "HUR-ry, HUR-ry!" Then, to the Kienzles' astonishment, he flew right to the gilded nest, though he had never seen a nest and couldn't possibly have known what it was for. As long as the tree was up, Robert returned again and again to the nest.

The Kienzles' grandchildren came for a holiday visit that year. The little quail, it seems, had firm ideas about how human children should behave. The first night, the children kept getting out of bed on various excuses. Finally, small pajamaed Thomas III tiptoed toward the table where the grownups were playing bridge. Only Robert, sitting on Dr. Kienzle's shoulder, noticed him. Rising to his full height, Robert read the riot act to the boy. He scolded, he squawked and very clearly implied that if nobody else would take care of this situation *he* would. Thomas III stared in bewilderment, then turned meekly and went back to bed—for good.

Spring came, and with it a gnawing fear in Robert's human friends. Would he feel the mating instinct and return to the wilds? Quail appeared in pairs around the house, but Robert ignored them. Then one day he gave a little scream. Mildred and Tommy dashed to see what was wrong. Robert stood up, shook himself, gave a contented little chirp and walked off—leaving an egg! After accomplishing this feat, Robert went to his (excuse me, *her*) tray, and ate and drank as never before. She completely ignored the egg, and seemed glad the whole business was over. Since the egg was not fertilized, it did not hatch. We wondered if she would lay more; a quail's clutch usually runs from 12 to 15 eggs. Robert, however, laid only that one—apparently just to keep the franchise. A discussion followed about her name: finally it was decided that Robert she had always been, and Robert she would continue.

Then a problem appeared. For years the Kienzles had dreamed of a trip to Europe. Now their younger son, who was in West Berlin starting a career in the State Department, had fallen in love and wanted his parents to meet his fiancée. So

I offered to board Robert while they were away and plunged into preparations. I had a wire-enclosed patio built beside my house (there were many cats about), loosened the soil in my geranium beds for Robert's dirt baths and planted several clumps of chickweed.

During those three months, I learned many fascinating details about a Q.I.Q.—quail's intelligence quotient. For instance, I saw how a quail drinks dew; in the morning, Robert would search out a blade of grass laden with dewdrops, and deftly run her bill along the blade, scooping up every drop. She loved daddy longlegs, ants, inchworms, flies and mosquitoes; she caught honeybees, but avoided wasps, angleworms, grubs, earwigs. She had an unvarying technique for her dirt bath, working down into the dirt with head and wings, then staggering out, her feathers laden with dirt, to shake three—always three—times.

She feared other birds, perhaps as a result of an instinctive fear of hawks. If even a chickadee flew over the patio, she gave a little cry and flattened herself in the grass. Of four-legged animals, however, she had no fear. Once three cats with twitching tails watched her through the patio wire, and she paid no attention. She struck up a friendship with an old white poodle that a friend of mine often brought to visit, and developed an amusing game, stalking slyly behind the sleeping dog to grab a curl of his hair and yank it, making him yelp.

The local papers had declared her "our first citizen," and other papers across the country carried the story. The first Sunday I had her, 19 people came to call and sign her guestbook. In the following weeks they kept streaming in—300 in all, from 24 states and two foreign countries. Some came from curiosity, others from a real scientific interest in birds. None could resist the blandishments of this bouncy, five-ounce bird as she greeted them loudly, hopped on their shoulders and cuddled under an ear.

One visitor was a young artist who made and sold beautifully carved birds; he was astonished that he could touch Robert, and excitedly examined her as if she were a rare jewel. "I've carved lots of quails." he told me, "but now I see the mistakes I've made." Another visitor was a photographer; a picture he took appeared on a commercial postcard that sold thousands. Many people became shutter-happy over Robert, and she developed into a regular ham before the camera.

When the Kienzles returned, Robert welcomed them joyously. From then on, though, she had two homes and often visited me. In February 1964, NBC posed a bombshell question: Could Robert be brought to New York to appear on nationwide television? At first the Kienzles were enthusiastic; then doubts set in. Finally someone experienced in TV work advised them to say no—the intense heat from the lights would dehydrate Robert dangerously.

So a compromise was made. Professional photographs of Robert were shown on the "Missing Links" show, with comments from me. The result was a deluge of fan mail.

In May 1964, just before Robert's second birthday, she seemed to be trying something new in her vocalizings. Her head bobbed back and forth; her throat fluttered and swelled as she stood motionless trying to say something. Finally the true quail call came, loud and clear: "Bobwhite!" She appeared quite pleased with herself, and trotted off repeating, "Bobwhite!" After a week or so, however, she stopped and never said it again.

As the months and years went by, Robert experienced only kindness and affection. Approaching her fourth autumn, she had many visitors, as usual, but people remarked that she seemed less mischievous. Early in November a spur-like growth appeared at the corner of her beak and began to spread inside her mouth. Robert required much assistance in eating, and she could no longer preen herself. By Thanksgiving, she had become very weak. She took to leaving her shelf early in the morning, and Tommy would awake to find her cuddled under his chin.

On December 2, 1965, she wanted to be held a great deal. Early that evening, for the first time in her life, she tucked her head under her wing to sleep. Next day, Mildred called me, and I knew from her voice what she would say. "Robert finally went to sleep with her head still under her wing." I could make no reply.

In her own small way, Robert was a power for good. Young men, after seeing her, vowed never to shoot a wild bird again, and she inspired many visitors to an interest in birds and other wildlife. Hundreds had been entertained and touched by her, and the last guest to sign her guestbook wrote the ultimate tribute: "A joy to hear and see."

Coping With Civilization

Behold, The Durable Deer

by Jack Denton Scott

THE FOUR deer came daintily through falling snow and stood 50 yards from the window of my Connecticut farmhouse as if posing for a Christmas card—a picture of elegance and grace heralding a happy season. But as the cold December wind burred their cinnamon-gray coats and the winter sea of snow eddied about them, I saw these beautiful wild ones for what they really are: one of the gentlest, yet possibly the toughest, of animals.

The deer is a remarkable creature that most of us know by appearance, but few by ability. A delicate creature with soft brown eyes, slender limbs and timid Bambi ways, he survives the terror of winter that sends most other animals into hibernation, or into dens, hollow trees or holes in the ground. He thrives despite our farming, lumbering, road-building, our automobiles and guns, which have wiped out 63 species of wildlife and threaten 150 others. He is, indeed, the only animal whose continuing vitality we honor nationwide with signs on the superhighway: DEER CROSSING—TWO MILES.

How does he do it? By drawing on his high intelligence and outstanding physical assets.

One summer evening, as I was driving home from a neighbor's, a deer came hurtling out of the dusk toward my car. I braked to a stop and so did he. But then, from a standstill, he took off and sailed over the hood of my car with perfect ease. And, with a casual flick of his tail, he vanished in the night.

According to biologist William Monypeny Newsom, that jump over my car was no feat at all. He saw a buck soar over an eight-foot fence from a standstill. He watched another easily broadjump 30 feet. Besides the soaring leaps, slamming stops and quick turns are made possible by the deer's anatomy: the long bones of the foreleg are not directly joined to his skeleton. Instead, the shoulder blades are fastened to the body muscles inside the skin with springy tissue, allowing them a kind of free-floating, ball-bearing flexibility.

The best-known, most numerous and successful of our American deer is the whitetail (so-called because the white underside of his tail flags up when he's in flight), also known as the Virginia deer. Roving from wilderness to backyards, from the Atlantic to the Pacific, from Hudson Bay south to the Isthmus of Panama, he appears in 30 sub-species. These range from 100 to 200 pounds when full-grown.

Whitetails played a key role in America's development. These animals fed and clothed pioneers, supplied meat for our Revolutionary Army, helped sustain trappers and explorers as they opened the West. There were an estimated 50 million whitetails in colonial days. By 1900, wholesale market hunting had all but wiped them out in most states. But with passage of the Lacey Act in 1900, regulating the interstate sale of game, the whitetail rapidly rebuilt its thinned ranks. Even stepped-up lumbering operations haven't deterred the deer. Cutting big stands of hardwood trees has sparked the growth of woody vegetation that they eat in winter. Today there are an estimated 12.5 million whitetails in America.

In spring, summer and fall, the highly adaptable whitetails live almost anywhere, feeding on everything from twigs to wild mushrooms. They have even been seen fishing, expertly pawing suckers from a creek, then eating them head first. Being a ruminant with four stomachs is also an asset: when food is plentiful, a large amount can be stored in the first stomach and digested slowly as it passes through the other three.

Winter, though, is the great leveler. Then whitetails live mainly on tree and bush growth (buds, branches and bark) up to six feet above ground. If the snow gets more than two feet deep, the deer "yard"; that is, they gather in small groups—usually along streams or lakeshores where thick growths of conifers help shelter them from the bitter winds—and trample the deep snow into a communal yard in which they can move about. They use this same teamwork to open food trails, packing down the snow so they can travel within 48 hours after a snowstorm. But the snows limit their feeding range to about a mile—a fifth of normal—and in severe winters many die of exposure and starvation.

Withal, nature has given the whitetail excellent equipment for survival. For example, the coat, shed twice a year, is a perfect camouflage for all seasons. Chestnut-red and comfortably light in summer, it becomes in winter a gray-brown and insulates so efficiently that its owner can sleep in the snow all night, compressing it without melting it.

The whitetail's senses are so acute, hunters say, that he can detect a flicker of movement or smell a cigarette at a distance of half a mile, or hear a hidden man blow cigar smoke. He also has special scent glands to send signals and mark trails. One pair, the tarsal, inside the hind legs at the hocks, discharges a strong musk to call a fawn or warn of danger. Another gland, between the toes on each foot, he uses to find and recognize his own kind, and as an aid in retracing his tracks through unfamiliar territory.

Whitetails can sprint 40 m.p.h., then dash at 30 for four miles—through rough country. Even half-grown fawns have been clocked pacing a car going 35 m.p.h., then pulling away. They are also at home in water, their air-filled hairs giving them considerable buoyancy. They have been seen easily swimming the 3½-mile width of New York's Cayuga Lake, and paddling more than five miles out in the ocean off the coast of Maine—apparently just for the fun of it.

Whitetails also use water to fight flies and heat, and as an escape hatch. In *The Deer of North America,* edited by Walter P. Taylor, is a description of a fawn being chased by dogs. The young deer doubled back, leaped into a water-filled ditch, ten feet wide, four feet deep—and vanished. Searching dogs and men lost the trail. But a half hour later the observer noticed faint ripples. Below a jutting bank he found the patient little deer, completely submerged except for nostrils, forehead and eyes.

Also in the deer's survival kit is a skill of silence that is nearly unbelievable. Sipping tea late one fall day on our terrace, my wife and I looked up and saw two does about to join the party. No more than 50 feet from us, they had come across a broad yard littered with parchment-dry leaves—without a sound.

In *The Deer Hunter's Guide,* Francis E. Sell tells of using binoculars to follow the precise put-and-take of the feet as a buck silently crossed a glade cluttered with dry leaves. With each cautious step, the point of his hoof was aimed directly at the ground, then brought a bit forward and positioned gently—under, not on, the leaves. Then the foot was brought back, high above the leaves, before it was placed forward again. Examining the deer's path, Sell found that not a single leaf had been crushed!

Mating begins in November, and a whitetail doe usually gives birth to her young in May, in brush on forest edge or in deep swamp. There are from one to three offspring. Male fawns average seven pounds, females five pounds. They arrive in full red coat with over 200 white spots that break up body contour and blend the fawn into its background. Although able to walk at birth (and at three weeks to outrun dogs and men), the fawn stays close to the ground, dropping at the slightest noise. This instinct and perfect camouflage, plus the newborn's complete lack of scent, give him excellent protection. Observers have seen dogs jump inches above a bedded baby deer without smelling or seeing it.

The doe hides her fawns separately, then watches from a distant vantage point so her own scent won't betray her babies. She remains near enough to lead off threatening predators. She has been seen appearing just in time to beat off a lurking fox with her horny hoofs. One of wildlife's most diligent mothers, she nurses her young for two minutes at three-hour intervals. Her milk contains twice the solids of a Jersey cow's, three times the fat and protein, its richness producing a spectacular growth. Fawns double their weight in 15 days, quadruple it in a month. At three weeks they browse lightly, also taking some feed from their mother's mouth. In a month they can handle acorns and beechnuts, and at four months they are weaned.

At six months the fawns of the larger subspecies weigh about 125 pounds. If they were the usual wild youngsters, they would now be on their own for the rest of their ten-year lifespan. Not deer. Their doting mother still pampers them. The young bucks stay with her for one year, the does for two, keeping company with her newer offspring—a close family, the young learning by association and imitation, especially the art of hiding.

Several years ago, a study was conducted in the Cusino Wildlife Experiment Station in Michigan, in a high-fenced square mile of hardwood forest and conifer swamp. Thirty-nine deer (7 bucks, 14 does, 18 fawns) were released there, and six veteran hunters were asked to try to locate them. It took the men *four* days to see a single buck! During a continuing four-year period, with at least 34 deer within the fenced mile, the best sighting record by experienced stalkers was 14 hours to get within "shooting" distance of *any* deer, including fawns, and 51 hours to locate one buck.

In another experiment, in South Dakota, researchers attached a radio transmitter to a buck so that they could "beam him in" and follow his movements, and tied long orange streamers through his ear tags so he could be more easily seen. Then they released him in the Slim Buttes area. Five skilled hunters searched for seven days without finding a trace of the buck.

The experimenters then sent three of the hunters into the exact area where the radio transmitter showed the test buck to be. They made a careful bush-by-bush search, all morning and all afternoon, but they couldn't find him. The following day, with the radio zeroing him in precisely, all five keen-eyed men searched. Finally, in the evening, returning from the area, one hunter almost stepped on him before he saw where he hid, cocooned in underbrush.

With such talent, deer, to the delight of us all, seem in the wildlife world to be proving the Biblical prophecy, "The meek shall inherit the earth."

The Clever Coyote's Will to Survive

by George Laycock

SOME years ago, government trapper Bill Pullins arrived at a ranch in South Dakota to dispatch a sheep-killing coyote. "I didn't think it would be any big job," Pullins recalled. His trapping technique had worked well on hundreds in the past.

Finding the coyote's much-traveled trail, Pullins set a trap and camouflaged it with a cover of dirt, litter and grass. Returning later, he found that the trap had been carefully dug up and sprung. For weeks the two old-timers—coyote and trapper—waged a battle of wits. Time and time again Pullins reset the trap; each time the coyote dug it out.

Then Pullins shot a prairie dog, placed it partly under a flat rock near the trail, and buried four traps around the rock. Later, he found every one of the traps dug up—and the coyote had carried off the prairie dog. "It seemed like a game with him," Pullins said in admiration.

After six months, Pullins finally caught his nemesis. "When I found the coyote in the trap," he said, "he just looked up at me like he was saying, 'I sure pulled a dumb one this time.'"

Pullins' regard for the coyote he hunted so relentlessly is shared by others who know the animal best. Indeed, the coyote may be the most remarkable wild creature anywhere in North America. Other wildlife—wolves, grizzly bears, black-footed ferrets and southern bald eagles—have almost vanished in the wake of plows, fences, fires, traps and guns. But the adaptable coyote has not only survived, he has prospered.

With an inherent intelligence and an uncanny sensitivity about threats to its welfare, the little "song-dog" of the prairies has gone tiptoeing over the landscape, exploring new places, sampling new foods, testing new hazards, to become the central figure in a compelling wildlife success story. He has expanded his territory southward into Central America, northward to the Arctic coast of Alaska, eastward to the Atlantic seaboard. Today, few states are without some coyotes. Furthermore, the animals have moved steadily closer to cities (or cities closer to coyotes). Residents of Toronto are no longer surprised when they hear the coyote's song. And probably no city has more coyotes than 464-square-mile Los Angeles, where the song-dogs howl nightly from the Hollywood hills and on occasion sip chlorinated water from the world's most costly swimming pools.

The average male coyote stands 21 inches high at the shoulders and weighs 25 pounds. The female is somewhat smaller. A bit on the shaggy side, the coyote has pointed, erect ears and a bushy, drooping tail. It is mostly gray, with a tinge of yellow on flanks and neck, and black on forefeet, tip of tail, and at the tail's base.

As evidence of the coyote's high intelligence, field observers cite some of its hunting techniques. While one coyote chases a rabbit, another may wait behind a bush to leap upon the prey as it runs by. Folklorist J. Frank Dobie described a coyote that leaped stiff-legged into the air and clowned for the benefit of a spellbound jackrabbit, while another coyote crept up and surprised the rabbit from behind.

Retired trapper Lloyd W. Hutchison, who once supervised all government trappers in Wyoming, is convinced that a race of super coyotes has emerged. Their dens are harder to find now, he says. In some places where coyotes were killed by eating poisoned carcasses spread by trappers, coyotes no longer eat carrion. "They're the smartest wildlife we have," Hutchison says.

After watching many coyotes, mammalogist Victor H. Cahalane believes they have a sense of humor. According to a story told by Dobie, it would seem likely. A ranch boy, who used to drive a horse and wagon to town, regularly saw a coyote by the road at a particular point. One day the boy's fat old shepherd dog leaped from the wagon to chase the coyote. Instead of coursing off across the prairie, the coyote began to run around the wagon in a wide circle. It gained on the dog so fast that after a few laps the shepherd was running full-speed to keep ahead. Finally, the dog cut across the circle and jumped back into the wagon. It cringed there in disgrace while the coyote sat down beside the road and watched the wagon move out of sight.

Although not strictly monogamous in the midwinter breeding season, if left undisturbed coyotes will maintain their family ties. Male and female stay together until one of them dies. They may hunt together, and both help provide for the young. When the female is in the den with her newborn pups, the male delivers food to her. The gray, woolly pups—an average litter is five to seven—are born by mid-April in northern states, somewhat later in the South. Many perish before they are one year old, victims of traps, highways and hunters. The survivors may stay with the family group or disperse into new territories, depending on food supplies and social pressures.

A coyote raised by other coyotes will be forever fearful of people, but if captured early enough can be domesticated. A young female raised by the family of F. Robert Henderson, extension specialist in wildlife-damage control at Kansas State University, was removed from the den when her eyes were still sealed. The tiny, furry pup knew no coyote parents, no dark cavern in the hillside, no melodious ballads sung of an evening under wild prairie skies. At the sight of her owner, she bounded joyfully about her pen. When turned loose, she stayed with the people who had reared her, romped with the children and responded to her name.

The strangest of all the coyote's relationships is that with the badger. Ever since the times of ancient Indians, men have seen these two predators traveling and playing together. "The coyote on his long legs can travel a lot faster than the badger," says trapper Lloyd Hutchison. "But pretty soon he stops and turns around and waits for the badger to catch up." There is an obvious advantage for the coyote in the association: the badger, with its long, powerful claws, digs out burrowing rodents, and any that escape are pounced on by the waiting coyote. What the badger gains from the partnership is not clear.

Although rabbits, carrion and rodents make up the largest part of the coyote's diet, it eats almost anything, including berries, pears, mesquite beans and fish. Cowboys learned long ago not to tie up their horses with rawhide lines, for a coyote might free them by eating through the leather. Some coyotes are so fond of watermelon that they constitute a major threat to melon farmers in the irrigated valleys of the West; they choose only ripe melons, and take only a bite or two from each. Occasionally, coyotes attack and kill large animals—adult pronghorns and deer.

But it is the coyote's appetite for lamb and mutton that keeps him in hot water. For a century the sheepmen of the West have reviled and hunted him down as a killer. In 1915, Congress appropriated $125,000 to enable the Bureau of Biological Survey to begin predator-control service. Over the next 30 years, federal trappers poisoned, trapped or shot 1,780,915 coyotes. Now part of the U.S. Fish and Wildlife Service of the Department of the Interior, this predator-control service is still very much in business. But, in 1972, after conservationists became concerned about the many species of birds and mammals falling victim to poisons intended for coyotes, an executive order was issued banning the use of poisons on public lands for predator control except in emergency situations. The order was followed by Environmental Protection Agency action making it illegal to ship such poisons across state borders.

Then, in 1976, Executive Act 11917 (1976) permitted the use of sodium cyanide heavily monitored by the EPA, to control the coyote population in western states. Sheepherders were glad to see the ban relaxed, but are still not satisfied with coyote control; they think more extensive measures should be taken. The feeling of some sheep ranchers toward coyotes is best expressed by a South Dakota sheepman of 40 years: "The best control we ever had was poison, and those misguided people in the East had the gall to deprive us of it. We're not telling them how to control their riots and run welfare, and we don't think they should tell us how to run our business. Balance of nature? To hell with that."

Cattlemen, however, often have a different view of the coyote. Although they may report occasional losses of calves—and such losses are said by some to be increasing—many cattle ranchers consider the coyote a friend who eats the rodents and rabbits that eat the grass their cows need. Rancher-writer Dayton O. Hyde, of Chiloquin, Ore., testifying before a Senate subcommittee in 1973, placed the savings per coyote at $88—more than double the price of a lamb at the time.

Until the seventies, there had been little scientific effort to unearth the *facts* about coyote habits. Now, however, so many government bureaus, universities and private agencies are studying the song-dog that no one knows for certain how many investigations are under way. A list compiled in 1974 identified 127 such projects.

Hundreds of sheep and coyotes have been wearing miniature radio transmitters and have been tracked electronically by field agents. In 328 locations in 17 western states, a newly devised system uses special scent posts on 15-mile-long lines to measure coyote density. A number of experimenters are studying ways to frighten, disturb or disgust coyotes enough to discourage them from killing sheep. These include the use of electrical shock, chemicals and special fences. One test will involve placing repellents like cayenne pepper on collars worn by sheep.

As for the effectiveness of massive coyote-killing programs, there is evidence that coyotes possess an inherent capacity to compensate for unusual population losses. In south Texas, where coyotes were abundant, biologist Frederick F. Knowlton found years ago that coyote litters averaged 4.3 young. But in the Uvalde section of south Texas, where coyote numbers were drastically reduced by intensive control efforts, the average litter size was 6.9. Furthermore, in areas where coyotes suffer depressed population levels, females appear to begin breeding at younger ages than elsewhere.

Similarly, Colorado State University researcher Franz Camenzind found that coyotes in one Jackson Hole, Wyo., area where the population is relatively free from traps, gunning and poison have litters averaging 4.5, as contrasted with six or seven pups in areas where heavy control is practiced. Camenzind concluded, "The more coyotes that are removed from the area, the more pups the remaining adults will produce." Perhaps the ancient Indian tribes who believed that "Brother Coyote" would be the last animal on earth were truly prophetic.

The Koala—
Nature's Animated Toy

by Fred Dickenson

PLACED in the corner of a nursery, the koala of Australia would appear perfectly at home. Soft fur covers his chubby body from tiny feet to rounded ears; bright, shoebutton eyes and a patent-leather nose make him resemble nothing so much as the traditional Teddy bear. When he moves, the temptation is to look for a windup key on his sturdy back.

The similarity does not end there. The koala, once accustomed to man, is the most trusting of all wild animals, and if you pick one up he will nestle docilely against you and even put an arm around your neck. He is also the most helpless. He can neither fight very effectively nor run, and if fire comes he will only climb to the top of a tree and wait for death. Yet he has survived unchanged for a million years and today ranks as a "living fossil."

Scientists theorize that the ancestors of the koala and other primitive marsupials—such as the kangaroo and duck-billed platypus—reached Australia millions of years ago by ancient land bridges, since covered by the sea. These marsupials roamed the continent, free from large carnivorous animals, evolving peacefully but slowly as burrowers, climbers, hoppers or even gliders. When Australia became separated completely, they were cut off from the rest of the world. In those chaotic days the land was alternately flooded with fresh or salt water, and the koala learned to stay in the trees.

Almost everybody refers to the koala as Australia's "native bear." Even his scientific name, *Phascolarctos ciner-*

eus, means "pouched bear of ash-gray color." In fact, as a marsupial, he is not remotely related to the bear family. But nobody seems to mind the misnomer. His chunky form, his slow, lumbering gait on the ground, and his striking resemblance to the nursery favorite make it seem right.

The koala, who seldom drinks water—he gets enough liquid from the dew on leaves—has been accused of being a secret tippler—because of his sleepy appearance. Explains David Thomas, keeper in charge of koalas at Taronga Park Zoo, Sydney, "There is a sweet substance secreted by eucalypt tree leaves which can ferment. But I don't believe the koala is intoxicated. He *is* drowsy. Remember that he's a nocturnal creature, and most people see him only in the daytime."

Slaughtered by the millions for his pelt only 60 years ago and brought to the brink of extinction, the koala is now the object of intensive conservation programs. In refuges on Phillip and French islands, Victoria, koalas have increased so rapidly that thousands have now been moved to controlled areas on the mainland. There were 1500 koalas left in Victoria 15 years ago. There are now 50,000. So jealously is he guarded as "rare fauna and property of the Crown," that no one may make a pet of him without government permission.

The only koalas living outside Australia have been in California since 1959—ten at Balboa Park in San Diego and one at the San Francisco Zoo. Each zoo has more than 25 different species of eucalypts—"gum" trees—because the koala must switch species at certain times of the year or risk poisoning by prussic acid which, for unknown reasons, his free lunch counter suddenly generates. Only he knows when to make the change.

Propped in low, arboreal notches, the creatures sleep most of the day, awaken at dusk, climb higher, and begin to feed on the leaves and tender bark. Though clumsy afoot, one may travel many miles in a night to find food. Or for other reasons. A fancier of the opposite sex, little *Phascolarctos* collects a harem of from three to seven wives, and still enjoys the freedom of a wandering bachelor.

Papa Koala's love call is startlingly harsh—it has been likened to a saw going through a thin board. Thirty-five days after it has been answered, a cub no more than three quarters of an inch long emerges from the mother's womb. Unlike that of other marsupials, the female koala's pouch opens downward, and it is up into this warm pocket that the tiny newborn crawls. At the top, the pouch tunnels to the left and right. Each cavity contains a teat, and in one of these the baby will remain and nurse for six months.

The cub is about seven inches long and well-furred when he emerges and clambers to his mother's back. There he will ride for another six months, while she teaches him to climb and select the leaves he needs to live. Ultimately, he may grow to about 30 inches and weigh some 30 pounds.

The female koala is a loving but strict mother. Spectators have been astonished to see her place a misbehaving cub across her lap and spank him soundly, human fashion. In retaliation he wails piteously (a sob so childlike that it has been known to start hunts for a missing human youngster). If he keeps it up long enough, she will rouse and spank him again, until he decides to keep quiet. She then takes him in her arms and they go to sleep together.

A female cub is allowed to remain with her mother until serenaded and won by a visiting bachelor, but a male, on reaching maturity, will be "invited" to leave—sometimes with a swift cuff—by mother's latest lover.

Cubs raised by humans become the most affectionate and dependent of pets. Mrs. Oswin Roberts, of Phillip Island, once noticed several koalas gathered solicitously about a crying baby—the cub would not eat, or accept any of the volunteer mothers that sought to hold it. She brought the cub into the house where she calmed his fears, got him to take some warm milk, and named him Edward.

Mrs. Roberts collected leaves from a dozen different gum trees. Tiny Edward turned away from 11 of them, happily devoured the 12th. His favorite perch soon came to be on top of his benefactor's head, and here the little orphan rode contentedly while she went about her housework. Given a special government license to keep the animal, Mrs. Roberts raised Edward to sturdy koalahood and he lived to a ripe age. (In captivity, this usually is the early teens, but in the wild, perhaps 20.)

In 1788, when Western man first came to Australia, countless millions of koalas lived in eastern Australia. Then, early in this century, hunters discovered that the animal's pelt could be sold abroad. The slaughter reached a peak in 1924 when two million skins were exported. The koala all but vanished.

Aroused conservation forces moved into action. One by one, states of the Australian Commonwealth passed laws levying fines up to $100 for trapping or shooting a koala. An appeal was made to President Herbert Hoover, who had spent several years as a young mining engineer in Australia, and soon the U.S. Treasury Department initiated "Decision No. 44413" which still prohibits the importation of "koala bearskins" into the United States. The slaughter and shipments stopped.

But the fight to save the koala was far from won. Because he must have so many different gum trees for his diet, the encroachment of farms and suburbs threatened him with starvation. What he required was natural, heavily wooded and fire-controlled refuges. These he now has—in New South Wales, Queensland, Victoria and South Australia.

One story told in Australia is that when President Theodore Roosevelt sent his Great White Fleet around the world in 1907, the sailors visiting Sydney saw a resemblance between the koala and their commander in chief, and so gave the "Teddy bear" its nickname. In fact, the sailors were merely noting the koala's resemblance to a cloth toy bear cub already associated with Teddy Roosevelt.

However, there was no doubt in the mind of the orphaned baby koala raised by Mr. and Mrs. A.S. Faulkner of Northern Queensland. They kept their tiny charge alive with fresh milk and blue gum leaves. But she would sleep only in the arms of a large toy Teddy bear!

Although many dangers still threaten the enchanting little creature, his future seems assured by the protective regard Australians show for him. Visitors to the land "Down Under" smile when they see this sign along many highways: DRIVE CAREFULLY—KOALAS CROSS HERE.

Speaking of Sparrows

by Mike Tomkies

AS HE WATCHED the ten-foot-tall oil-beam pumping unit clunking away in the fields east of McPherson, Kan., John Tatschl could not believe his eyes. Two house sparrows with food in their beaks flew to opposite ends of the moving pumping bar—and promptly disappeared.

He went closer. The sparrows were feeding young in three nests that had been built in the head, the fulcrum and the drive-shaft end of the bar, which was seesawing two feet up and down every four seconds. His astonishment increased when a look at eight other working pumps nearby revealed a nest of sparrows on each. The oil-field supervisor told him that, except for minor repairs, none of the bars had been stopped for two or three years.

John's discovery that English sparrows—as house sparrows are often called—could build nests, lay and incubate eggs, and rear their young on constantly moving objects was the first reported case for this species. It is just one example of the cunning resourcefulness of these incredible 1¼-ounce morsels of cheek, whose ability to exploit the ecological niche created by modern man has helped make them the world's most widespread land birds.

Measuring but 5¾ inches from beak to tail tip, house sparrows are pushy, hardy, noisy and gregarious. Perhaps the most human of all birds, they are happiest in man's company—preferring occupied rather than empty buildings. They live, like us, by strong social codes, centering their lives on a permanent home—their nest.

Unlike most other small birds, house sparrows pair for life. I recall a pair I used to feed every evening on my windowsill in London. When the male was killed by a truck, his mate sat on the sill, head hunched into her shoulders, a swaying ball of dejection, oblivious to wind and rain. Only by giving her milk and tidbits of boiled egg could I help restore her interest in life.

The house sparrow, *Passer domesticus*, belongs to a group that probably originated in tropical Africa 10 to 20 million years ago. Some of these birds spread across southern Asia to the Far East, giving rise to jungle and tree sparrows; others went north and west, becoming house and Spanish sparrows.

House sparrows are now found throughout Europe and in much of Africa and Asia. They first reached North America in the 1850s, imported by European settlers who wanted reminders of home, and by farmers who wanted something to help combat insect plagues. By 1886, the house-sparrow invasion was fully under way; they had been introduced to a hundred places in 32 states. They soon spread out, often hopping rides on empty boxcars of grain trains. Today the house sparrow lives in most major American cities, and there are so many millions of them in North America that it's impossible to give an accurate estimate of their numbers.

The sparrow year begins in late February and March (earlier in southern states and Mexico). While young males search for nest holes, the adult cocks sit on the sites they have kept all winter, leaving no doubt as to which are occupied, calling out a constant refrain of loosely strung, strident chirps. Then in late March and April come the "sparrow weddings."

The male must court the female assiduously. Quite a dandy in his spring courting outfit—rich chestnut upper parts streaked with black, a black breast, gray rump, blue-black beak and fawny white wing bars which flash in flight—the cock hops and bows stiffly before the dowdier hen. His wings are held down rigidly, as if at attention, and his tail is fanned out. Soon other cocks fly down to join in, all hopping around the hen like a troupe of mad marionettes, chirping hysterically. If she flies off, they all follow in hot pursuit. Although cock sparrows may fight over a hen, a threatening posture by one cock—feathers puffed, black chest thrust out—is usually enough.

House sparrows are opportunists, especially at nesting. When the new planned city of Columbia, Md., was built and the human population leaped from sparse in 1966 to some 30,000 in 1971, house sparrows moved in, too, exploiting construction flaws in the new buildings, such as gaps between gutters and roofs. "County building inspectors discovered they could readily detect flaws in construction in spring and early summer by merely noting the activity of house sparrows and starlings," says urban-wildlife specialist Aelred D. Geis.

In their untidy nests, varying from football size to a small hole lined with straw, grass, hair and dried weeds, the birds rear from one brood to four broods a year. In April (March in the South) the hen lays her first clutch of three to six whitish eggs, spotted with gray and brown. When they hatch, 12 to 14 days later, the cock plays the dutiful father, doing most of the feeding in the first days.

After about 15 days the young are ready to fly, and the parents urge them from the nest with loud cries. Soon the hen is ready to lay again; she may even lay in a second nest before the first brood has become independent.

House-sparrow parents are devoted to their young. At Poole, in Dorset, England, when a pair were seen still carrying food to their nest long after the rearing season, a curious observer climbed a ladder to see why. He found a fully grown young sparrow held prisoner by a piece of thread twisted around its leg. Rather than abandon it, the parents had fed it lovingly for months.

House sparrows are also exceptionally clever. Psychologist J. P. Porter found that they were as quick to learn and remember, in maze tests, as higher vertebrates like rats and monkeys. And only sparrows would *swim* 12 inches under water to try to escape from a trap. Out of 820 house sparrows trapped for banding by Denis Summers-Smith, a world authority on sparrows, a mere 26 were caught twice. Indeed, some used his traps for their own benefit. They waited until more acrobatic chickadees took the bait, then dived at the lighter birds, forcing them to drop their booty.

When living around big-city parks, markets and gardens, house sparrows seldom move more than a mile or two from their birthplace, but those in suburbia often flock to outlying hay and grain fields in the summer. Once the harvest is in, and grass and weed seeds are gone, they fly back to town.

Shelter in winter is essential, for a sparrow without a roost and food will die after 15 hours at freezing point. Indeed, a house sparrow's life is fraught with hazards. Only one fledgling in eight survives to breed, and few sparrows in the wild reach senility. The oldest recorded was a bird ringed in Belgium in August 1929 and recovered dead 11 years and 3½ months later.

Automobiles are the biggest cause of accidental house-sparrow deaths, especially for unwary young birds at feed. Hawks and cats—even dogs and rats—will kill sparrows, and one study indicated that they may be the biggest single bird item in the diet of suburban owls. Some sparrows are killed by large hailstones; others die in heavy falls of snow from roofs. One house sparrow won renown through getting himself killed at Lord's Cricket Ground in England in July 1936—by a fast ball from a Cambridge University bowler.

Through the centuries, house sparrows have often been regarded as pests. How much harm do they really do? They will sometimes tear and partly eat garden flowers (especially those with yellow petals), pull up a few new-sown peas, uproot seedlings and nip off fruit buds. Yet they also eat weed seeds and feed their nestlings on insects and grubs—weevils, grasshoppers, caterpillars—that man considers pests. On balance, town sparrows probably do as much good as harm, country birds more harm than good.

Yet would any of us want to live in areas devoid of house sparrows? No birds need us more, but surely they repay their debt. Our cities would be duller, more sterile places without these cheeky comrades who invade our picnics, factories and windowsills, feeding from the hands of those they've learned to trust.

For city folk, the house sparrow is one of the few links with that great, free, natural world outside a metropolis. Noisy, cocky and impertinent he may be, but no one other wild creature does so much to cheer us up. And out of the whole living world we are the ones he has chosen to be his friends.

The Town That Hosts Polar Bears

by Richard C. Davis

ONE FALL not long ago, when Maurice (Moe) Bellerive was repairing his summer cabin a few miles out of Churchill, Manitoba, he spotted a polar bear sniffing at the doors of nearby cabins. A stone's throw from his door is an aging phone booth, its door long gone, and Moe hurried to it. With the bear just outside, eyeing him closely, Moe dialed the operator, who summoned the Mounties, who rescued Moe.

At the town's Legion Hall, a polar bear walked in at midday and ambled toward a crowd of dart players before being evicted—by an indignant shout from the club steward. Not far away, another bear leaped through a house window at dinnertime and started helping himself at the family table. The homeowner beat him off with a two-by-four.

For several months a year, polar bears walk the streets of Churchill at any hour of the day or night. Sometimes they are followed by a crowd of children and dogs and picture takers, taxing the efforts of Mounties and conservation officers to keep man and beast a safe distance apart. The task would be easier except that no one wants to shoot the polar bears; in the world there may be no more than 12,000 of the splendid animals still alive.

Nowhere are polar bears more concentrated than at Cape Churchill in central Canada, about 700 miles north of the Minnesota border. In winter, bears can range over the ice for 100 miles or more to hunt seals, their primary food. But constant winds and currents move pack ice south and, along with it, the bears. In summer the last of the melting ice hangs up on the shallow flats of southwestern Hudson Bay and here, in July, the bears are forced ashore. Most follow the coast 200 miles north toward Churchill for a simple reason: the pack ice—which means seals and a resumption of hunting—forms weeks earlier there because of dense freshwater ice that freezes in the Churchill River and is discharged into the bay's salty waters.

Big males wait for the freeze-up at the Cape, 40 miles east of town. Young bears and females with cubs are pushed into Churchill itself, a village of 1600 on the western shore of the bay. The situation is incredible: a town on the migration path of one of the most dangerous carnivores in North America.

When I flew into Churchill's airport that October, the same bear that had beleaguered Moe Bellerive was wandering idly about. Later that morning, as I rode in the bear patrol truck with wildlife-development specialist Roy Bukowsky, the radio crackled warning of another bear in town. We found him asleep beside a house, looking no more dangerous than a child's oversize toy. He was chased off with a device like a giant firecracker. Two nights later the Mounties helped answer a bear call: when they came to the last house on the street, a bear came to the window to look out. Routed with noisemakers, it played hide-and-seek with the officers for the next half hour, finally hiding inside an abandoned bus.

At the Cape a day or so later, we watched 25 big males from a 40-foot observation tower. They seemed bored, most either strolling through flocks of willow ptarmigan or sleeping. In an hour in a plane, we saw 67 beautiful animals, loafing on the water's edge or curled asleep in beds of kelp.

How dangerous are these polar bears? Polar-bear mothers will attack anything in their cubs' defense, but it is probably more curiosity than aggression that makes most bears draw closer when they see a man for the first time. "It is possible that polar bears would avoid men if they knew what we were," wrote Arctic explorer Vilhjalmur Stefansson. "But they frequently mistake us for seals."

In all, there have been two mauling incidents and one death at Churchill since 1966. In one instance a young bear attacked a 12-year-old boy, and the next year another attacked two Cree Indians. In 1967 a young male bear killed a 19-year-old Eskimo. All the bears involved were killed by conservation officers, and a researcher investigated each case. The autopsy of the first bear showed that, on the day of the attack, the animal had been shot repeatedly with a .22 rifle. The second bear had been loafing around town for two months and had little fear of men. The third had been asleep in the rocks of the schoolyard when the young Eskimo and two friends—not seeing it—all but fell on its back.

Several years ago an airport employe narrowly escaped death. Guiding a plane on the ground, he was mystified that the pilot kept blinking his lights. He shone his flashlight over his shoulder and saw a bear charging. Just as the bear took a swipe at him, the pilot revved his motors and the bear, a mother with young, took off and rejoined her cubs.

Despite the very real dangers of polar bears, most Churchill residents wouldn't have it otherwise. Dr. Sharon Cohen of the Churchill Health Center said: "Nothing unites the people of this town as much as polar bears." Moe Bellerive said, "I've seen hundreds of bears, but never a belligerent one." And though they ate his ducks and broke into his cabin, he says, "that was only once in 15 years."

Resident Doug Webber said, "I only wish they'd go out the same hole they come in." His goose-hunting cabin was broken into six times in one winter. Invariably, he says, the bears make a new hole in the wall or window or door when they leave.

At the town's only café, you hear comments like these: "Bears were here long before people," and "Dogs are more trouble here than bears." The village council has no intention of eliminating the bears, which add flavor, distinction and excitement, something frontiersmen have always cherished. And a research team studying the animals finds its subjects literally come to the doorstep.

In the fall of 1977 the first organized polar bear tour of a dozen Americans flew along the coast in helicopters, and their enthusiasm for what they saw may prompt Canada to create bear-watching towers for tourists.

A few businessmen see the potential in tourism, but for the most part, Churchill simply likes its bears and is determined that bears and people shall coexist. To that end, slide shows

Fearless, Powerful, Cunning Hunters.

Polar bears are magnificent animals, with a dignity born of an utter lack of fear. Big males weigh half a ton, measure eight feet long and five feet high at the shoulder. Yet for all their size, they glide across the ice with a fluid grace. Standing erect, as they often do, big ones are up to 12 feet tall.

A grown male is powerful enough to snatch up a 200-pound ringed seal with the ease of a cat catching a mouse, or to kill a 500-pound bearded seal with a single blow of its 50-pound paw. And bears are swift. A young one was clocked galloping along a road at 35 m.p.h. They can swim at six m.p.h. and can go non-stop for 100 miles or more. Their sense of smell is legendary. Eskimos maintain bears can scent a seal 20 miles away.

They hunt by lying in wait at the breathing holes of seals, pouncing and retrieving them through the smashed ice. When open water appears and seals bask on the ice, a bear may stalk them, creeping forward as the seal dozes. Eskimos say that a bear may push a chunk of ice ahead of it when there is no other concealment. A bear can ease itself into the water with scarcely a ripple, swim under water or with only its black nose showing, and surface silently beside a sleeping seal.

and lectures have been organized, and bear-alert numbers are widely publicized.

Garbage remains the major problem. Bears love its smorgasbord of smells and tastes. Last fall a bear ambled into an industrial kitchen at the harbor, spurned a fortune in pork chops, and walked out with a bag of garbage. A garbage incinerator has been built, but bears addicted to the dump have climbed over trucks, barricaded the entry and several times sent workers scurrying up ladders until help arrived.

Visitors are full of solutions. Move the dump far inland or, better yet, move the town. Fence the town with high netting or electric wire. Fly bears away. (This last is done at $500 a bear, paid for by the International Fund for Animal Welfare.) At present, troublesome bears that keep returning to town are being trapped and released far from the area. As a last resort they are killed. Several years ago, 15 were shot by a conservation officer and another nine by frightened residents; in the fall of 1977, only four were shot. By September 1981, a Quonset-hut holding pen for 50 bears may be ready; there troublemakers can be confined until freeze-up when, it is hoped, they will take to the ice.

The Way of the Wild

Encounters in a Winter Wilderness

by Earl W. Hunt

THE WOLVES feared few creatures of the Northern Minnesota forest, but they did shun the intruder who walked on two legs and carried a stick that killed from a distance. To avoid him, the old wolf and his family traveled at night, hunting large prey as well as squirrels, mice and other small animals. The old wolf, his mate and their four hungry pups—not quite a year old and each already weighing 60 pounds—developed into a smoothly operating pack, hunting and traveling as a single unit.

It was a clear night when the wolves spotted a group of white-tailed deer moving along the forest's edge. The frantic deer turned and ran in headlong flight, moving with long powerful strides. The old wolf quickly gave up the chase. In a long run he would grow lame from injuries received during his 12 years of hunting—the terrible blow his shoulder had taken from the hoof of a thousand-pound moose, the near-fatal goring of his chest by the antlers of an angry buck.

Later, as they topped a small ridge, the wolves spotted a large group of deer lying in some bushes. As the wolves advanced, the deer rose and ran—except for one old buck who hesitated. His sluggishness told the wolves that he was weak and tired, and the pack soon surrounded him. The end was violent but quick, and then the wolves feasted.

THE MAJESTIC great horned owl, a skilled night hunter, found that the snow gave sanctuary to many of the creatures it normally ate. Frequently the owl searched around the bases of trees where the wind would leave a dished-out area of snow which the sun quickly melted. Mice came to these places to feed on the seeds of grass and weeds, followed by shrews and weasels to feed on the mice.

In mid-January the first major blizzard of the season struck. Unable to hunt, the great horned owl sheltered in a dense grove of evergreens. When the three-day storm finally abated, hordes of creatures came out of hiding to look for food. The weakened owl—his wingspread reaching five feet across from tip to tip—quickly swooped down to feast, and his strength soon returned.

FOR AN ELDERLY female muskrat, snow and ice provided insulation and protection against hawks and owls, and served as a barrier against the dreaded mink.

One of the muskrat's winter chores was to prevent too thick a layer of ice from forming on the surface at the entrances to both her home (a house of weeds and mud built in the marshy part of the lakeshore, with two underwater entrances) and a small one-room feeding house a hundred yards away, where she would eat water plants gathered from the lake bottom. Should the ice become too solid, the muskrat could not break out and would be doomed. The muskrat made the trip out to the feeder several times a day to clear its entrance of ice. The underwater swims that followed to gather plants would have been a simple task had it not been for an arthritic stiffness in her hips.

By mid-January the ice on the lake was more than two feet thick. As the pain in her hips worsened, the muskrat made fewer trips to the feeder, and on one particularly cold day she was unable to break the ice that blocked the entrance hole. Now, having lost the use of the feeder and the food that grew around it, she would have to rely on the limited supply of roots and weeds within swimming range of her home. These were rapidly depleted and, to avoid starvation, she began feeding on the inside of her plant house. And in her weakened condition she allowed one of the exits from her two-room home to freeze over.

The cold and hunger had a pleasant numbing effect. Her only desire now was to sleep. She had just closed her eyes when a mink invaded her house. With the other exit frozen solid, she was trapped. She made a gallant effort to defend herself, but didn't have a chance.

When the mink left the muskrat's den, he headed across the lake. A half-moon shining through a thin layer of clouds gave just a trace of light. Suddenly the mink felt needle-sharp talons piercing his side and neck and whirled to defend himself. A great horned owl had attacked him downwind from behind.

Squealing with rage, the frenzied mink twisted and squirmed like a bundle of steel springs. The owl lost his grip on the mink's neck and, hissing and snarling, the mink repeatedly sank his long, pointed teeth into the bird's leg. The owl tried to release his hold on the savage fighter, but could not. Then a deep-sinking talon pierced the mink's heart.

The winged hunter's victory was won at great cost, for his leg was mangled. With much difficulty, the owl took off from the lake in awkward flight, leaving the mink in the blood-spattered snow—a carcass to be picked clean by scavengers, many of whom the mink had once stalked.

Unlike the confinement that winter brought to the muskrat, the woodchuck and the chipmunk, it gave the rabbit new freedom. A six-month-old male cottontail, who had rarely ventured outside the bounds of his home range, was now able to hop across ice-covered surfaces to places inaccessible by land. His main danger lay in his gray-brown fur, which silhouetted him against the white landscape.

In mid-January, when the blizzard hit, the rabbit holed up for three days under a thick clump of speckled alders. When the storm finally ended, he emerged from his shelter with one goal in mind: to satisfy his now-ravenous appetite. To his delight, he found that food was readily available: with the added height of the snow to walk on, he could reach twigs and berries previously beyond reach.

By the end of January, the cottontail was in excellent condition. He had already beaten the odds, for of the young cottontails born the previous summer, only about one in six was still alive. Yet he must remain lucky if he was to produce offspring—the mating season was more than two months away.

One day in February, without warning, he felt the searing pain of an owl's talons slicing into his back. He kicked and twisted as hard as he could. One of the owl's feet held him but the other seemed maimed and useless—if both talons had penetrated him there would have been no hope. Then a wolf rushed toward them. The owl relaxed his hold on the cottontail and the victim tore free.

THE LAST GOOD CATCH for the wolf pack had been the tired old deer. The pressure to find more food was greatest on one of the young pups with an enormous appetite. Alone, he climbed atop a small hill and froze when he saw a cottontail moving straight toward him. As he waited for the prey to draw nearer, a great horned owl, one leg hanging limp, dropped out of the sky.

Seeing his prospective dinner being taken away, the pup raced downhill. The big bird immediately released the rabbit and stabbed at the wolf, tearing a gash near his eye. But with a crunch of the young wolf's powerful jaws, one of the most commanding creatures of the sky was crushed. The wolf dropped the owl and went after the wounded cottontail, overtaking him with ease.

ONE NIGHT in February, after a fresh snow had fallen, the wolf pup was hunting along a riverbank when he picked up a familiar scent. Tracking it, he came upon the lifeless body of a rabbit in the snow. He circled it twice, sniffing as he moved closer. He seemed to detect another odor that reminded him of the two-legged intruder. Cautiously, he moved toward a hillock a few feet away to look the area over. As he stepped onto the mound he felt steel jaws close on his foot. The intruder, knowing the wolves might be wary of his bait, had set one of his traps at the highest point of ground nearby.

By morning the temperature had dropped to 35 degrees below zero F., and the river below the hillock on which the wolf lay froze over completely. By nightfall of the second day, with his foot badly swollen, shivering, his energy almost drained, he fell into a fitful sleep.

Early on the morning of the third day, he awoke with a start. Panic gripped him as he saw the two-legged animal with the long, terrible stick walking along the opposite bank of the river. The wolf leaped to his feet and lunged against the trap. The trapper saw him and hurried across the river, running hard over the newly formed ice. Summoning all the power within him, the wolf made one final desperate lunge for freedom and found himself tumbling over in snow, his foot wrenched out of the trap.

Before he could get to his feet, he heard a piercing scream. Looking up, he saw the two-legged animal breaking through the ice into the rushing water. The pup lay motionless, but the trapper did not emerge from the black hole. All that remained of him was his stick, which lay on the ice beside the hole.

Slowly, painfully, the wolf made his way to a thicket of spruce trees where the dense branches had caught the snow to form a roof over a cozy hollow. Here he licked and nursed his foot for three days. On the fourth day he moved out along the riverbank and began working his way upstream. He found two mice and gulped them greedily—but they did little to ease his hunger.

The next night he heard something familiar in the distance—wolves on the trail of a large animal. Later the pup came upon the remains of a freshly killed deer. He knew at once that this was the work of his pack—there was no mistaking the scent. He ate his fill, then lay down to rest, knowing they would be back.

Suddenly an urge came over him. Ever since the pup had stepped into the trap, he had been too dazed and sick even to think about singing. Now he raised his head and sent a loud howl into the night. From not too far away, the howls of other wolves came back to him, and he settled down to wait. He was home.

Birds Live in Nature's Invisible Cage

by John and Jean George

"FREE AS a bird," we say; yet nearly all birds and most bird watchers know how mistaken that saying is. The conduct of birds is so rigidly fixed that they are prisoners to the land they fly over, slaves to the air they fly through. Once we watched a bird go to his death because he was not free to fly 700 feet to safety.

We were returning home along the Huron River near Ann Arbor, Mich., where we were studying birds and mammals, and stopped to visit a cardinal we had named Red Click because of a special clicking note he used at the end of his song. We found him stranded on the piece of property where he lived; the land had been scalped that day by bulldozers so that only a few stumps and roots remained. As we watched, Red Click flew about 400 feet, then suddenly back-winged as if he had hit an invisible wall. After flopping to earth he flew off in another direction, only to smash into another invisible barrier.

"What's the matter with that crazy cardinal?" Jean asked. "He'll be killed by a hawk or an owl if he doesn't fly to the woods."

"He can't fly to the woods," John said. "His 'territory' is in the middle of the cleared land. The bulldozers have taken away his trees, his bushes, his grasses, but the boundaries of his home that he and his neighbors carefully established in their bird minds are still there and he can't fly through them."

"Perhaps we could carry him to safety," Jean suggested.

"And turn him loose on some other cardinal's territory? He's a prisoner precisely because he is more terrified of intruding on another male's land than he is of remaining here without shelter."

A screech owl called from the wood lot behind us. "Hear that?" John said. "That will probably be the last chapter in the biography of Red Click."

Next morning, at the roots of a maple sapling in the wasted field, we picked up the blood-red feathers of our cardinal.

This devotion unto death to a piece of ground is probably more intense in birds than in any other vertebrate. Strongest during the breeding season, the territory fixation serves to aid in the formation of pairs, to provide shelter for the young and to ensure perpetuation of the species by spreading its population over a wide area.

By simply walking behind chickadees, pushing them around their property in the spring, we were able to map some 200 of their territories in the woods near Poughkeepsie, N.Y. The chickadees would fly to the extremities of their lands, then circle back around the edges, revealing their unseen fences. Sketched on a map, a chickadee community looks like an exurbanite settlement of people, with the size of each property varying according to the "social standing" of the occupant; the older the male, the bigger, the stronger he is, the more land he gets.

Birds which are year-round residents tend to retain the same territory for life; migrants have both summer and winter properties. The birds that stay around your home all winter may seem to be in flocks, and therefore trespassing, but they are not. They are a well-ordered bird society made up of old-timers and young, complete with a leader or "boss bird." In these winter societies the defense of the breeding territory has given way, in certain species, to the common defense of a community territory against neighboring groups of the same species. Birds will tolerate trespassers of a different species on their land, since they are not competing, but not intruders belonging to their own.

Birds' property lines are established by song. If a male bird, returning in the spring, can sing from a tree without being challenged by a neighbor, he has it as his own, to mark the limits of his real estate. If, however, another male comes winging at him and puts him back a tree or two, he knows that this land is already claimed.

By taking the best land he can and as much of it as he is able to defend, he assures himself not only a good food supply but also a mate. Female birds pick their mates by their attractive voices (each bird's voice is as distinctive as your own) and by the quality of the nesting sites in the land they have staked off. The weaker males and the late-comers, pushed into submarginal land, often go through the season as bachelors.

A bachelor song sparrow we called Mike sang so beautifully that Jean couldn't understand why the girls would not set up housekeeping with him. John said, "Your friend's territory is very small and in the woods. Song sparrows like some open fields and brush borders on their property. Getting a female to nest on Mike's territory would be like asking a debutante to live in Siberia."

Territory varies with different species from several square miles, as in the case of the horned owl, to only a square foot or so around the nest, as among the colony nesters such as terns and gulls.

Once boundary lines are settled, the feelings of the bird toward his territory mount with the progress of his nest, until he seems to do desperate things particularly near the nest site. Flying at windows and the shiny grillwork of automobiles is not bird hara-kiri. It is territory defense. His reflection in a window or grille is another male on his property, and he will fight this adversary until exhausted.

Territorial disputes, though constant in the bird world, are normally resolved by singing duels, almost always between males of the same species. Sometimes a disputed territory touches off a breast-to-breast battle in the air; the battlers seem to be rising and sliding down an invisible wall. The fight will usually be brief, and afterward each contestant will fly to a tree limb on his side of the property line and click in agitation. Usually there is a compromise and both birds will sing, in a full and exuberant song.

The female ordinarily stays within the boundaries established by her mate, but occasionally a blundering or frivolous wife can cause trouble. One season we observed a tragi-comedy in a community of vivid indigo buntings. A little female, a first-time mother, had by error built her nest on another male's property. She would fly happily to her nest, expecting her husband to usher her home, only to find that he had stopped at the edge of his territory. There he was, turning around in circles, torn between two powerful impulses: to follow his mate, and to stay off his neighbor's property. Apparently property rights proved stronger than family love. He never once crossed the barrier during the nesting period. When the young hatched, the father would catch insects for the babies, call his mate and give her the offerings. Taking them eagerly, she would return to stuff her bottomless young. We were all (including the frustrated father) greatly relieved on the day the little mother coaxed her fledglings over the border to their father's estate.

A territory boundary is not the only restraint in a bird's life. Even within their own property birds do not fly around their land on any random course, but stick to routes or "sidewalks." A bird will take the same path daily from his night roost to his feeding spot, from his nest to a certain singing post. We once saw impressive evidence that birds can map the fixed routes of other birds in the interest of safety.

A Cooper's hawk in our Michigan area staked off two square miles and soared elegantly around to attract a mate. The presence of this bird-eating intruder threw the small birds into a dither. But soon things quieted down and we wondered what adjustment they had made to the predator. In time we discovered the answer.

The big hawk, too, was a slave of habit. He nested in their woods, but always hunted in a far wood lot. Each morning he took an aerial sidewalk to the wood lot, returning home along another fixed path. The small-bird population figured out his habits, for they used fewer and fewer alarm notes to announce his coming and going. They knew he stayed on his sidewalks and never dipped down into their woods for food.

These invisible sidewalks can easily be noted in any back yard where there is a feeding station. A bird will come to the station every day about the same time from the same direction, and by way of the same sticks and twigs. There is generally a sidewalk in and another one out. We once put up a post on a bird's sidewalk, and he almost struck it, he was so confined to his route.

Each night the bird returns faithfully to his bedroom or roost, which he picks as carefully as his nesting site. In a world teeming with enemies, its loss can mean his undoing.

A woodpecker roosted in a hole in an apple tree outside our window. He went to bed at the same time every night, depending on the amount of light. As the days grew shorter, our clock showed him returning two minutes earlier each night, but our light meter registered exactly the same light value. On cloudy days he came to roost early.

One night a white-breasted nuthatch went into the woodpecker's bedroom a few minutes before he was due home. The woodpecker performed his night rituals according to his heritage. He squawked from the top of a maple. He defecated in the same spot he had used for months; he flew to the apple tree, spiraled up it and winged into his hole—where he hit the intruding nuthatch head-on.

Out they both tumbled and fought briefly. The nuthatch departed, with the woodpecker in pursuit. Sometime later we caught a glimpse of the woodpecker. It was late, but probably he could still see to get into his hole. However, he had to repeat the rituals of retirement all over again and so he went back to the maple tree. The night grew cold but the woodpecker never returned. Now it was very dark, well below his accustomed level of light. He squawked but did not fly to the apple tree. One twilight a few nights later the nuthatch cautiously investigated the empty hole and moved in. He had finally won the contest, probably because he upset the woodpecker's evening retirement habits, and the woodpecker, unable to change, was literally left out in the cold.

Almost all birds live and love and die behind the bars of nature's compulsions. They are captive in cages of their own instincts, from which, with rare exceptions, they cannot—and have no desire to—escape.

Jaguar in the Jungle!

by Franklin Russell

THE BLACK JAGUAR'S amber eyes looked upward, into the majestic canopy of the Amazonian jungle. He saw thick liana vines snaking upward like giant ropes, orchids growing from cracks in tree trunks, columns of ants climbing the huge trees, leaf insects so well camouflaged that their wings glistened with marks like droplets of water.

Blood dripped from the jaguar's nose. Blood ran down his flanks and hindquarters. His lustrous black pelt was torn with a score of wounds; his ears were tattered with claw rips. His last fight, with a much larger male jaguar, had sent him fleeing south from the higher, more open woodlands down among the forest giants along the Amazon itself.

This was alien territory. He had been reared in country teeming with deer, pigs and other succulent animals. There, born in a shallow lair clawed out of rocks and stones, he had spent his first two years under the protection of his mother. Now, 150 pounds in weight and able to take care of himself, he must find his own way as a solitary hunter.

But most of the jungle was owned by other cats. He had been beaten a dozen times in a month. He had seized a snuffling anteater, only to be nearly killed when the powerful creature's low, clawed arms gripped and nearly crushed him to death. When he was a cub, he had seen his mother flipping over the crocodile-like caimans along stream banks to eat out their tender undersides. When he had tried the same thing, a 15-foot-long caiman had knocked him into the water and then come after him. Only the jaguar's superb swimming powers had saved him.

Now, after traveling all night, he sought only a place to hide, rest up and lick his wounds. He heard the chuckling sound of a nearby stream. The enclosing network of lianas, canopy foliage, secondary trees and shrubs was so complete that it was as if he were moving inside an enormous and dimly lighted covered amphitheater where plants had triumphed over animals. From 150 feet above came a soft whisper of wind touching the highest branches.

The jaguar spent so long watching, motionless, that he became a mark for one of his enemies, a 25-foot-long anaconda stretched above him like a liana vine. The cat had scant warning—only a menacing slithering sound—before the snake knocked him to the ground, writhing at high speed all around him. Biting deeply into a massive coil wrapped around his neck, the jaguar wrenched his head free. Other coils encircled him and tightened. Slowly, using all his strength against their suffocating constriction, the cat drew the hissing tiny head toward his mouth and crushed it between his jaws. The giant snake loosened its hold and fell away.

Back legs dragging, the jaguar lurched through the undergrowth toward a hidden stream. Screams and cries rained down on him. Flocks of brilliantly colored parrots dashed among the treetops. Garish Morpho butterflies winged along the thickly matted vines. Carefully, the jaguar moved through a dense mass of 60-foot-high bamboos to the edge of the water, drank, and then draped his long black form along a fallen tree trunk. After licking his wounds thoroughly, he dozed, but never far from wakefulness.

By late afternoon, the jaguar was rested, his wounds no longer bleeding. As he stretched from his slumber, a deep, rich humming noise rose above the other sounds of the jungle. Cautiously, he lifted himself into a crouch. Now the sound transformed into the wrenchingly loud roaring of fighting jaguars. The black cat growled, then cried out himself a series of choked "chuff-chuff-chuffs," and leaped off the log, the stiffness of his hindquarters unfelt.

He had not seen the red howler monkeys, but they, the guardians of the jungle and imitators of its sounds, had seen him. They were broadcasting his position. He leaped, clamped himself to the trunk of a nearby tree, and ascended it rapidly.

The tumult of the monkeys was now vibrant with power, a veritable chorus springing from scores of throats spread all through the upper branches of the trees. The jaguar paused. The monkeys' cries died away, to rise again in subtle trilling, like many small birds singing. Now another change; the cries were interspersed with imitations of the clicking noise of jungle pigs, the peccaries.

This finally provoked the big black cat. His own cry, a deep, throaty roar, the most ferocious sound in the jungle, silenced the monkeys. Some howlers fled to higher branches. Others clung to each other. In one smooth, powerful leap, the jaguar lifted himself ten feet higher into the trees. One howler had found refuge among a cluster of branches from which he could neither jump higher nor leap sideways. The jaguar fixed his steady gaze on this monkey.

At first, the terrified creature tried to look away. But gradually his eyes locked with the jaguar's. Frozen with fear, he whimpered, remaining motionless as the cat easily climbed up and approached him. The jaguar killed with one blow of his paw, then stretched out on the branch and ate his victim.

As dusk fell, the roar of another jaguar cut through the jungle. The black jaguar waited, careful to make no sound that would betray his presence to the enemy whose territory he had invaded. Millions of insects began their nocturnal hunting. Large flying beetles shone tiny beams of light ahead of them as they probed through the thick foliage. The jungle floor teemed with night-hunting ants and termites.

Then the stench of peccary came to the cat. Ferocious little pigs, about three feet long, they were jaguar prey, but dangerous in a pack. Moaning, clicking and rattling their tusks like castanets, the peccaries burst noisily into a clearing beneath the jaguar, their suspicious little eyes squinting all around them. Immediately, they saw the cat, milled and formed a compact bunch.

At almost the same instant, the other jaguar—a spotted cat—appeared on a branch across the clearing. His rasping growls of rage sounded over the clattering of the peccaries, which now formed themselves into both an attack and defense formation. At the front of the herd were the younger males, eager animals that would not hesitate to launch a mass suicide charge against their enemy. But as they milled, they became aware of the second jaguar, and this confused them.

Normally, a fight between two jaguars would involve a lengthy ritual of snarls and intimidations, mock attacks and bluff. But this time the spotted jaguar sprang from his branch and scaled a trailing vine, plunging directly on top of the black jaguar. The cats grappled furiously, claws scrabbling, then fell together more than 20 feet to the ground.

In a second, the young boars were upon them, tusks and teeth ripping at their hides. The cats screamed, killed pigs all around them with blows of their paws, and catapulted themselves back into the tree. Both animals now strove to contain their fighting to one branch. The black jaguar gripped one side of the spotted cat's face and with his hind legs raked his enemy's flanks. The two animals swayed precariously and, suddenly, the spotted cat again fell among the waiting pigs.

The black jaguar heard the massive whacking of the spotted cat's paws killing and crippling the ravening pigs. He heard squeals and grunts as bodies spilled over each other. The spotted cat's head appeared out of the mass of pigs, then was overwhelmed again as the uproar increased and finally died away.

For another hour, the pigs milled around, rooting among the bodies of their fallen comrades and glaring suspiciously up at the black cat, before finally forming a line and trotting off into the dark jungle.

The black jaguar waited through the night. At dawn, a distant chorus of red howler monkeys began; it throbbed and waxed and waned through the jungle, but the jaguar paid no attention. On the ground, a shaft of sunlight revealed brightly colored tufts of skin and scattered bones.

The black jaguar waited, and the voices of the jungle swelled all around him, in a territory that was now his alone.

Astonishing Acts of Courage

by Alan Devoe

A TINY WREN, hardly more than thimble size, had been perched for an hour on an arbor post near the bird box, pouring out such a tumult of cascading melody that I had been listening entranced. Abruptly the lilting rush of notes stopped. There was a second's silence. Then there burst forth a staccato chattering that in wren talk means *something wrong!*

I walked toward the arbor, watching. Father wren was dancing on the post in a spasm of agitation. Mother wren had poked her little head through the door of the bird box, her bright eyes fixed on something below. Then I saw it. A milk snake as long as my arm was climbing in a steady glide up the arbor.

These snakes, relentless catchers of field mice and baby birds, can climb like a cat and clean out a bird's nest in seconds. Though not venomous they strike savagely, and when they bite they hang on viciously and chew.

I grabbed a stick and hurried forward. It turned out I needn't have. This snake had picked on heroes.

With a screaming yatter, father wren dived from the arbor post and smacked the marauder just behind its head. The snake lunged, but its jaws hit empty air. In that instant mother wren slipped from the birdhouse door, plummeted, and caught him in the backbone with a lance-like thrust. The snake's body quivered and slackened. It took only about two minutes and some 20 furious blows of fearless little beaks before it was all over. The reptile lost its hold and dropped to the ground. But the tiny feathered defenders of their babies were not finished. Again and again they struck and flailed until the big snake lay dead in the grass. And from a nearby post of the arbor there rang out a flooding cascade of triumphant song.

I since asked a famous zoologist what had been the most outstanding action he had ever seen a creature of the wild perform. Casting around among his memories of valiant big-game animals, he suddenly smiled and said he thought his outstanding hero was probably an insect.

He had been standing on the bank of a small Pennsylvania stream when he noticed a digger wasp on the ground near him. It had paralyzed a huge spider and was trying unsuccessfully to lug it to its burrow. The wasp couldn't get into the air with its heavy load and the overland haul was proving impossibly difficult.

Finally the wasp dragged the spider the short distance to the stream and floated it onto the water. Taking a firm grip on the now buoyant body, the wasp buzzed its wings at top speed. Slowly, like a helicopter towing a barge, the wasp towed the spider some 70 yards downstream, while the absorbed zoologist kept pace on shore. Suddenly the wasp turned inshore and in a moment was heaving its sopping treasure up the bank. There, within a few inches of the water, was its burrow. Exhausted but triumphant, the insect dragged its hard-won prize into its doorway.

"In that unforgettable glimpse into the insect world," said the zoologist, "I came to know that they too have their Columbuses and Galileos."

I had never thought of heroism in connection with the slow, plume-tailed skunks that prowl around my woods, but one day I met a big fellow who had managed to get himself hung by the tail on a barbed-wire fence. He was dangling head downward, his forepaws just clear of the ground. He had been there a long time, I'm afraid; he was desperately spent and weak. (I was tempted to help him but, remembering his effective weapon, I decided to watch.)

The usual animal way in a strange catastrophe is to thrash and struggle in panic. What makes heroes is the capacity not to be usual. My skunk was acting with an unusual kind of heroic discipline. Instead of wasting his dwindling strength in a furious struggle he would hang for long minutes as inert as a dead animal; then in a wild swing contortion he would whip his body up and around until he could grab the fence wire in his forepaws. Hanging so, bent almost in a circle, he attacked his tail with his teeth, just below where it was snarled in the wire. He was intent on an amputation.

He could work only for seconds at the grim job; then his strength would fail and he would have to drop back to hang limp again, hoarding his powers for the next go. Then up and at it again, controlled as a surgeon, not uttering a sound.

He made it. With a six-inch stump of tail instead of a foot-long plume, he dropped to earth, his legs buckling, and he was off into the woods.

Heroism is contagious. To see it blaze up in one exceptional individual and spread from this leader to a group, sets a watcher's heart singing. An outstanding instance was witnessed by Enos Mills, a naturalist of the American West. He was watching a band of seven mountain goats climbing a canyon in Alaska.

They had started up an almost sheer wall of rock following a cleavage line in the rock face. Tiny ledges and root clusters afforded precarious footholds. Suddenly they stopped, only a few feet from the top. The cleavage line had petered out. In single file, hugging the rock face, they were trapped.

Mills turned his binoculars on the old billy in the lead. He saw the way a hero acts. Slowly, with infinite care, the leader pawed with his front hoofs at the rock wall. He reared higher, higher, on stretching tiptoe, his front hoofs feeling and grappling until he found an infinitesimal hold. Then, with front hoofs hooked into it, he hunched and sprang straight upward. Hind hoofs caught where front hoofs had been, and in that split second the big body hunched and sprang in a second upward leap.

The mountain goat had done the impossible. On the cliff's summit he whirled and stood for his comrades to see—a symbol of triumph. He had done it; they could too. One by one the others made the heroic leap.

The heroes of the wild make a shining company!

Night of the Hyena

by Franklin Russell

THE OLD hyena lay smothered in mud, motionless except for one brown eye watching vultures falling from the evening sky. Around her stretched the grasslands of East Africa, region of lion, leopard, elephant and antelope. The sun dropped into a red haze, and five angular acacia trees were silhouetted on a stage now set for a night of hunting.

The hyena stood, and shook off showers of mud. Her flat sides, spotted with dull brown blotches, were scarred by bites, lion claws, the horns of desperate victims. Her ears were ripped and torn, and her right eye stared sightlessly into space, a scarred white disc canted upward. Her top lip was split so that her teeth showed in a perpetual snarl. She limped from old injuries, and her head was still ringing from the kick of a zebra two days before. Ten years is a long life on the plains for a hunting animal, and the weight of this age pressed down on her.

She could last days without food, but now, with two hungry cubs in a den more than 40 miles away, she was anxious to replenish her supplies of milk. Because the autumn rains were late, the antelope and zebra had moved south in search of grass, and she could not hunt near her den.

Her clumsy-looking body, powerful in the legs, and her untidy, hangdog appearance did not mark her as the great hunter she was. As purple night stole into the vast grasslands, she gave a whooping cry, soft but penetrating. Low whoops answered her from all sides. Dark shapes loomed up out of a nearby dry creek bed, melding into the tribe of more than a dozen hyenas which the old female dominated. Powerful males, younger females, youngsters, all submitted to her.

She had become dominant not only because she was big and powerful—all female hyenas are bigger than any male—but because she had special skill in darting under snapping teeth, and her terrible bites at tender zebra underparts often killed, even though her 150 pounds were dwarfed by the 600 pounds of her victim. The other hyenas did not yet suspect that she found each night's attack a little harder than the last. She was stumbling, even falling, in high-speed chases—chases that demanded the strength and heedlessness of youth.

Now she headed down a path flanking the dry creek bed, the others loping behind her in a loose, straggling line. A leopard's guttural cry and the staccato bark of a baboon did not turn a single head. The moon rose and shone silver light in the female's good eye. She began running, perhaps on impulse, perhaps as her acute ears picked out one tiny sound. Stiffness dropped from her limbs. Racing blood surged new confidence into her.

The pounding feet of zebras sounded ahead. They cantered easily at 15 miles an hour, each stallion behind his family of mares. The hyenas, running at an effortless 30 miles an hour, overtook them. The stallions turned at bay, with ears back, teeth bared, whirling, lunging, kicking, biting. Two hundred hoofs hammered the grass as the mares herded behind them. The night exploded with sound: gasping, braying zebras, the hoots and howls of excited hyenas. A young male hyena was kicked, his body catapulting vertically, his moans dying away as the others charged on.

Then the old female hyena's determination weakened. She failed to make her lethal thrust, and suddenly, gasping, she turned away. Her retreat blunted the enthusiasm of the others. Limping hyenas came out of the smoky-white dust and collapsed, panting. Soon the only sound in the night air was their heavy breathing.

In the long experience of the female hyena, even in the best of times, only one such hunt in three succeeded; when drought or disease stalked the grasslands, a dozen hunts might bring no food. Once, she would have been first away in the next chase. But tonight impatient youngsters drifted off while she lay exhausted. A silent hour passed. Then a distant cry, pounding hoofbeats, a howl told her that the youngsters had cut a wildebeest out of its herd and had it on the run.

At full speed, the old female joined the chase. When the moon slid behind a cloud, experience cautioned her to slow down. No animal could safely run at top speed over earth littered with termite mounds and pitted with the holes of bat-eared foxes, jackals, honey badgers, hyenas, warthogs. One misstep into a mongoose hole could snap a hyena leg. Thus, she was trailing behind when the wildebeest, with hyenas on either side, dashed into a streamside thicket and, with a last desperate effort, plunged into the dark water.

Hyenas poured into the water after him. The old female hung back, remembering crocodiles. But the sounds of eating and squabbling became irresistible. She was poised to jump when a great splash sent all the hyenas churning for safety. Crocodile. For a second, the wildebeest's head reared up. Then, with a powerful swirl, it disappeared underwater.

Indecisive, and ever more ravenous, the old female slumped down. Midnight came and went. She slept—as always, so lightly that by day the sound of a vulture dropping from the sky to feed a half-mile away could waken her. During her own cub life she had starved for days while her mother hunted. Her brother and sister had been dug out and eaten by a hungry male hyena; she herself had dug deeper down and so escaped.

Now she was aroused by a lion's heavy footsteps. Fully alert, she stood up, tail hushed and curved over her back. Old memories made her tremble. Lions had once killed a big eland almost on top of her cub-filled den, and taken five leisurely days to eat it. She had been forced to circle the bloated group, listening to her cubs crying supreme hunger until one by one their voices went silent. Lions enraged her, terrified her. Yet she often followed them and waited for 50 or 60 hours if necessary—for scraps from their kills. Her powerful jaws could crunch bones that the lions could not eat; her strong stomach juices could dissolve hide and skull, intestine and hoof, that are unattractive to other hunting animals.

The steadily plodding footsteps told her of a solitary lion. If he made a kill, he would be vulnerable. She moved toward the sound. This was no time for patience, for only two hours remained before daylight. Her udder was slack of milk. The cubs had been two days without food already.

For an hour she followed, crossing shrunken streams, passing the stark moon shadows of candelabrum trees, moving silently through thornbush thickets. Hyenas appeared at her side, sniffed her, and disappeared. Distant whooping told of a chase, but she would not be diverted.

Then the footsteps stopped. She stopped, too, ears upthrust, tail trembling. A zebra's whistling alarm call brought a response of galloping feet. A brief silence. Another alarm call. Furious galloping, a violent crash, then high-pitched screams.

This was her signal to race forward. The screaming stopped. The lion's teeth now clasped the zebra's nose, and the big animal was suffocating. More hyenas appeared out of the gloom. Silently, they encircled the lion and his kill.

The female's impatience grew quickly. Fur bristling, tail curved tensely, she began a slow, half-sideways advance on the lion, whooping and uttering tense, low snarls. The lion ignored her. She bared her teeth, scarcely six feet from the big cat. He brought up a menacing rumble from deep in his throat; she was too close. He got up. Instantly, the female darted forward, gripped a piece of zebra meat and ripped it free. The lion's great flat paw came whacking down—but she had wheeled away.

Her success brought the other hyenas closer. The chorus of their cries became deafening. When the lion rushed at her, a dozen hyenas grabbed mouthfuls of meat. The lion whirled to drive them off, but the female bit his leg to the bone. He roared, and caught one of the hyenas a glancing blow that bared white ribs. He charged back to the carcass, now covered with giggling, whooping hyenas, whose cries seemed to have a scornful ring.

Swiping only empty air for all his efforts, the lion was bitten again and again, and his hind legs streamed blood. All at once, with 20 hyenas facing him, he fled. Fifteen minutes later, the zebra was devoured, the grass licked clean.

Shortly after dawn touched the eastern sky coral pink and the harsh cries of bustards rasped in the still air, the female hyena was back in her mud pool, too bloated with meat to travel. She would digest her meal, make the milk, and then begin the long run home.

Her solitary brown eye watched the sun leap into the golden sky, saw vultures making giddy climbs in the still clearness of morning. Then her eye closed. The perils of the night dissolved into sleep, and in her dreams she became young.

Observations Close to Home

Our Bear Affair

by Eileen Lambert

IN THE night, we heard thumps and a wrenching scrape at our back door, and next morning we found the wooden platform-step pulled away from the house. Heavy nails had been jerked out and bent. In the exposed dirt were tracks suggesting human feet, but heavier.

It was hard to believe that we had bears for neighbors at our new home in Virginia's Blue Ridge Mountains, just two hours by car from the nation's capital. But the tracks were unmistakable. And my husband Darwin and I were to see a lot of these neighbors, not without apprehension.

Sometimes they came in daylight. More often they came invisibly and left only signs of their hunting and eating—big tracks, impressive droppings, boulders turned over, anthills and yellow-jacket nests excavated.

I was doing breakfast dishes when I saw our first cubs. They paused at the thick stone fence that separates the gnarled orchard from the forest. The largest cub, glossy black with a white streak on his chest, lifted his turned-up nose and swung it from side to side, reconnoitering. The other shrank back. The leader advanced toward my window and found a windfall apple.

Our young dog, Sourdough, caught the scent and ran out barking. The timid cub vanished like a puff of mist, but the bold one bounded onto the stone wall and stopped, not even dropping the apple. The dog came prancing back, proud of having done his duty. Two minutes later, Boldy, as we immediately named him, came for another apple.

A drought and late spring freeze had reduced forest foods that year, and the wild creatures were hungry. During September and October, bears ate our apples around the clock, sometimes more than one bear at a time.

Individual differences in bears were obvious. Boldy would show off in plain sight, swinging an apple in his mouth as if saying, "Just try to take it away from me." Then he'd steady it with his front paws and eat it a bite at a time. His sister would sneak into the orchard, and flee at the scold of a bluejay. A few adults ate greedily, crunching one apple and immediately grabbing another. One lanky adult would get down on his elbows to hold apples in his forepaws against the ground but leave his back end standing.

Black bears live up to 25 years or so. The best age indicator from a safe distance is size; Virginia's adult bears usually weigh from 250 to 500 pounds. Cubs are born in late January or early February. They're blind, helpless and almost naked, weighing less than a pound, but grow fast. The mother nurses and trains them for about a year. Our cubs were yearlings, maybe 20 pounds heavier than Sourdough, who weighed 60.

Boldy was an untiring tease. He'd seek Sourdough out again and again, approaching until the dog couldn't help being aroused to pursuit. Each time, Boldy would flee from Sourdough, but only fast enough to keep barely ahead—"Catch me if you can!" Sometimes Sourdough was hard put to *avoid* catching him.

Bears don't sleep the winter away in Virginia, but they usually stay secluded. Boldy did. It wasn't until one evening the following summer that I saw him again—his face at our bathroom window. When I floodlighted the back yard, he ran to the garden and pulled up a cornstalk. Lying on his back, he used all four feet in an effort to keep it flying. When Darwin ran out, yelling and flailing his arms, Boldy bounded over the fence. But he came right back. He looked toward the window as if soliciting us, not only Sourdough, as playmates. Then, with a sassy look over his shoulder, he took his cornstalk and went into the woods.

Boldy matured rapidly (males usually mature at age four, females at three). He had more than twice Sourdough's bulk now, and it worried us that summer when he perfected two distinct forms of the tag-bluff game. When Sourdough gave chase, Boldy would simply stop, often before reaching the fence, whereupon Sourdough would return to his corner. Each would go about his business, pretending that the other wasn't within a thousand miles. But, sooner or later, Boldy would tease the dog into chasing again, and the game might go on for hours. Sometimes Boldy chased back. Yet, no matter who chased whom, they never seemed to touch, and the game could be terminated at the wish of either player. The dog simply went into his house and let the flap fall—indicating "Do Not Disturb"—or the bear just disappeared into the forest.

In autumn, Boldy escalated the game. He began making surprise visits in the dark hours of morning. Sounds suggested this sequence: Boldy would pad softly up to the doghouse and poke his rubbery nose in the doorway; Sourdough, growling, would ricochet from wall to wall trying to make another door. By the time we got the floodlight on, Boldy would be padding innocently away. Often he would look back over his shoulder and lift a lip as if to say, "Just kidding."

The real rub came when older bears began following Boldy's lead, and robbing us of sleep. Sourdough would chase any bear fiercely now—until the bear remembered that it was, after all, a bear. Then it would turn and charge Sourdough—far enough to restore bear morale. Sourdough changed strategy; he made himself a different bed every time he snoozed, often in the forest's fringe. When a bear came to surprise him, he surprised the bear. With a new note of authority, then, he'd drive the bear entirely off. We had to bring him inside when we wanted to observe wildlife, and we felt such confidence in the bears' harmlessness that we began venturing outside even when bears were in the yard.

But bears are individuals, unpredictable, as we should have remembered. A strange female, seeking ants near the garden, was so intent on her business that I took my camera and ventured a dozen steps from the back door to get an unobstructed view. Suddenly, the bear growled and charged me. I dashed for the door. Darwin hurled a stick at the bear, and she ran off.

Boldy was the first bear to come in the spring of '73. It was after dinner, and our living room was full of guests. Sourdough, who'd been napping on the front porch, exploded in his most urgent bear-warning and ran way out front. Darwin went for a spotlight. One eager guest started outside, hoping for a glimpse before the fugitive faded into the forest. The screen door wouldn't open, and the guest leaped back—"The bear's here—on the porch!" I snapped on the porch light.

Yes, our Boldy! But so big now, surely 300 pounds! He blinked in the sudden light, then ambled to a nearby tree and sat down, teddy-bear style, paunch exposed. The mood was of quiet fellowship—for what seemed ten minutes. Then Boldy lifted himself to all fours—and slowly, looking back once as if saying good night, he left.

For weeks there was no further sign of Boldy. But, one evening last June, a bear we hadn't seen before came through the orchard, eating honewort and wild lettuce—a glossy female with a small white spot high on her right front leg. She walked out under a clothesline, sniffing at a nylon mesh bag holding a mix of birdseed and ham fat that I had tied on the line. She stood on hind legs, but couldn't reach the bag. Then, without hesitation, she walked 20 feet over to higher ground where she *could* reach the line. Holding it down, sliding it through her forepaws, she moved on hind feet over to that bag. Clever! We named her Beauty. But where was Boldy?

A few mornings later, I put a batch of granola in to bake. Windows were open, and the lovely aroma wafted down-hollow. When I went to turn off the oven, I found Boldy. His front feet were on the stone floor of the little porch, his turned-up nose stretched toward the screen door. My excited exclamation brought Darwin from his desk. Boldy looked in through the flimsy screen.

"Better forget the granola, friend," Darwin said, keeping his voice calm and low. Boldy moved slowly off, stopping at the big dining-room window. There he stood up and put his nose to the glass, and then a forepaw. I yelled, "No!" Darwin roared.

Boldy dropped front feet to ground. Sourdough charged. Boldy bounded into the forest. Immediately we felt badly about chasing him off. He could have broken the glass so easily—but he'd been delicately gentle. Prints of his paw and nose remained there. I wanted to keep them forever.

Three mornings later, Beauty came across our orchard, pausing at intervals to eat honewort. And there, following her, was Boldy. They walked side by side around our garden.

Sourdough didn't make a sound. Beauty and Boldy glanced at us, but were mostly interested in each other. They soon disappeared into the forest.

Again, in mid-July, Boldy and Beauty came into our yard together, looked toward us at the window, and left. Sourdough didn't bark this time, either.

Neither of them came the rest of that year, or early the next year. But, several months later, when we were starting to walk for our mail, Sourdough barked. As we called him back, we saw a small bear cub run to a tree beside a stone fence and embrace the trunk as if to climb. Our insides leaped as we whirled to see if we'd blundered into the classic danger position, between mother and cub. But—no. The cub just stood watching us over its shoulder.

Then we saw Beauty, not 50 feet from us, sitting as if she'd been nursing the cub and hadn't bothered to get up. We watched her and she us, and after a while she seemed to speak softly. A second cub came tail-first down a nearby tree. The family reassembled and moved slowly toward our house. We continued down-hollow, hoping that the cubs have inherited Boldy's sense of humor and will visit us often.

The Saga of Patsy and Oscar

by Harland Manchester

DRIVING UP the hill to open our Vermont farmhouse one spring day some years ago, my wife and I stopped to say hello to a neighbor who kept a friendly eye on the place. He looked a little gloomy. After matters of health and weather had been settled, he gave us the bad news. "Your dam washed out," he announced.

We went and looked. The shimmering five-acre mirror which once echoed the red sunset and the wind-tossed pines and birches was now a dim eye of water sunk in a murky socket of mud and sedge. Freshets from melting snows had chewed a gaping hole around the concrete core of the earth dam. We turned away from the dismal sight, speculating about contractors and repair costs.

For the next two weeks we stayed away from the lake. Then early one morning Laetitia returned from a walk. "Something odd is happening at the dam," she said.

Sure enough, the washout was partly blocked with rocks, mud and bits of log and twigs, and the water was a little higher. Fresh green leaves showed that the work was only a few hours old. Next morning we noticed that the dike was higher, and water covered more of the marshland. Apparently the mysterious engineers were working at night. At sundown I smeared myself with insect repellent, took the binoculars and crawled through the bushy pines to a point overlooking the dam.

The repair crew was hard at work. A big beaver was plastering mud over the break. Another beaver was pushing a rock into place, and a third, only his nose showing, was swimming down the lake with a section of log. Each night at dusk they came and did their stint. The water crept over the flats to the forested shores. I painted and launched our small rowboat, and repaired the pier. Once more we had our shining bit of sea.

At first we hardly ever saw our hydraulic maintenance crew. There were only their lodge—an island hummock built of sticks and earth—and occasional fresh twigs on the dam to show their presence. Then one hot afternoon when we were lying on the pier near the dam my wife suddenly grabbed my arm and pointed down the center of the lake. A curious dark-brown dot, just skimming the surface, was coming toward us, leaving a long wake. Behind the leader, to left and right, two other dots appeared, trailing their rippling V's. Assured and precise, the committee advanced in symmetrical formation. Soon we could see the noble head of the chairman. He looked enormous. When he was some 50 feet away, his entourage submerged and gave him the stage. He turned and described a wide circle, completing the maneuver with an arrogant tail-slap which rang against the hills.

It was a magnificent picketing job. Obviously they wanted to inspect their project, so we meekly took our towels and slunk to the other side of the lake like gate crashers ordered from a beach club. But it was not enough—the leader followed us, and repeated his circle-and-slap demonstration. Emboldened by his example, the others copied his routine, and the three-ring beaver circus proceeded to put on a 15-minute act that lesser beasts would have spent whole winters rehearsing in Sarasota. They would submerge, leaving the water still and quiet for long minutes, pop up in unexpected places, circle again, slap and recircle. Finally, having made their point, they swam off into the sunset, three fading dots.

"Maybe they don't like summer people," I said.

"You can't tell about Vermonters," said my wife. "Maybe they want to be friendly."

She turned out to be right. They never lost a certain aloof poise, but on days when they had no pressing chores they came down the lake to see us. Sometimes the chairman came alone. We thought he should have a name, so we began to call him Oscar, first behind his back, then to his face. He became more jovial and frisky. One day when Laetitia was swimming I saw Oscar serenely escorting her, only a few feet away.

About this time Patsy, our black retriever-clipped poodle, discovered the beavers. Patsy, a descendant of Norman Thomas's late lamented "Jester," was about half Socialist, and fervently egalitarian. Some of her best friends were cats, and not even sad encounters with skunks and porcupines could dent her grinning faith in all God's creatures. We had been told that beavers distrusted dogs, and had been known to drag them under water and drown them. Yet Patsy, true to her breed, loved to swim. The inevitable happened—she took to chasing the beavers.

I was working in my study one day and my wife had gone to the lake when I heard a triple blast from the jeep horn—a family signal of distress. I ran puffing to the pier. Halfway up the lake, Patsy was pursuing Oscar. Whenever she got close, Oscar would submerge, leaving the bewildered poodle splashing about at her wit's end. Jumping in the boat, I rowed to the rescue.

Little good it did—the next day Patsy was back for another round. The wily Oscar, with three dimensions at his command, evaded her with infuriating ease. But it became clear that he meant her no harm—he was having the time of his life. While Patsy was swimming west toward his last vanishing point, he would pop up in the east, deal the water a resounding crack and lead her off on another wild beaver chase.

This went on day after day. When Oscar was late, Patsy climbed to the top of the beaver lodge and barked, tapping an impatient paw. After time enough had elapsed for a beaver to rouse from his siesta and exit through his subterranean tunnel, the familiar brown dot would break the surface, and the chase was on.

When Oscar finally got bored and retired to quarters, Patsy would stagger home, eat her supper and go to sleep. As the summer progressed, she slept more and more. She seldom barked at birds any more or dug for woodchucks beneath pasture walls. She seemed to be living only for her daily workout. One afternoon it lasted longer than usual, and my wife got worried. "Let's go and get her," she said. "She's an old dog—she'll wear herself out." So we broke up the act and hauled her into the boat.

After that, we tried to keep Patsy in the house when we went swimming, but she scratched the paint off the door and acted miserable. One day she disappeared and came back wet and exhausted. That night she didn't touch her food. The next morning she lay in the kitchen and didn't rise when we called her.

The vet shook his head. Her heart was leaking, he said. We put her away beneath a young birch tree. The next spring, Oscar was gone. Our neighbor said he had seen men with traps.

For several years, although the dam was kept in perfect repair, no beavers came to see us. Sometimes we spoke about another poodle, but during winters in town they have to be taken out on a leash, and somehow . . .

Then last spring when we arrived we jeeped down to the pier and looked at the fresh, gleaming water. Far down the lake, a brown dot appeared—then another and another. A veritable armada of five submersibles advanced in stately procession. At their head swam a majestic young beaver, worthy heir to Oscar the Great.

Up on the hill the young birch tree had shot high against the dark pines. Its lacy foliage, laughing in the breeze, seemed to take the shape of a retriever clip.

Salute to Old Blue

by Jean George

IN THE dead of winter when the raccoon sleeps in the bole of a tree, when the skunk has plugged himself in his burrow with a stopper of leaves, and the beaver is frozen in under the ice, the world of nature seems quiet, deserted. But in the stillness there is activity. Each day at my window—at anyone's window where there is a bird feeder—there is an explosion of excitement as a flock of chickadees bursts upon seed and suet.

For years these tidy, approachable acrobats of the bird world meant little to me. Then one day my husband, John, who is a naturalist, announced that he was planning a seven-year study of the chickadee. I stared at him in amazement. Wasn't everything already known about this commonplace bird? No, he told me; less was known about the chickadee than about almost any other abundant American bird.

I met my first chickadee in person on a December evening on the Vassar College campus in Poughkeepsie, N.Y., where John was teaching bird ecology. John stepped into our kitchen, placed a small bird in my hand and said, "Hold him while I band his legs."

The bird within my fingers cocked his head and put a blazing eye on me. Although a songbird, like a person, can focus using both eyes together, it sees more detail using them separately; that's why a bird cocks its head. A bird can sit in a tree, scanning the leaves for a caterpillar, the sky above for a hawk, the fence behind for a cat—and all at the same time!

As I held the black-and-white bird I was awe-struck by

the intricacies of his beauty. The feathers of the black cap lay like open ferns across the head, white cheek patches shone and the black bib rumpled like tissue paper under my thumb. My finger pressed the heart, which beat so fiercely that it shook the small body—1000 beats per minute, John told me.

With a puff I parted the feathers behind the eye, and there lay an open hole—the ear. I spoke, but the chickadee did not stir, for the human voice is usually pitched too low for his hearing.

And then we banded him—in the same way that John was banding every other chickadee in the area. I stroked the bird's breast and, as my finger tips caressed him, he stopped struggling and lay still, hypnotized. John slipped a blue plastic band on his right foot, and an aluminum band on his left which read: 48–53487. I lifted the bird to my cheek, smelled the leafy odor of his feathers and walked to the open window. As I held him into the dusk I felt his lightness, and understood how much buoyancy is provided by a bird's hollow bones. Now the cold wind touched him; he awoke from his trance, flipped onto his air-lined wings and flew lightly off. "Goodnight, Old Blue!" I called.

The campus was good chickadee country, with 15 tribes living within the 500-acre study area. The tribes varied in number from 5 to 15 members, depending on the wisdom and boldness of the leader and, more important, on the food supply. It was the tribe at our house—to which Old Blue belonged—that I cared about most.

John told me that Old Blue's tribe was of average size—10; it had about 20 acres of the best chickadee land—woods, small yards and dense thickets. Most of the tribe slept in Mrs. MacMahon's woods, came to our feeder when the members first awakened, went from our house to the beech tree at the powerhouse, to the owl woods, across to the English building, over to the faculty houses and back to our feeder at noon. On very cold days the birds fed in the protected woods, where John often found them resting in bushes, staring silently out at the snow.

The morning after I released Old Blue I arose early to watch my flock, for I was anxious to know where he stood in the hierarchy. Just at daybreak, like the burst of a Roman candle, chickadees descended on bushes, trees and vines. Yellow tried to feed first, but when Old Blue quivered his wings at him, he vanished. I thought Old Blue might be boss, until Green called out and my bird flew away. After an hour Old Blue had shown that he was second only to Green.

As December wore on, I came to understand the social world of the chickadee tribe: how some birds dominate others, but how the whole tribe protects each individual. Even a stupid bird can find food if he follows the gang, and a careless one can be warned to hide when a hawk goes overhead.

Late in January something happened to my birds: they permitted more than one at a time on the feeder. John told me they were selecting mates. All the next day I hung around the window to find out whom Old Blue was courting. Then, late in the day, I saw him low in the shadbush, preening and twisting toward Red-Yellow, an aggressive little female. Presently he deserted her and flew down near the power plant, where his beautiful "Hi, sweetie" song purled out. By singing he was establishing his exclusive right to that land; and before March was out, the two birds were inseparable in their own territory.

By then the tribe had broken up; some males had gone as far as five miles to find a territory. Every bird now had a mate except two young males. They hung around singing to mated females, were chased by husbands (chickadees are faithful for life), and finally were pushed to a neutral area by the college lake. Here they sang and waited for misadventure to befall a mated male so one of them might fill his vacancy.

A week passed and I did not see Old Blue. Then one day I wandered into his spring territory—four acres within the tribe's 20. By the power plant I heard a fierce hammering, and found Old Blue chopping a hole in a rotted aspen stump. Chips rained down. When Old Blue grew tired and hungry, Red-Yellow worked at the hole. When it was done, it was nine inches deep and lined with roots and hair.

A week later I looked out the window and saw Old Blue preening his feathers in the hemlock. A quiver above him caught my eye. Red-Yellow sat there as puffed as a dandelion, her drooped wings trembling, calling "Be my mate." Old Blue heard her and answered by shaking his wings. He twisted slowly like a dancer, pointed his beak—and then, lightly as wind, he flew upon her. As he did so, the egg that was descending her oviduct was struck with life.

During the next few hours this fertile egg moved downward, was encased in albumin and membranes and covered with shell. Early the next morning Red-Yellow, feeling the pressure of delivery, winged to the aspen cavity and laid the egg. Then she left it and quietly joined Old Blue. On the eighth day, after her eighth egg had been laid, Red-Yellow did not come out of the cavity, for she had completed her clutch.

Now Red-Yellow covered the eggs with her brood patch, a hot featherless spot on her breast, and stayed with them almost constantly for 13 days and 13 nights. During this long vigil Old Blue sometimes fed her. Often she was in a deep incubation state and difficult to arouse unless she heard Old Blue's nest call, a sound not audible more than ten feet away. This soft song brightened her eyes, made her open her bill. Old Blue poked in the worms.

Since the chickadee starts incubating all the eggs on the same day, they all hatch on the same day. May 9 was bedlam in the hole as shells were removed and baby birds ate their weight in green caterpillars. Many songbirds keep their nests clean by one of nature's ingenious devices—the fecal sac. These young birds excrete their waste matter into a thin membranous sac, which the parent carries off. That first day I watched Old Blue haul off dozens of these sacs, like a dutiful father disposing of diapers.

After 16 days the young were ready to fledge. I took my seat early.

About 8 a.m. a blowzy youngster wavered in the doorway. The rim of his yellow beak shone like a clown's grin from eye to eye. The beak would soon change color, for this yellow target is a mark for parents to hit when the young are nesting. The day they are on their own, the yellow disappears.

The bird in the doorway suddenly spread his wings and whammed off, lit on a twig, swung forward, then back, spread his wings and righted himself. Then he screamed for food. Soon the others followed suit.

By August, cats, snakes, owls and hawks had cut down Old Blue's family to three. And by early September Old Blue was alone. Following deep instincts, his children had left him to join other tribes on campus; this prevented inbreeding. Red-Yellow was dead, we knew not how. Then up from the woods, out from the brushlands came young birds to join together in a social winter.

This year the leader was Old Blue. Battles with song and wings and beaks proved it.

Over the following years Old Blue made a brilliant leader. He led his tribe safely around cats and sparrow hawks, took them to secret food supplies, and into the deepest shelter in sleet and storm. When a neighboring tribe leader died, Old Blue gathered a group of aggressive males and they flew into the area and claimed it. He expanded the kingdom by almost 20 acres. They were a bold and rich tribe.

Then came the seventh year. Old Blue's return to our feeder that winter astounded us, for never had we heard of a chickadee living that long. He was still in full command when John called me one evening to see him put his tribe to bed. They flew into Mrs. MacMahon's woods, where each sang, then flew off to various tree cavities and hollows. Old Blue was still up when the rest were gone. He slowly circled a tree, cocked his head to hear the last call of a crotchety nuthatch, buzzed his own "dee, dee, dee, dee," then slipped into a hole in an old apple tree. I visualized him inside his hollow puffing his feathers and closing his eyes, the lids coming up from the bottom to the top. The wind blew; it grew darker and colder.

At 3. a.m. a sleet storm struck the Hudson Valley; trees glassed over, bent and shrieked when the wind hit them. We listened and wondered about the birds in their hollows.

The morning was dark and long, and when the birds finally got up only a few came to our feeder. Old Blue was not among them.

I watched every day for a week, but he did not return. John said he might be out feeding in some area vacated by birds that did not survive that icy night. But neither of us believed it, especially since our tribe was fighting fiercely all day—a sign I recognized as a struggle for leadership.

One morning Orange chased all the other birds from the feeding station and ate without challenge. I knew we would never see Old Blue again. I went to the records and looked up Orange. "Grandson of Blue" was scribbled beside his name. My sadness lifted as I realized once again that nature loves to repeat her successes. There would be other "Old Blues" at my window.

The White Lady

by Leonard Dubkin

ONE JUNE EVENING, while idly exploring a clump of trees in a weed-grown Chicago lot, I made an exciting discovery. Under one of the trees was a huge dome-shaped structure. All sorts of vines had twined around the lower branches, forming an almost impenetrable mass of foliage that curved upward from the ground like an igloo, to a height of 18 or 20 feet. It was the kind of thing one might find in a tropical forest, but here in the city, with a factory nearby and with cars whizzing past, it was strange indeed.

Inside, this unusual grotto was even stranger. It was musky smelling and dimly lit, like a room with the shades drawn. And hanging head downward everywhere from the leafy, sloping roof were clusters of sleeping bats—more than 200 of them, I estimated.

That summer and fall I often returned to watch this bat colony. My entrance into the grotto, through the inconspicuous opening I had made, always excited the bats at first. But if I remained quiet they soon ignored me. About seven in the evening they would start to stretch and squeak. Soon they were whirling around the tree trunk in a mass of wings. Then, as at a signal, the whole flock, leaving their young behind, would swarm out of the foot-and-a-half opening at the top like a puff of smoke. For a couple of hours the air overhead would be filled with bats hunting insects. Then they would disappear, not to return until dawn.

The homecoming at dawn was a bedlam of squeaking,

darting figures; it was usually an hour before all the mothers had identified their young and were again hanging with them from the roof, composed for the day's sleep.

In mid-October that year the bats all left for some unknown place of hibernation. But early next May the first of them came back. A week later all seemed to have returned. They were restless and excitable—the young were being born.

On May 28 I found a bat hanging from a limb head upward instead of the usual downward position. She was clutching the vegetation above with her thumbs (located on the wingtips) and her feet clawed the air. She made no sound, but her lips were bared and her teeth moved as if she were gritting them. Suddenly she bent her feet up under her body so that the tail membrane which was stretched between them curled under her like a pocket. Soon a tiny mouselike creature, its wings crumpled around its head, emerged and lay motionless in the pocket. The mother licked it, turning it over and over, until it emitted a barely audible squeak. Now it twisted about in its cradle, brought one wing down to its side, then the other, and began crawling shakily upward toward its mother's stomach. The mother bit through the umbilical cord, picked the baby up by the back of the neck—exactly like a cat picking up her kitten—and placed it near one of her breasts. While it was suckling, the placenta emerged, then the mother grasped the roof with her feet, and, hanging head downward now, wrapped one wing around her baby. The whole thing had taken just four minutes.

So engrossed was I in the birth that I had hardly noticed that this baby bat was completely white. But now I realized that I had watched the birth of an albino bat—a creature very seldom found. This summer, instead of observing the colony as a group, I would be able to distinguish this one bat from the others and watch its individual development.

When the baby white bat was only a day old, it was already hanging beside its mother. Among the other bats it was as conspicuous as a bright star in a dark sky. That same day I edged forward in the grotto and closed my hand around it. Then, with the mother and a few other bats flying frenziedly around my head, I sat down to examine my rare discovery.

Her eyes were still closed, and she wobbled as she crawled across my palm, her folded wings trailing like silken garments at her sides. She sniffed as she went, and when she came to the end of my little finger she clamped her feet on it, swung herself over the edge and hung motionless. "Little white lady," I whispered, "you are a rare thing." From that moment she was always the white lady to me.

Just then there was a flutter of dark wings under my hand; in a flash the baby bat was snatched away by her mother. The action was so instantaneous that it appeared she had plucked off her baby in full flight. Yet there had been no pull on my finger. The mother had swiftly spread her tail membrane as the baby let go of my finger and grasped her fur, and off they sailed together.

Now, with the white lady to guide me, I discovered that the bats had a strongly developed, proprietary sense of position on the roof. Each day the white lady and her mother hung in a particular spot, part of a compact cluster of 26 bats, each of which had its own place in the group. And if a bat hung itself up in any group but its own, the others all turned on it, bared their sharp teeth and squeaked menacingly.

Until she was five days old the white lady clung to her mother when she flew abroad at night. But after the fifth day, when the white lady's eyes opened, she was left in the grotto—possibly because she could now hide from danger.

The first few nights the white lady hung for an hour or so after her mother left. In a few days, however, she began to spend her time with one or two other young bats—scrambling about among the vines, chasing or being chased with playful biting and squeaking. Still later, I often saw her among a group of 40 or more, all squeaking, biting, crawling over and under each other in what appeared to be some elaborate game.

I began taking the white lady home with me in a cigar box with air holes in the top. Transferred to the canary cage I'd fixed up with screen wire around it, she would at first crawl about on the bottom, sniffing at the screen, then climb up on a perch and hang downward for about half an hour. She did not sleep, and her eyes followed my every movement. Later she would embark on an exploratory tour, sniffing and trying to squeeze through every slight opening. Often I'd find the cage empty in the morning, although she was almost full-grown now and there seemed no opening large enough. It was sometimes a problem to find her—especially if she was hanging on white kitchen curtains, or from a white wall fixture.

I always took the white lady back to the grotto in the

morning on my way to work. As soon as the box was open she would sniff the air, then utter a faint, nearly inaudible squeak. Instantly the mother would leave her perch, swoop down and snatch up her daughter in one of those instantaneous pick-ups which always left me feeling I had witnessed magic.

When she was 23 days old the white lady flew for the first time. I had intended to take her home with me that evening, but when I reached to pick her up she launched herself out into the grotto, her white wings flashing around and around the trunk. While I watched—for almost two hours—she launched herself again and again, trying her newfound skill. Twice her wings brushed against my face, as though to be sure I was paying attention, like a child who cries, "Look at me, look what I can do." I did not take her with me that evening—not on this, her first night of flight.

The next evening I came to the grotto before the adults had gone out. There, whirling around with the rest, was the white lady. I knew that now, for the first time, she would be going out to hunt with the others. So I went outside to await their exit.

There was the usual black, smoke-like eruption as the bats left the grotto. Gradually the mass resolved into myriad pairs of beating wings, and soon above me I saw the white lady. She was zooming, diving and zigzagging as skillfully as the others, even though this was her first time aloft on her own wings!

This was not surprising, though. The wings evolved by the first primordial bats are still the most efficient on earth, bird wings included. The only control a bird has over its wing feathers is the ability to turn them slightly and to spread groups of them more or less. A bird's wing in flight is almost as rigid as that of an airplane with its ailerons. But the wing of a bat is skin spread along its arm and between its fingers. As easily as a man can bend his fingers a bat can flap the whole wing or any part of it, can change lift, pitch or angle of any part in any way it pleases.

Tonight I kept my eyes on the white lady. She was graceful, airy, insubstantial. As the sun sank, the whiteness of her body changed to rosy pink, and from her wings there flashed, as she tilted them, a shaft of orange light reflected from the sun. Then suddenly the air was empty, as though a magician had waved his wand.

From that day I came to the grotto every evening. If the bats were outside when I walked across the field, the white lady would welcome me by diving toward me and flashing her wings near my face as she skimmed by. (None of the other bats ever took such liberties.) One evening as I was examining a disabled grasshopper on the palm of my open hand, there was a sudden blur of white wings and the grasshopper disappeared. The white lady had taken it from my hand, just as her mother had snatched her from me when she was a baby. I found another insect—a brown beetle—and placed it on my palm. Almost immediately the white lady swooped like a dive bomber; the beetle, too, was gone. I fed her four more insects in this manner, the last one a tiny ladybird beetle. It was so dark that I could not see the insect as it crawled over my hand, but from 20 feet above the white lady swooped down and snatched it away without touching my hand.

One evening I came to the grotto early, caught the white lady in a net, and released her at home to photograph her. I had adjusted the camera and was waiting for her to come within range when, to my horror, she flew directly toward the revolving blades of an electric fan I had neglected to turn off. Powerless to do anything, I stood there, convinced that she was flying to her death. But she was not even touched by the blades. She flew into the fan and came out the other side as easily as a child jumping rope. Flying to her death, indeed—she had known exactly what she was doing!

After that first dash into the fan, she did it again and again, apparently glorying in her ability to fly through the whirling blades. I was tempted to try an experiment: I turned the fan from its low speed—800 revolutions per minute—to a higher speed—1200. She dashed toward it as before, but this time she did not go through. She zoomed up over the top of the fan.

Much as I had watched the bats, I had never before recognized any manifestations of "radar" which enables bats to fly in darkness and to avoid obstacles. Later I found that two Harvard professors (Galambos and Griffin) had proved that bats in flight broadcast sounds inaudible to the human ear, and guide themselves by the echoes returned. When a bat's mouth was stopped up it bumped repeatedly into wires strung across the room. The same thing happened when its ears were plugged and it could not receive the reflected signals. But whether its eyes were open or sealed shut made no appreciable difference.

This chance experiment with the fan emboldened me to try another that same evening. I decided to see if she could find her way back to the grotto. It was five miles from our home, and it was with some misgivings that I opened the window and watched the white flash as she darted away. But the next morning I found her hanging from her usual place on the grotto roof.

How much farther could I take her? One evening toward the end of August I decided to try another experiment. I waited until the bats were circling the tree trunk just before leaving, then caught the white lady in my net and drove 15 miles through crowded traffic to Jackson Park on the South Side, where I released her. As I watched her fly off I was filled with remorse: she was headed in the wrong direction. In a minute or two she would be over the lake, where she would probably fly until she became exhausted. What a fool I was to have taken her so far. Nonetheless, I decided to return to the grotto and wait, all night if necessary, to see if—through some miracle—she might return. When I arrived there by the quickest possible route I found the white lady out hunting insects with the others, none the worse for her experience.

Toward the end of September I had to drive to Milwaukee on business and I took the white lady along. Just as I started back I released her and then I drove directly to the grotto. There she was in her usual place. She had flown 90 miles over unfamiliar territory in less than two and a half hours.

From this time on, through the early fall, the bats became more and more lethargic. They slept more soundly, and many did not leave the grotto at night but continued hanging from the roof in deep sleep. One day about the middle of October I found the grotto deserted.

The next spring, on the first Sunday in May, with the warmth-laden breeze blowing a hint of the summer to come, I drove out to see if the bats had returned. But as I approached the place my heart sank. Where there had been a field with a little clump of trees, there was only a muddy plain. Where the grotto had been, there now stood a steam shovel, its great open jaws resting on the earth like some huge rapacious beast.

Now I would never know whether the white lady had a baby, or how long she would live, or what happened to her.

But at least I had learned that bats are playful and

friendly, not the malicious, spiteful little animals most people believe. And I had seen the birth of the white lady, watched her grow, and witnessed her first flight. It was as though I alone had been present at the production of a work of art, watching it grow from an insignificant beginning to a thing of beauty.

Born to Kill

The Fiercest Animal on Earth

by Alan Devoe

WHEN I was a boy I used to wonder, as boys do, what animal was the most ferocious in the world. Would it be the lion, perhaps? Tiger? Grizzly bear? When I grew up to be a naturalist and learned the answer I was astonished. The fiercest of all fighters and the most voracious predator is a tiny mammal, the common shrew. You'd have to put at least two of them on a scale to register one ounce.

A shrew is so savage that it will attack, kill and devour animals twice its size. It has such a prodigious appetite that it can eat the equivalent of its own weight about every three hours, and it burns energy so fast that if deprived of food it will starve to death in less than a day. A shrew uses up its life force so prodigally in preying and feeding that it dies of old age at about 16 months.

There are shrews of one sort or another in most parts of the world—in the tropics, deserts and the Arctic. The pigmy shrew found in Virginia, Maryland and North Carolina is possibly the tiniest mammal on earth. It is only about three inches long.

Probably not one person in 100 is aware of ever having seen a shrew, yet in many countrysides it is the commonest animal of all. It looks like a wee mouse with a sharp pointed muzzle, tiny eyes that are barely visible and velvety dark-gray or sepia fur. What we see is just a scurrying little blur as the shrew whisks through the grass in its ceaseless search for food.

In its grass-roots jungle the little assassin has to rely on sniffing out its prey or blundering upon it, for its pinhead eyes see little. It lifts its muzzle, sniffs, darts around a grass tussock, sniffs again, whizzes off at a tangent through the grass and suddenly makes a springing leap like a tiger. It has found a beetle, perhaps, or a butterfly, slug, centipede or cricket.

A shrew will eat almost anything, and it gobbles so fast—all the while shaking in spasms of excitement—that it devours its prey in a few seconds. The fact that it dispatches hordes of insects of all kinds makes it one of our most valuable animals.

It is afraid of nothing. When I was a boy I put a shrew into a cage with a young white rat, intending to leave it there for a few moments while I got its own cage ready. Instantly the furry midget reared up, bared his teeth and let loose a high-pitched chittering squeak of rage and hunger. In panic, his hulking adversary cowered in a corner. Then in a flash the shrew was across the cage, slashing at the rat's throat, swarming all over him. At the end, the shrew gobbled up every last vestige of the rat, including bones, claws and fur.

A naturalist friend of mine who keeps snakes and feeds them on mice once made the mistake of giving one of his charges a shrew. When he visited the reptile's cage next day it contained only the shrew, racing around looking for more snakes.

The life of this bloodthirsty creature begins in a loose ball of leaves and grasses usually hidden in a hollow stump or log. In this nursery is born a litter of four to ten pink, crinkly babies smaller than honeybees. They begin to creep around the nest when they are about a week old. At three or four weeks their mother weans them, changing them to a diet of flesh—usually earthworms.

A few days later she unceremoniously boots them out of the nursery, and each youngster is on his own. Twinkling the tip of his pointed nose in a frenzied alertness for a sniff of prey, he goes rushing off through the grass stems on the indomitable hunt to which his whole life will be given. Whatever small fellow creature he may meet, it will never cross his mind to think, "Is he bigger than I am?" There is just one thought in his tiny skull: "Let me at him!"

In periods of family-raising, father and mother shrew live devotedly together. But this is the only time in a shrew's life when its ferocity subsides, even toward its own kind. It is fatal to put two shrews in a cage, for in a few minutes there is just one shrew, licking its chops.

What of the shrew's natural enemies? Only a few strong-stomached hunters like the great horned owl, weasels and bobcats eat shrews. For on each of the animal's flanks is a potent gland containing a sickening musk that the shrew can loose when overwhelmed. The fox that pounces on a shrew in the tall meadow grass usually drops his catch in a hurry.

Tests of the short-tailed shrew have proved that its salivary glands contain a venom similar to that secreted by such poisonous snakes as the cobra. When its teeth slash an enemy the victim grows foggy-minded, then has trouble breathing, then is stricken by a numbing paralysis.

As far as naturalists can tell, the short-tailed shrew is the only species that carries such powerful venom. But every shrew carries a ferocious hostility, a ravenous hunger and reckless rage.

Piranha: Minijaws of the Amazon

by Emily and Per Ola D'Aulaire

ONLY A HANDFUL of creatures on earth carry the dread title "man-eater." The great white shark is one, quick at times to snap up swimmers and shipwrecked sailors. People have been meals for lions and tigers. But perhaps no creature is more blindly savage than a small fish of South America's inland waters—the piranha.

At first glance, the piranha (pronounced pee-RAHN-yah) seems harmless enough. Deep-bellied and flat, it looks like a sunfish a youngster might catch on a lazy Sunday afternoon. It is actually a close relative of the silver dollar—an ornamental and placid fish prized by aquarium enthusiasts. But toward the business end of a piranha, any similarity to its more docile brethren ends.

The head of the piranha is massive by scale, its raked-back skull armored by thick bone. Its large, round eyes are sometimes blood red, its mouth is armed with triangular teeth as keen as razors. When the lower jaw, thrust forward bulldog-fashion, snaps shut, the upper and lower teeth mesh perfectly. The result on anything caught in between is that of surgical steel on butter. One bite and out comes a neat piece of flesh the size of a quarter. Indeed, the name piranha comes from the Tupí-Guaraní Indians and means "tooth fish." In some Spanish-speaking countries it is called the caribe, or cannibal-fish.

We had a chance to see those dread jaws in action ourselves when we hired a guide to take us fishing out from

Manaus, in Brazil's jungle. An hour after we left the city, Jorge cut the engine in an inlet off the muddy Amazon, and baited a hook with raw meat. Almost immediately something struck, and Jorge hauled the line back in, flipping a struggling fish about 12 inches long into the bilge. "Red piranha," he warned. "Watch your hands and feet."

Thrashing in the narrow boat bottom, sunlight glittering off its vermilion belly, it looked as handsome as any tropical fish we'd seen. The fierce-looking jaws, however, were snapping wildly at the air. Jorge reached for an oar to deal it a blow just as the hook worked loose from the fish's mouth. With a lightning-swift snap, the piranha chopped a neat semi-circular chunk from the wooden oar—then flipped over the low gunwhale into the water. We now understood why so many fishermen in piranha country are missing fingers and toes.

Since piranhas often feed in large schools, sometimes in groups of hundreds, the damage they can do—and the speed with which they can do it—is astounding. One Brazilian vaquero told us of wounding a 125-pound capybara, the world's largest rodent, whose flesh is prized in the Amazon Basin. The animal galloped toward the safety of a nearby lake and plunged in, trailing blood. As the cowboy watched, the water turned white with activity, then scarlet, and within minutes there was nothing left of the capybara but bones.

Ever since Theodore Roosevelt brought back an account in 1914 of a man stripped to a skeleton while fording a Brazilian stream on a mule, piranhas have had an awesome reputation the world over. Though actual cases of piranhas eating people are rare, when they do occur, the results are nightmarish. In November 1976, a bus tumbled into the piranha-infested Urubu River at a ferry crossing 125 miles east of Manaus. When rescue workers arrived nine hours later, they found most of the 38 passengers who died in the accident skeletonized by the fish.

In spite of such incidents, many experts think the threat piranhas pose to humans is exaggerated. They point out that natives of the Amazon Basin often swim in rivers where fishermen are hauling in piranhas by the dozen. The Indians are, in fact, much more afraid of sting rays, anacondas and the *candirú*, an insidious little parasite fish that swims into body orifices and lodges there, often necessitating surgical removal.

But as George S. Myers, professor emeritus of biology at Stanford University, points out, the piranha's danger, like that of the shark, is real—a matter of being in the wrong place at the wrong time. "Neither sharks, lions, rattlesnakes nor piranhas automatically kill a person who enters their habitat," he says. "But anyone who claims that any of these is not a deadly animal is foolish."

It is in shallow waters that the piranhas are most dangerous—in oxbows, inlets or lakes and ponds that shrink with the summer's sun. As the waters recede and the piranhas' natural food supply (mainly other fish) is exhausted, they become particularly aggressive. In cattle country, they often attack livestock, even swimming beneath cows wading in shallow water, nipping off teats and tail tips. The *Dicionário dos Animais do Brasil* reports that in Mato Grosso State alone during one year, piranhas killed 1200 head of cattle.

It is probably not one, but a combination of factors, including hunger, low water and high piranha density, that drives the fish to attack. The piranha is sharp-eyed and uses vision, smell and a sensitivity to vibrations in the water to find its prey. The scent of blood maddens them, sending them knifing to the source, mouth agape, at speeds that make them a blur to the human eye.

There may be more than a score of piranha species—ranging from several inches up to about two feet—that infest lakes, rivers and ponds throughout most of South America east of the Andes between the Caribbean-facing nations and northern Argentina. Some are little more dangerous than goldfish; others, like the red piranha, are killers.

Oddly, even the most dangerous of the species make solicitous parents, unusual among the family of fish (Characidae) to which they belong. The females lay their eggs on strands of aquatic vegetation, hundreds at a time. The males fertilize them and then hover nearby. When the young fish hatch, they remain attached to the vegetation for several days, until the yolk sacs of the eggs are absorbed. The tiny larval fish would be tempting morsels to other passing fish if the male piranha did not deal with intruders savagely. Only when the fry are free-swimming does he leave—and then it's every fish for itself.

Like sharks, piranhas are feeders of opportunity: both

as loners and in schools they will attack and eat anything available. Unlike the shark, who is usually intimidated by size, piranhas will attack creatures many times their own size, if such victims are wounded or behaving strangely. If the prey is a large fish, the piranha may snap off its tail and immobilize it. While eating, each fish bites, then pulls back to rip off a mouthful of flesh, leaving an open space. Another fish quickly darts in and repeats the maneuver. Feeding in this "conveyor-belt" fashion, they polish off a quarry with incredible speed. Not even birds are safe when these fish are hungry. Herons, egrets and wild ducks flying low over the water have suddenly vanished in foam and blood.

There is at least a measure of poetic justice regarding piranhas: the Indians find them eminently edible, catching dozens of them by spreading the crushed bark of the poisonous timbo vine on the water, then roasting the catch over hot coals. Dinner over, the jaws are used as scissors for cutting vines and skins. The teeth, sometimes tipped with curare, become arrow points.

Although Indians find the piranha useful, conservationists in areas that don't have it decidedly don't want it. In southern Florida, where there is an ideal climate for piranhas, scientists are particularly on the lookout. The reason: a thriving trade in tropical fish, including piranhas, from South America to the United States. Authorities fear that some of these "pets" could somehow end up in Florida's waterways.

That fear was actually realized in 1972, when a piranha was caught in a pond near Miami. The Florida Game and Fresh Water Fish Commission poisoned the water, but no other piranha surfaced. Since then, according to Vernon Ogilvie, a biologist with the Commission, there have been recurrent rumors of schools of piranhas, west of Miami. "We've never found any evidence," says Ogilvie, "but I do know that, biologically, they'd do just fine here."

There is one small solace, however, even where piranhas abound. When piranha and man collide, it is generally by accident or because there has been an error in human judgment. Take the case of the Indian chief on the upper Tapajós River. He had been cleaning a chicken on the bank of a lake, carelessly throwing the entrails into the water. Then he sloshed his hands around to wash off the blood. There was a sudden dash beneath the surface and a yelp from the chief as he jerked his hands back—minus a neatly severed index finger. "The villagers were very philosophical," the missionary who witnessed the incident told us. "They said it was his fault for putting his hand in the water, not the piranha's for biting it."

Prince of Cats—
The Lethal Leopard

by Jack Denton Scott

FOR SIX motionless hours we had been sitting in a big kowa tree in the jungle of India's province of Madhya Pradesh. On that chill February night many years ago, my wife and I had been called from our camp to come quickly to the village of Dhega, where a pair of tigers had been killing cattle; we were the only people within 50 miles with rifles. Now, the moon gone, we were still waiting for the tigers to return to a buffalo kill they had made.

"We will hear them when they come," said Rao Naidu, our guide. "When I flash the light, you and Mrs. Scott will shoot."

At last the barest scuff of sound came from the darkness. Rao Naidu flashed his light. Directly below us stood, not the tigers, but a large tawny leopard, eyes shining like topaz as he looked up at us. He had deliberately bypassed the dead buffalo to stalk a fresher meal—us. Growling, he suddenly stood with front paws on the trunk of the kowa tree. My shot hit its mark before the leopard could charge.

That was my introduction to the regal spotted creature, the prince of cats. Cleverer than the tiger, fiercer than the lion, pound for pound the strongest of carnivores, the leopard is the most beautiful and graceful animal in the jungle. He is also the most dangerous. One seasoned forest officer observes, "A leopard can hide his whole body where a tiger can't hide his head. He can leap on your back from a tree that a tiger or a lion could never climb."

Leopards are not normally man-eaters. Some become so by accidentally killing a human being and, finding how easy it is, concentrating on it. At times physical incapacity or old age forces the cats to prey on human beings, but usually the leopard is such a master hunter that he has no need to attack man.

Deadliest of all man-killers was the "Man-Eating Leopard of Rudraprayag." From 1918 to 1926, in the 500 square miles of Garhwal, India, this fearsome animal killed 125 persons before he was shot by Jim Corbett, the famous big-game hunter.

Rao Naidu told us that three days before we arrived at our jungle camp a leopard had stealthily entered a village compound and killed and carried away a girl who was sleeping between two other girls—without awakening the two. Rao Naidu thought it was the same cat that stalked us in the tree. Seldom is there more than one man-eater in a territory.

I once had the opportunity to observe that the leopard is the cleverest of predators. Armed with binoculars, I waited several hours a day near a grassy clearing in the Indian jungle to see a sight Rao Naidu had told me about. Often chital, or spotted deer, came here to graze. Then one day I saw something rolling on the ground, playing with its tail like a house kitten. Chital are creatures full of curiosity and, as I watched, three came out to investigate. When one of the deer was within striking distance, the "kitten," a full-grown leopard, was off the ground and on the chital's back so fast that I could scarcely follow the motion.

Like human fingerprints, no two leopard skins are identical in their markings, or rosettes. Coloration varies from the normal buff or straw color with black rosettes, to a heavily coated gray in Persia and a rusty brown in Java. African leopards differ from Asian in having slightly smaller spots placed more closely.

The Indian jungle animals are the largest, with tawny coats and fewer rosettes. An average male measures about six feet, eight inches in length, weighs 110 pounds. But many large cats measure over eight feet, weigh as much as 180 pounds. Since the tail often stretches another three feet, the cat appears enormous. Size, however, has little to do with a leopard's ability. This amazing animal has a variety of hunting tricks. In Kenya, a leopard was once observed stalking a buffalo calf. To disguise his own body scent, the leopard rolled in buffalo dung so he could get close without frightening his prey.

I saw a pair of leopards using perfect teamwork as they hunted langurs in the trees. Almost as agile as these monkeys, the cats jumped from tree to tree, finally herded nearly all the monkeys to a large mahua tree, a giant creeper so isolated that the monkeys had to jump from tree to ground to reach it. As the last langurs hit the ground, a leopard leaped from the tree and easily killed one. The other cat calmly joined its mate in one of their favorite meals while the terrified monkeys sat in the tree, howling.

Nature has equipped the leopard superbly to be the perfect killing machine and the faultless hunter. It has "radar" chin whiskers and bristle tufts on its forearms. These tactile organs instantly flash impressions to the brain. The upright ears are extremely efficient, picking up the slightest airborne sound, and the sense of direction in respect to sound is remarkable. After I had waited eight hours over a bait one night, a leopard approaching cautiously heard me—200 yards away—slip a notebook from my pocket. His head went up, and he bounded off. Yet the person sitting beside me in the tree hadn't heard a sound.

Success as a hunter lies in stealth and the ability to surprise. The leopard walks on his toes in the graceful manner of a ballet dancer, and can leap 40 feet. His feet are so heavily cushioned with noise-muffling pads that his sinuous movement has been described as "the flowing past of a phantom." This gliding walk is effected by setting the hindfeet precisely in the tracks of the forefeet, a perfect method of moving his 150 pounds silently across even the driest leaves.

The leopard's principal weapons of attack are claws—five on forefeet, four on hindfeet—and these have an ingenious device which leopards share with most of the cat world and which prevents the claws from blunting by contact with the ground: in normal position the clawbearing joint lies folded back over the preceding joint, so that the claw is off the ground and completely covered by a sheath of skin. When the leopard extends his paw to strike, a tendon connected to the limb muscles immediately pulls the reverted joint, drawing it downward and forward. Claws emerge instantly.

Even the leopard's strikingly beautiful coat, glowing with "black roses," aids in the cat's profession of killing—and surviving. This spotted hide is such perfect camouflage that U.S. armed forces in World War II copied its pattern for jungle warfare. By repeating broken lights and shadows, the rosettes deceive the eye and obscure body contours.

Yet with all these marvelous physical endowments the leopard's most important single asset is his intelligence, which ranks high in the evolutionary tree. There is evidence that the leopard has the ability to reason. Naturalist Dunbar Brander noted that when a leopard was caught in a trap, the only sound was the closing clack of the trap itself. The cat would silently and intelligently work to free himself, seeming to realize that noise would attract man, his enemy.

A leopard takes only one mate, and the pair show strong affection for each other. A hunter once put poisoned bait out for a female that had been killing a settler's stock. Next morning he found the leopardess dead, her mate beside her, his head across her body. The leopard refused to leave his mate; he stayed there until he was shot.

The young—usually from two to four cubs—come into the world blind, after a gestation period of three months. Home is usually a cave, a hidden place under a rock ledge, or a hollow tree. From the time they are weaned at four months, until their death 16 to 23 years later, leopards devote their lives to hunting. The leopardess starts training her offspring in the art as soon as they can waddle. She teaches them to stalk her moving tail. As they attempt to attack the tip of the tail, she quickly flips it out of their way, keeping them at it until they can finally catch it.

When the young are about the size of a fox terrier, the mother takes them stalking in forests or rocky areas. An Indian has watched a female with three cubs carefully kill a goral, or wild goat, exaggerating all her movements—the crouching stalk, the leap, the kill—while the youngsters watched, much as students observe a teacher's lesson on the blackboard.

At the sign of danger leopards freeze to the ground instantly, never run and expose themselves. An English tea planter observed an Indian leopardess teaching this important lesson. When her cub broke and ran at an unexpected noise, the mother picked the cub up by the scruff of the neck, brought it back to the place where it had started to run, then placed her paw on it, pushing it to the ground. When she removed the paw, the cub lay still for a long time, lesson apparently learned.

The dazzling beauty of the leopard has threatened its future. In 1968 and 1969 alone, 17,000 leopard skins were imported into the United States. In 1972, in response to this heavy exploitation, the Department of the Interior placed the leopard on its list of endangered species, banning importation of leopards and leopard skins.

Since then the leopard's status has stabilized in Africa, though conservationists stress that he is not yet out of danger. Let us hope that the world's most beautiful four-footed animal continues to survive in spite of his beauty.

The Savage Predator of the Sea

by William J. Cromie

STANDING near the edge of the antarctic ice, Herbert Ponting, official photographer of the British Terra Nova Expedition, was focusing his camera on a group of killer whales out in the bay. Suddenly the three-foot-thick ice heaved up under his feet and cracked. There was a loud blowing noise, and Ponting was enveloped in a blast of hot, acrid air that smelled strongly of fish. Eight killer whales had come up under him, broken the ice with their backs and isolated him on a small floe. Now the floe began rocking furiously, and the whales shoved their huge black-and-white heads out of the water. One ugly toothfilled snout was within 12 feet.

The photographer leaped to a nearby floe, then to another and another. The killers followed him, literally snapping at his heels like a pack of hungry wolves. By the time Ponting gained the last floe it had drifted too far from the solid ice for him to make the jump. Then, by an extraordinary stroke of luck, currents pushed the floe back so that the gap was narrowed.

Still clutching his camera, Ponting made a life-or-death leap. His boots hit solid ice and he took off running. He glanced back just once. He saw, in his own words, "a huge, tawny head pushing out of the water and resting on the ice, looking around with its little pig-eyes to see what had become of me."

With his intelligence, speed, size and power, Orcinus orca is one of the most terrible predators on earth. Unchecked and unchallenged by any creature, including man, he roams every ocean and eats anything he can catch—fish, seals, penguins, walruses, porpoises. Porpoises can swim 25 miles an hour, but killers have been clocked at 34, making them by far the fastest swimmers in the sea. They are primarily fish eaters, devouring barrels of them at a "sitting," but they also enjoy warmblooded animals. The stomach of one 21-foot killer was found to contain the remains of 13 porpoises and 14 seals.

In 1957 I went ashore in Antarctica as a member of an International Geophysical Year scientific group. I had seen killers on a previous trip to the arctic, had watched them swim under floes on which seals were sunning themselves, tip the floes with their mighty backs and dump the unsuspecting creatures into mouths full of razor-sharp teeth. I had seen baby walruses, taking refuge on the backs of their mothers, get butted off and tumbled to their doom.

Years later, on a January morning, I had another example of killer voracity—plus their astonishing agility. A friend and I were studying a herd of Weddell seals on the ice. There was a large, solitary seal asleep near the edge, a fat fellow about ten feet long and six or seven feet around the middle. As we watched him, we saw a formation of saber-like fins slicing through the calm water about a half mile out.

I ran over and kicked the sleeping seal as hard as I could. He did not stir. Seaward, six or seven killers broke the surface and spouted in unison—a low, bushy spout. I planted my heavy ski boot on the seal's sensitive nose. With that he awoke, staring and blinking at me in astonishment. I shouted at him and, gesturing toward the rapidly nearing fins, I turned and ran.

I was satisfied that I had saved the beast's life, but when I looked back he was still in the same position, sleepily unmindful of the menacing fins. Seconds later a head shot vertically out of the water a few feet in front of the ice. Hurling a third of its body length onto the ice, the killer sank its three-inch teeth into the seal's hide and dragged the 1000-pound animal over the edge as if it were no more than a stuffed toy. A few convulsive jerks of his body, a frenzied beating of his flippers, and the seal disappeared. The other fins converged on the spot.

Killer whales are two to six times as large as dolphins and porpoises, reaching a maximum length of about 30 feet. Like porpoises, they are hairless, and streamlined for rapid movement through the water. They have rounded snouts with 10 to 14 pairs of heavy interlocking teeth in each jaw. A killer's body tapers back to two broad, horizontal fins, or flukes, which with the fore flippers and coördinated body movements provide silent propulsion and great maneuverability at high speeds.

Orcinus orca can easily be recognized by his distinctive two-tone coloring. The adult's belly and throat are livid white, as is a lens-shaped area just behind and above the eyes, and the color usually extends up onto his sides in a saddle shape. His back is midnight black. He is also easily distinguished by the recurved triangular fin located halfway along his back. In the old males this fin is often six feet high. The females are much daintier in every respect, reaching only half the size of the males, or about 15 feet.

How do killers find their food? They cannot see more than about 100 feet and they lack the acute sense of smell that sharks have, but like all whales they can hear very well. They hear sounds inaudible to humans and can pinpoint the location of a sound source.

Like porpoises, they probably locate their prey underwater by built-in sonar. Porpoises make sharp clicking noises producing sound waves that bounce off objects in their path, and they home in on their food by means of these returning echoes. Tapes made by the U.S. Navy reveal that killers also make clicking sounds. And they "talk" to one another in creaky-door sounds and high whistles.

Killers travel in packs or schools of from 3 to 40. When the pack is hunting or traveling, the females and young usually swim together in close company while the males travel alone or in smaller groups, some distance away. They are often seen to leap clear out of the water.

An example of a coöperative attack by killers is given by a whaler, Frank T. Bullen, in his book *The Cruise of the Cachalot*. While on a whaling voyage in the North Pacific, he spotted a bowhead—a slow, big-headed whale. The whale was close to the ship and obviously in trouble. Bullen at first could not see what was the matter. Then a killer leaped completely out of the water and landed with its full weight on the bowhead's back. Again and again the aggressor cleared the water and fell onto the larger whale as if trying to flail it into submission.

The big whale did not seem to be able to swim away or fight off the leaping killer, and when it lifted its enormous head out of the boiling foam, Bullen saw why. Two more "furies" were hanging onto the bow head's huge lips, as if trying to drag its mouth open.

The most active of the three kept up the tremendous pounding until the bowhead was exhausted. When its gigantic bulk lay supine on the surface, the leaping killer joined the others at its lips. After a short struggle they succeeded in dragging open its mouth, then devoured the defeated whale's tongue. "This had been their sole objective." Bullen wrote, "for as soon as they finished their barbarous feast they departed, leaving him helpless and dying."

Normally a female gives birth to only one calf at a time, after carrying it for about a year. Since the killers are mammals, they suckle their young (the mammary glands are enclosed in a sort of pocket so the calf can nurse without shipping sea water). The newborn calves are large and well formed, and as soon as a baby is born the mother pushes it to the surface for its first breath of air. From that time on, it is able to swim along with the group.

Killers are splendid parents; they produce only a few young and are extremely solicitous of them, giving them the best of care and attention. They have, like wolves, strong family and group ties: if a cow or calf is injured, the other females in the school will push the injured one to the surface or to safety.

These great predators are at the peak of the food pyramid. At the base of the pyramid are countless billions of microscopic plants floating on or near the surface of the sea. They are eaten by tiny animals like shrimps and copepods, which constitute one higher and narrower tier on the pyramid. It takes hundreds of pounds of these shrimp to keep ten pounds of mackerel, herring or halibut alive. Ten pounds of mackerel per day will support only one pound of large fish, shark, seal or porpoise, which in turn becomes food for Orcinus. Since killers have no natural enemies, it is well that they cannot reproduce at a high rate. If they did they would very soon eat themselves out of house and home.

Fortunately, killers pick the remote polar seas for their principal hunting grounds. But they also abound in the Gulf of Alaska and along the coast of British Columbia, and are occasionally seen from ships on Atlantic and Pacific crossings. They sometimes visit warmer coasts. They have appeared off

Florida at least five times since 1921 and more than 13 times off California. In 1954 they were sighted off Port Aransas, Texas, in 1956 off Massachusetts.

Since then killers have been captured and domesticated. There are an estimated 80 to 90 of these whales in Puget Sound, Washington, and between 20 to 50 along the California coast.

Since everything in the ocean flees these piebald whales, it has been asked what they are good for. Actually, the killer whale fills an important niche in controlling the balance of nature in the ocean. He is not a predator in the same sense that man is. As Dr. Carleton Ray, professor of Environmental Science at the University of Virginia, pointed out: "The most rapacious predator on earth is the two-legged one, man. But man seldom serves nature's purposes. As a fisherman he kills indiscriminately. As a hunter he 'takes off the top,' usually slaying the prime animal. In contrast the natural predator takes off the bottom. The wolf takes the weakling, the stray. The killer whale does the same in the sea, leaving the best and strongest to survive and breed."

Cycles of Life

Love Among the Insects

by Max Eastman

WE ALL KNOW that the cricket sings on the hearth. And some of us know that you can tell what the temperature is by measuring the rapidity of a tree cricket's bursts of song. Count the number of his chirps in 15 seconds, and add 39—this will give you the temperature in degrees Fahrenheit.

A less-known fact about all crickets is that their song changes when they are in love. They have a file and an edge, or scraper, on each cover, and their song is made by rubbing the wing covers against each other. In his everyday song the male (who is the only real singer) uses about 47 percent of the teeth on his file. But when he is in love, this percentage rises to about 89; and, moreover, the song becomes so irregular that you can't tell the temperature or anything else by it, except that he is courting.

While he is singing, the female lingers near and gives him an encouraging nudge from time to time. Finally, he stops scraping his wings together and lifts them both up. If she has been sufficiently moved by the song, she climbs on his back and proceeds to eat out of a cup-like gland, placed just behind the joints of his wings. This gland secretes a substance which she finds delicious, and may be compared, perhaps, to the gift of a box of chocolates. This process of singing and nudging, giving and receiving, continues for about half an hour before she is satisfied, and he is silent. Then the nuptial union takes place.

There is often a connection in nature between sex and

the pleasures of eating. These pleasures are simultaneous in the female of the praying mantis, who sometimes devours her sweetheart while he is mating with her. Starting at the head, she often gets him half eaten before their amour is over. He surrenders his life to love and posterity without a quiver of hesitation.

A more edifying mixture of love and nutrition is the practice pursued by some species of the Empid fly, who hunt up some tempting morsel, possibly a smaller fly, or perhaps the petal of a flower, wrap it in delicate silk strands spun from glands in their forelegs, and formally present it to their chosen females. Hardheaded biologists suspect that the industrious little fly adopts this manner of wooing in order to avoid the fate of the praying mantis, for he doesn't wait for the lady to exclaim over the delicacy of his gift but proceeds to mate with her in something of a hurry while she is busy unwrapping it.

The grayling butterfly puts on an act that seems to require solemn music. He alights in front of his inamorata, displays his beautiful wings and waves his antennae until she is *almost* in the mood of consent. Then, at the critical moment, he dips his head in a courtly gesture and enfolds her antennae in his wings. He carries a sort of sachet bag on his forewing, and during this ceremony a bit of the perfume is brushed off on her sensitive antennae. This delicate gift of perfume overcomes the last remnant of her coyness; the courtship is over; impregnation follows as a matter of course.

It was long thought that the colors of moths, their tiger hues and the great luminous eyes painted on their "deep-damask'd wings," were designed primarily for courtship. Experiments have shown, however, that it is largely the moths' vivid sense of smell which brings them together in the mating season. In species where the female has a scent gland, a female visible under a bell glass is of small interest to the males in the vicinity, but a female in a less than airtight container will, if she is in a lovelorn condition, bring males fluttering to her through the dark from almost incredible distances. The males of the emperor moth are thought to be able to find females of their species from distances up to three miles. Forty or 50 males will often assemble, as though out of nowhere, around a latticed box containing a lovelorn female.

The female's scent gland is specially designed for attracting suitors. She "calls" by raising the tip of her abdomen and vibrating her wings so rapidly as to drive the air over it and disperse the scent in all directions. Her instincts are so precise that she never calls except when weather conditions are suitable for a wide dispersal of the scent. About her lovers she shows less discrimination than about the weather; it is a case of "first come first served." This indifference to the suitor's appearance has been a surprise to those biologists who had assumed, along with Darwin, that the gay colors of many male insects were developed through the ages of evolution by billions of discriminating choices on the part of the female.

Sight *is* involved in one of the most human-seeming of all modes of courtship among insects—the communal song and dance. The dance of the midges and mayflies inspired three lines of one of the most beautiful poems in our literature, Keats' "To Autumn":

> Then in a wailful choir the small gnats mourn
> Among the river sallows, borne aloft
> Or sinking as the light wind lives or dies.

The scientists cannot make you see and hear this happen, as Keats does, but they have a more romantic explanation of it. "In due season, and at certain times of the day," says Maurice Burton in his *Animal Courtship*, "mayflies [and midges] swarm over or near rivers. Their dancing consists of a quick fluttering ascent followed by a more leisurely descent, repeated again and again. The dancers are almost entirely males, and they are rejoined every now and then by one or a few females. Each female becomes paired with a male, and the couples fly away."

So it is not the light wind, after all, but love that puts on this rhythmical pageant. Some biologists, of course, will shudder at the use of the word "love" in discussing the behavior of the simpler forms of life. But in studying the courtship of insects you will find examples of every mode of amorous behavior known to man: bowing, curtsying, kissing, snuggling, fondling, embracing, giving of presents, seducing with perfume, serenading, dancing—even rubbing of noses and brazen exhibitions of sex appeal.

Just why these things happen remains a mystery. It remains a mystery why the slender demoiselle dragonflies link themselves together and fly around tandem for hours before mating, and why they continue in this position long afterward, the male bringing the female along behind him as though on a flying bicycle-built-for-two, until she has laid her eggs on the leaf or stem of some plant growing in the water.

We'll probably never have any scientific knowledge about the conscious feelings which may accompany these activities, but no scientist can stop us from enjoying the poetry in them!

The Egg of the Emperor

by Franklin Russell

THE GIANT EMPEROR PENGUIN stood on an ice floe, facing the red midnight sun as it dipped into the Antarctic horizon. The January sun dropped, touched the ice with yellow light. Within 30 minutes, it had risen again, now brilliant white. The emperor balanced his 3½-foot-high body on powerfully clawed feet and dived.

Underwater, he was transformed, plunging fish-like into the gloomy depths. Faster than most fish, he would stay underwater, hunting, for 20 minutes. A man would die in a matter of seconds in this frigid water—but the penguin was insulated by a layer of air trapped under his tight, oily plumage. In total darkness at 700 feet, the big bird sensed the vibrations of other creatures moving in the blackness. Suddenly he darted into a school of squid, his pointed beak snapping up victims. Then he headed for the surface.

The water shimmered as he drove himself three feet into the air and flopped, belly down, on the ice. Hundreds of other emperors left the water with him. They stood upright—a congregation of headwaiters in white, boiled shirts and black tail coats. The big emperor, at 100 pounds, was the largest bird among them.

Here was one of the more extraordinary creatures of earth, a flightless bird of the trackless Antarctic waters who could span thousands of miles of the open sea in his hunting, a creature for whom the worst cold, the strongest winds, held no fears. His species had developed extraordinary capacities to combat the coming winter. They could draw on their excess fat and sustain themselves for weeks, even months, without eating. Huddling together for mutual warmth, utilizing their specially developed dense feathers, they could survive hurricane-force winds that few other creatures could endure.

The big emperor dived again. He heard the whistling cries, grunts and gasps of whales and seals fishing the same waters. His life was interlocked with countless other lives in this hostile world of ice and cold. Diatoms, tiny microscopic plants of the sea, were preyed upon by krill, quarter-inch-long, shrimp-like creatures which, in turn, became food for millions of predators—whales, seals, seabirds, squid. The summer months of January and February were the best hunting time of the year and the emperor continued to feed voraciously on squid and small fish, growing ever more fat.

At the end of February, as fall approached and increasingly powerful storms swept sea and ice, the big emperor penguin stopped feeding and began walking south, with thousands of his comrades falling in behind him. The migration to the ancient breeding area had begun. Each year, instinct drove them back to the same low hollow of ice near the continental shore.

He had made this journey six times in his eight years of life. One year the rookery lay within a mile of open water. Another year, he had walked over 25 miles of ice to reach it. This year, the ice had broken up in early February, then refrozen in tumbled, up-thrust masses which formed a series of barriers. He stopped at a big chunk of ice, and the birds behind him stumbled into one another, squabbling, jostling, and crying out in rage until all were halted.

After half a day's delay, the big emperor finally scrambled over the last jagged barrier and sped away on his belly across clear flat ice, skidding himself along with kicks of his powerful feet. Within an hour, he had reached the rookery. There, he called repeatedly, letting out blasting trumpet cries to signal his mate of last year. He would recognize her with the help of her song. Each day, many females sang in front of him. Some fought among themselves for his attention, but he ignored them. He waited and walked slowly among a growing chorus of cackling, singing, courting penguins. The temperature dropped. Soon, the sun would barely rise above the northern horizon—there would be 7 hours of pallid daylight, 17 hours of night. The sea had frozen steadily and now open water was more than 40 miles away to the north.

One evening in a savage gale he came upon a lone female standing in the lee of a block of ice. He sang, then so did she. The big emperor bowed, expanded his neck and sang again. He and his old mate stood close, their breasts pressing together. A grumbling roar from a splitting iceberg came to them in the wind.

That night the temperature went down to 40 degrees below zero, and the penguins formed themselves into long, oval-shaped masses. The big emperor and his mate were packed in among thousands of other birds. The wind raged all night, but they were warm together.

The courtship and mating of the penguins continued during April and early May, through the worst of the early-winter storms. Then silence enveloped the colony. The days shortened further. By the middle of May, the flaming tip of the sun appeared above the horizon for only a few minutes, the nights lengthened to 23 hours. One day, shortly before dawn, the female laid her egg. The big emperor joined her in a joyful duet. Around them, other pairs were singing in celebration of newly laid eggs, their voices warbling and whistling in the dawn wind.

The triumph of the egg, however, marked a temporary end of the betrothal of the big emperor and his mate. Soon after laying, she bowed to him and revealed the egg by folding back the loose skin of her incubating pouch. The emperor sang and bowed, touching the egg with his beak. She stepped backward. The egg lay exposed on the ice.

The emperor shuffled forward and drew the egg back with his beak so it lay on top of his flat, webbed feet. He doubled his powerful claws under his feet so that the egg was lifted from the ice. Then he closed his own incubating pouch. The female sang, bowed and turned away. She joined other females headed north for open water.

During the next month, the big emperor, guarding his egg, suffered the worst of the Antarctic winter. Some of the weaker male penguins lost the will to live—when the wind blew them down, they were rolled away across the ice. Other males abandoned their eggs in the almost constant darkness and headed north for the ocean; their eggs were often commandeered by bachelor males.

Then one day a spark of light touched the northern horizon briefly, as the tip of the sun showed above the ice. The mood of the rookery became electric. The first eggs were hatching. Chicks screamed in hunger, but without avail—the food-laden females were still struggling toward the rookery across more than 70 miles of ice.

In the middle of July, the big emperor felt his own egg stirring. He bent down and opened his incubating pouch to reveal the cracked egg, now jiggling violently. He closed the pouch and the egg rubbed against the bare skin inside. At dawn the next day the egg broke. The tiny creature cried out and sprang from under the emperor's belly. The emperor bent down and fed the chick a small bit of milky secretion—the last of his reserves from the hunting months before. The chick's survival depended on warmth, the tiny amount of food from its father, and a remnant of yolk in its own stomach. The emperor preened the chick's feathers and pushed it into his brood pouch. Now he must hang on, hungry himself, until his mate brought him relief.

The females began appearing at the end of a blizzard a week later. Fat and sleek, they walked forward as an uproarious cackling spread throughout the rookery. Penguins kicked themselves in tobogganing slides through the snow. The big emperor, who had been incubating nearly 65 days and had lost more than 40 pounds, finally heard a familiar song. He sang back, and his mate responded.

But he could not easily give up the chick, even to her. On the second day, she attacked him with powerful blows of her beak. The chick screamed, fell out of the incubating pouch and sprawled on the ice. Both birds tried to recover it. A bachelor male then attempted to steal the chick. When the confusion was over, the female had the chick in her pouch. She fed him with some half-digested squid. The emperor hesitated for 24 hours, then left for the sea.

While the big emperor feasted in the spring awakening of the sea, the female sparingly doled out to the chick the food she had brought back inside her body. In late August, the big emperor, fat and sleek again, returned. The worst storms had passed and the chick would now grow quickly, tended by both parents. By the end of October, when the sea ice had retreated to within a mile of the rookery, he was ready to begin hunting for himself. One morning, his mother left for the sea. The big emperor stayed on and fed the chick irregularly. One day, the chick, too, was gone. He would learn instinctively to fend for himself.

The rookery, now a long, oval-shaped yellowish stain of pock-marked ice, started to break up in November. Ice floes crackled, groaned, and split in explosive gouts of water. The big emperor stood on a floe with a group of comrades. He raised his flippers, swelled his neck and uttered his great bugling cry, as though in anticipation of the brief, rich summer of hunting in the open sea. Then, as the gloom grew, he disappeared into the bountiful Antarctic Ocean.

Mothers of the Wild

by Alan Devoe

HIDDEN in a hedgerow, in the fragrant summer dusk, I had twice seen a rabbit come hopping cautiously to the same spot among the tall grass stems. On her first trip she had remained there, nearly invisible, for an hour. The second visit was shorter, but long enough to make me positive about the guess I had made. There must be a nest of baby rabbits there.

But how could there be? After seeing the rabbit's first stealthy visit, I had crossed and recrossed that area of the field, staring at every foot of the ground. I had found nothing.

Now, marking the point with my eyes and never losing sight of it, I again began slowly combing the tall grass. Suddenly, in the dim light, I saw a tiny stir of motion, as if a patch of earth beside a tussock had moved. I bent down. What had seemed to be only a bit of grass-grown earth was actually a tiny, soft, felted blanket. Gently I lifted the little coverlet. Tucked under it were four rabbit babies.

I had learned mother rabbit's secret. The blanket was a quilting made of her own fur and matted wisps of grass. Every time she left her youngsters in the nest after a feeding, she pulled this warm, soft covering over them, leaving them perfectly hidden and secure against the evening chill.

This practice is only one of many wonderful devotions and ingenuities by which mothers of the wild bring up their little ones. Baby animals are born in all sorts of situations: caves, burrows, hollow trees, nests. Whatever the circumstances, the animal mother has the mother-wit to give them the special care they require, and a mother-love that lights the world of woods and fields with one of its loveliest radiances.

Nature's simplest nurseries are "built-in" ones: the body pouches of animals called marsupials. Kangaroos belong to this company. Marsupial babies are born incredibly tiny. A big kangaroo stands man-high and may weigh 200 pounds; but mother 'roo's little one at birth is only an inch long.

Tiny and undeveloped as they are at birth, baby kangaroos instinctively head for the nursery pouch. The mother watches intently, ready to give a fondly helping nudge. With her brood safely cradled she uses special muscles to pull the pouch securely closed.

As baby kangaroos grow up, their mothers use many protective ingenuities to look after them. When "Joey" (as Australians call a kangaroo youngster) is old enough to leave the furry nursery periodically and hop along beside Mother, any sudden appearance of an enemy sends him diving back head-first into the pouch. He rights himself, peeps out, and Mother instantly takes off on a jouncing race to safety. If the hunter is gaining, her one thought is for little Joey. Dodging for a second into underbrush or behind a boulder, she flips him furtively out. Then she leads away the enemy, mile after bounding mile. Only when she is sure she has shaken off pursuit does she come back circuitously and rescue her charge from his hiding place.

Animal mothers that do not have "built-in" nurseries make many kinds of nests and dens to give their babies security. A mother bat arranges her childbirth by hanging upside down by all four feet and spreading her wings and body to make a receiving cradle. While baby is still small and helpless, she carries him everywhere with her on her flights through the darkness. He holds tight to the fur of her breast with his milk teeth.

Mother gorilla builds a tree-cradle of leafy boughs which father gorilla can keep constantly under watch from a shelter he constructs at the base of a nearby tree.

Mother polar bear tunnels out a nursery in the snow. At the end of the tunnel she scoops and shapes a comfortable cub-room, as secure against the arctic blasts as the inside of an igloo.

Mother coyote takes over the abandoned burrow of a

badger, woodchuck or some other digging animal, and renovates it specially for her babies' needs. She cleans it out and enlarges it, and equips it with an air-hole that provides cross-ventilation.

In fashioning underground nurseries, even such small mothers of the wild as meadow mice and gophers are scrupulous about constructing special "sanitary rooms." Animal children are trained early to obey the law of cleanliness. I have dug up many nurseries in which various four-footed little ones have started their adventure of life: snug little rooms lined with leaves, made soft with fur. To find a messy one has been a rare exception.

One of the most delightful nurseries is the work of the common white-footed mouse. Mother mouse gathers fine grasses, rootlets, shreds of soft leaves, strips of pliable cedar bark. Working and reworking the material, she weaves an almost perfect sphere. At one side she leaves an opening just large enough for her to squeeze through. Darting in and out, she performs innumerable turn arounds, hollowing a cozy chamber in the center of the ball. She lines it with the softest materials she can find, bits of moss, wisps of plant down. The finished nest is at last given a final extraordinary detail—a door-stopper. In bitter weather, or when she is away from her babies, this tight little plug of grass is inserted in the doorway, closing it against any intrusion of foes.

A heroic chore of many animal mothers is the task of moving the family. Squirrel mothers often decide they must leave a frail old hollow tree when they sense a bad storm coming. One by one the youngsters are picked up, mother squirrel slinging them upside down under her chin. With her teeth she grips them by their stomach-fur, and the difficult trek is made to a new and safer location.

When a mother bear must transport her cub she seizes the young one's entire head in her mouth. It looks alarmingly dangerous, but somehow she is so gentle that she does not harm the baby.

Animal mothers often impart to their babies lores that we may imagine to be inborn. Baby seals, for example, have to be taught to swim. Pleading, persuading, enticing, mother seal generally ends by pushing her reluctant young one adrift. Mother otter, too, must induce her offspring to learn the art of their "native" element. She often resorts to trickery. With a youngster on her back, she swims out into the stream and then suddenly submerges.

Animal mothers teach chiefly by drawing their youngsters into creative play. Mother lioness twitches the tip of her tail, inducing her children to pounce on it. Mother raccoon flips frogs and crayfish to her young ones. On evening excursions by the brook she lets them make a game of what will later be serious business.

Perhaps the most moving of all such devotions is the superb courage of mother animals in giving protection when emergencies arise. I have seen a mother woodchuck, when a farm dog was pawing furiously at her family burrow, throw up earthworks as fast as the big, powerful dog could dig. Down would go one barricade. Within seconds she would fling up another. Then another and another, yielding the tunnel only inch by hard-fought inch. I thought her heart would burst, but it was the dog that grew exhausted first, and went off defeated.

I have seen a tiny chipmunk mother, defending her young, stand firm against a weasel, rearing on her hind legs, boxing, lunging, snapping, until that most implacable killer of the fields and woods had had enough. I have seen a white-footed mouse mother smaller than my thumb, whose nursery in an old bird house I had inadvertently disturbed, make six laborious trips, within two feet of me, carrying her babies one by one to safety. She was fairly shivering with fear; but there are things even in a mouse's world that are greater than fear.

We talk of valor that is like that of a tigress with her young, or a she-bear with her cubs. Actually that same blaze of heroic devotion burns in every mother of the wild, even the least.

The Cradle Shall Rock

by Jean George

IT IS spring. From seashore to mountain, on the northern half of the globe, the birds are launching a building boom more unbelievable than man's raising steel girders into the sky.

The previous spring I had witnessed the astonishing formation of a Baltimore oriole's nest—that spectacular gray basket that rocks in space from the tips of branches. No tool but a beak; no material that the wind could not carry away; and yet when done it was stronger than a thunderstorm, more intricate than a child's cradle. And it hung in my tree all summer, a testimonial to nature's timeless intelligence.

As I watched my oriole building, she fluttered on wing to strip from my orange milkweed plant an almost invisible strand of silk. With this she flew to my elm limb where she hung the strand in scallops from the springy tip and, weaving in flight, wrapped it with spindle-neatness around the twig. Then she flew down for another thread, and another. After her day's work I could see a misty rope draped in three loops between the forks of the twig—the beginning of my oriole's solution to warming and rearing her eggs in a hostile world.

The oriole sewed for 12 days on her creation. As the nest took shape the very sight of it stimulated the reproductive activity within her body, and this in turn drove her frantically on to complete it. She worked from the top down, and as she neared the bottom she wove only from the inside, turning, twisting, fluttering in that basket until it fairly Charlestoned with the thrashing of her body. When her job was done, my milkweed plant was frayed like an old rope, but the nest was an award-winner for beauty.

All nests built in the spring are here because, one day a hundred million years ago, an ancient reptile-like sea bird accidentally laid its eggs on sticks washed up by the tide rather than on the sand. Because the sticks kept the eggs from becoming either as cold or as hot as the bare sand, more hatched than ever before. The offspring, when it became their hour to lay eggs, remembered the sticks they saw the day they hatched, and sought the same conditions for their young. And so began a new trend in survival—the nest.

Some birds today, like certain of the sandpipers and killdeer, still lay their eggs on the ground. They have extremely precocious youngsters who break out of the egg, dry off in the sun and immediately run to safety. Other nestless birds, like the murres, lay top-shaped eggs that cannot roll off the cliffs and ledges they choose to put them on. Still others, like pheasant and quail, offset the high mortality rate in their eggs by laying greater quantities. But birds like the orioles, robins and swifts, that have evolved further, with better-developed feet, bones, wing feathers, nervous systems, have improved the nest as they themselves have improved.

A unique nest in the entire bird world is that of the Indochina swift, which men collect to make bird's-nest soup. This crystal jewel springs from the mouth of the female swift. As the nesting season nears, glands under her tongue begin to swell. She flies to a cave, stands against the wall and presses her beak on the rock. The viscous fluid fonts crystal-clear from her beak, and she weaves it back and forth, lacing it to the walls of the caves by the whipping of her body. The air hardens it, and it is complete—a delicate glasslike receptacle for her precious eggs.

Other swifts also spin with "glass" drawn from under their tongues, but they generally add to it sticks and twigs, as do the chimney swifts of our own country. In their case the viscous juice is just glue. The tree swift of the Orient also spins a glasslike nest—so delicate that she cannot sit upon it. It is laced to the side of a limb, and in it she lays but one egg. Two would break it, for it is but one inch wide and less than an eighth of an inch thick. Unable to touch her crystal creation, the female sits on the limb and puffs her feathers so that they lie like a warm scarf over the egg.

Few other birds have materials for a nest so readily available. In fact, some will travel half the globe to find their construction materials. The parula warbler prefers either the Spanish moss of our Southland or the mosslike lichen called "old man's beard" of the Canadian north. Even mud, a favorite material for many—the robins, swallows and phoebes—can put limits on a bird. These birds cannot live in parts of the world where the clay is not right.

The success of mud homes depends as much on the weather as the clay. A robin in our yard one spring was held back from nesting for four weeks by the rain. I watched her eye the earth, try to get a beakful, and then drop the flowing mess. Finally she found mud of the right consistency beside the back porch, but no sooner had she formed a base than a downpour washed it away. Some robins and almost all barn and cliff swallows have learned to let their mud cups set a day or two before lining them. I have seen a barn swallow, in damp summer weather, test the nest for three days before trusting her eggs to it.

The barn swallow not only limits himself by using clay but demands chicken feathers for warmth and décor. And they must be chicken feathers. A Michigan farm we often visited had a colony of barn swallows. One year the farmer sold his chickens, leaving the nearest poultry three miles away, an impossible range for a barn swallow. In June the swallows returned. They scooped up clay and carried it from the stream bank in their bills. Then they circled, wider and wider, looking.

Hours later we noticed their nests again. To our astonishment chicken feathers were neatly tucked into the clay. We followed their flight to a woods, and saw the swallows circling over the nest of a Cooper's hawk! On the nest was a dead young chicken purloined from some distant yard. At the risk of their lives, answering an instinctive drive so old it cannot be changed, the swallows were diving into a hawk's nest to pluck chicken feathers.

Straw and grass, world-wide materials, make an abundance of nests, from the house sparrow's mess to the vireo's tidy teacup. But some grass builders, too, demand special trimmings. The bowerbird of Australia, whose nest itself is drab, nonetheless requires a blooming forest floor for courting. Building a waterproof grass tent, he then surrounds it with moss, and lays on it colored flowers, bright fruit, vivid fungi. Brilliantly hued insects are brought until his castle glitters with natural gems. All of these are lovingly replaced as they fade.

Of all the nesters, those that have chosen holes are the most successful. To keep their numbers high, they need not raise two or three broods a season like the sparrows, robins or warblers, or lay great quantities of eggs like geese and pheasants. In their hidden tree holes they can just have one small secure brood a season.

The hornbill of Africa and Asia, a bird with a bill nearly as big as its body, is a spectacular hole nester. In spring the gaudy female finds a suitable hollow tree, and the male walls her in with mud until only her beak can reach out. Sealed in, she sheds most of her feathers and uses them to line the nest. Flightless and helpless, she remains imprisoned for weeks while the male feeds her fruits from the jungle.

The cowbird of North America and the cuckoo of Europe have discovered how to get out of the responsibilities of nest-making and young-raising. They simply lay their eggs in the nests of others. Such experts are they at finding nests that, when we were looking for sparrow and bunting nests for a scientific study, we had only to follow cowbirds.

Though the coming of man and civilization has been the doom of many birds, it has also benefited many. The barn owl originally was a "hollow-tree owl." But when European man arrived in the New World, this owl happily gave up the highly competitive tree for the mouse-filled barn and the church belfry, and increased his numbers. Starlings and house sparrows shifted from tree hollows to the abundant eaves, rainspouts and house trimmings of man. Perhaps the happiest adaptation of bird to man was achieved by a pigeon of Wall Street, which, according to naturalist Edwin Way Teale, used paper clips and rubber bands to make her nest.

With the coming and going of the horse in our culture, the birds have adapted and readapted. The chipping sparrow, once desperate for horsehair with which to line its nest, has been forced back to its original material, fine rootlets. Other birds that once demanded horsehair have shifted to facial tissue.

In India, unchanged by man or time, lives the most ingenious bird of all—the baya bird. This nester weaves two flask-shaped baskets, not unlike orioles' nests except that the entrance is below. The bigger basket has two rooms: a nursery and a family room. But the other flask—that is a sanctuary for the male alone; and this does not conclude the baya bird's genius. Around the walls of the nest are daubs of clay, in which, the Indians insist, the baya bird fastens lightning bugs to illuminate its home!

The creation of a bird's nest requires so much time and energy that it was with a sense of waste we watched our oriole nest, at summer's end, swing emptily in the autumn rain and wind. One cold twilight I saw that it was shifting crazily and I opened my window and peered into it. Two bright eyes emerged from a mound of string and cotton as a deer mouse peeked out.

By March the nest had fallen to the ground. Then one spring day I noticed a goldfinch struggling at its remains. She was salvaging the thistledown-like fibers, for a lining in her own new home in the tree.

Year of the Whale

by Victor B. Scheffer

IT IS early September when Little Calf first sees light—a blue-green, dancing light. Like all whales, he is born tail first, slipping easily from his mother's body somewhere beneath the surface of the Pacific Ocean, 200 miles west of Mexico. He trembles; the water is cold and he has lain for 16 months in a warm womb. He gasps for air, and his mother nudges him anxiously to the surface, where he breathes rapidly and desperately, puffing up a small cloud of vapor with each breath. Only minutes old, he is an amazing 14 feet in length, and weighs more than a ton.

As mother and calf roll in the wash, the five-foot umbilical cord snaps. Little Calf opens a pink mouth with toothless gums and seeks blindly for his mother's nipples. They are hidden in two deep slits, one on each side of her belly, far behind the navel. Finally locating one, he positions his mouth and presses hard. His mother extrudes the nipple and squirts a strong flow of rich milk, one-third pure fat, against the back of his throat.

Little Calf will continue to nurse for two years, gaining an average of seven pounds a day. By the end of his first month, he is already able to match the speed of his family—20 knots in panic, under 6 at ease.

Little Calf's family—never the same from one month to the next—is a loose social group of about 30 whales which is, in turn, part of a greater school of many families. The present group includes very young males and females, pregnant cows, nursing cows and an old bull who is usually several hundred yards to windward of the nursery. Bachelor males, fat and warm under a 12-inch blanket of blubber, are still feeding far to the north in the Bering Sea, while virgin females, responding to the September chill, have already turned slowly south.

As the nights grow longer and the morning fogs give way to clear autumn winds, Little Calf begins to recognize members of his family. There is a great-aunt whose lower jaw was horribly twisted in a fight with a killer whale. Another old cow has a strange, calloused ridge on her back; years before, she collided with an 800-pound swordfish whose long blade slipped cleanly into her back—and then snapped at the base. The entry wound closed in a few weeks and the sword remained entombed. Other members of the group are less plainly marked, but Little Calf can identify them also. Each has a special skin pigment, click-voice and scar pattern (all older whales have been repeatedly scratched and bitten around the face by the beaks of giant squid).

On a drizzly day in November, Little Calf's family loses one of its members. A small, ten-ton female, dozing peacefully at the surface, is caught in the vortex of a ship's screw. Mortally injured, she sends out a wild call of distress. Two of her companions move in, put their shoulders under her body and try to support her at the surface. Others come from all sides—showing the instinctive care-giving behavior of cetaceans that biologists once scoffed at but now accept as real.

In December, Little Calf's family, increased now by the arrival of the mature bulls, moves by easy stages southward to a feeding ground between Mexico's mainland and the Islas Revilla Gigedo, where cold and warm currents bring together a great variety of food. Little Calf's father—the great 60-foot, 60-ton guardian of the family's perimeter—has been here often. Now he dives for an hour and a quarter, as long as any sperm whale can hold its breath.

More aware of his world now, Little Calf is fascinated by his father's mysterious movements. The bull draws a dozen deep drafts of air, then dives on a long, slanting course to utter darkness, where the water is deathly cold and the pressure is 100 tons to the square foot.

Blood retreats from the bull's skin and tail, keeping alive

his massive brain. (The world's largest known brain, weighing over 19 pounds, was taken from a sperm whale.) The beat of his 400-pound heart drops to ten strokes per minute, pumping five gallons of blood at a stroke. The bull continues down. The pressure grows. His body goes in debt for oxygen. Now the spongy blubber cells relax and offer up their air, while his red-black muscles pour their own hidden stores of oxygen into his veins.

At 3000 feet, the bull levels off and begins to search for prey, the sonar device in his great dome operating at full peak. Within a quarter hour, he reads an attractive series of echoes. His gate-like lower jaw swings open and 60 massive teeth seize a giant, 300-pound squid. It writhes and tears at its captor, and its rasping beak succeeds in cutting away a chunk of black skin. The whale shakes his prey in irritation, crushing its central spark of life, then devours it. The bull's appetite is insatiable. He stows away a ton of food every 24 hours!

In early January, Little Calf and his family move aimlessly north and west, overtaking in a few days a large group of 200 or more sperm whales. Little Calf has been aware of their presence for some time, having heard the clicks and creaking of their whale-talk.* Late that month, Little Calf is witness to a frightful scene: a full-scale battle between bulls. A young, 15-year-old bull has cut loose from a bachelor group of timid males cruising a mile or so behind the larger herd. For a week he has cut in and out among the females. Now he swims toward Little Calf's father, who is outriding the harem 200 yards to windward. A vast, irritating tension powers his strokes.

The old bull recognizes the familiar rasping signals of challenge and reacts by rote, diving to 200 feet before he turns and shoots straight to the surface, his snout rising into the air like a black barrel, until it is 15 feet above the water. There he hangs, circling slowly, while his tail and flipper beat the water in strong sculling motions.

*Though little is known about underwater communication and range-finding by whales, it is clear that their hearing is extremely sensitive. Their vision, however, is on its way to obsolescence, being poor under water, myopic and astigmatic above. A whale's eyes stare from padded slits above the corner of his jaw—which means he can gaze only right or left, never straight ahead. He has no sense of smell.

The young whale charges, and the first impact of the huge bodies throws up a towering geyser of green water. The pair sink, break apart, race in opposite directions over the tortured surface of the sea. They turn, charge, collide, clapping jaws violently. Strangled, bellowing noises rise from the vortex of battle. The third exhausting round is the last. The jaw of the old bull locks firmly with that of the younger and the two sink below the surface.

Suddenly, the young male is done. One side of his jaw is broken and three ribs are fractured. They will heal in time, but now his body is strangely awkward. He sinks horizontally, then swims a mile before rising painfully to take a solitary position at the rear of the herd.

As spring arrives, a restless spirit begins to stir through the whale herd, now numbering several hundred. The white sunlight of longer days excites a gland no bigger than a crab apple in the whale's brain. The gland secretes a chemical messenger to the sex organs, rousing the ovaries of the females and swelling the testes of the bulls. The grand ritual of the breeding season is about to begin.

One stormy afternoon, Little Calf notices a bull turn aside to follow a cow. Hour after hour the pair swim side by side, touching flipper and flukes or simply rubbing sides. Presently, the male moves to a position above the female, gently stroking her back. He withdraws and chases her, then speeds up and rubs against her in a burst of motion. Now he races ahead, shooting through the water with his flippers held stiffly at right angles to his sides, throwing his body into odd shapes to attract the female.

The cow turns responsively upside down and the bull swims across her inflamed belly. They return to normal swimming positions and the bull locks his jaw in hers. They nuzzle and then slam their heads together. The love play continues for half an hour before the pair at last rise high from the sea, black snout against black sky, belly to belly, flippers touching. In the midst of the wind and the rain, they mate in seconds, then fall back heavily into the rolling waves.

Pacific sperm* whales usually reach sexual maturity at

*A misnomer. The sperm whale is one-third head, and its entire massive dome is brimful of a strange oily substance called spermaceti—which early whalers mistook for its seed, or sperm.

about age nine, full body-size at perhaps age 30 to 45, and extreme old age at 75. The most common cycle of reproduction seems to cover a four-year period. A female conceives in May of year I; gives birth in September of year II, after a gestation period of 16 months; nurses her calf for two years, or until September of year IV; rests for eight months and then is reimpregnated in May of year V.

By late May, the herd begins to dissolve. Whales of like age, sex and breeding disposition go off together. In June, Little Calf and his mother are feeding 400 miles at sea off San Francisco. They will go no farther north this year, although many of their companions are already far on their way to the Bering Sea.

Little Calf and his mother swim on day after day. They glide for hours in solitary dignity, then join in line with other whales like cavalry horses of old. They leap, descend, rise and spout together in joyous mood—easy, regular, majestic.

An hour after sunset, on a day in July, the mother of Little Calf arches her back and begins a deep descent. In less than a minute she finds herself at the edge of a cloud of tiny, luminescent squid. They are attracted to the pale cavern of her mouth; as they come within range, she bites them easily. When she rises at last to the surface, Little Calf is excited by the ghostly fire that gleams from her jaws, for he has seen it before and associates it with food. On her next dive he follows her uncertainly.

Hugging his mother's flank, Little Calf seizes a pale fragment and finds it good. He cleaves the water and his toothless jaws clamp firmly on two of the squid. Now his lungs are feeling the strain and he moves upward. Up and down he travels for a long while, feeding and breathing, making four round trips to his mother's one.

Quite suddenly, he is full. He floats at the surface under the stars, drifting now into sleep and then briefly out to move a flipper idly, bringing his nostril into the cool sea breeze. Toward daybreak his mother approaches and tests him with the quiet humming of her inner voice. Then she retreats. For the first time in his short life, the young whale will not awaken for his morning milk.

Late in August, as this first year of his life comes to an end, Little Calf and his mother are feeding on the deep Pacific, halfway between San Francisco and Oahu, 1000 miles from the nearest land. The form of Little Calf leaves a thin track on the flat immensity, a swirling punctuation. A cool wind moves. Late in the day, a red light gleams on the wave at his brow. Then the sun sinks below the sea and the yearling whale fades from sight.

Unraveling Nature's Mysteries

In Pursuit of the Loch Ness Monster

by James Stewart-Gordon

SHE IS PERHAPS the most enduring mystery in the world. Indeed, there have been well over 2000 reported sightings of Nessie, the Loch Ness monster since 1967, but there is remarkably little agreement on what she looks like. To some observers, she has appeared to resemble an upturned boat; a long-necked, elephant-hided sea serpent (with and without humps); even a creature allied to the Plain Belly Sneetch created by Dr. Seuss.

On film, Nessie remains equally confusing. In some shots, she looks like the rear end of a swan ducking for apples; a fuzzy version of Dino, the family pet of the Flintstones; or the half-submerged head of an African elephant with an extra-long trunk.

What's more, while it has, until recently, been assumed that there was only one Nessie in the Scottish Highlands' Loch (Gaelic for lake), Prof. Roy P. Mackal, a biochemist of the University of Chicago, is of a dramatically different opinion. After pondering the problem of the multiple sightings (sometimes almost simultaneously at different parts of the Loch), he has concluded that there is probably a whole herd of between 150 and 200 Nessies in the lake, which has enough migratory salmon in it to support them in Lucullan style. Although no one has yet been able to prove that theory, one keen monsterologist, considering the matter at the bar of the Clansman Motel overlooking Loch Ness, found it full of merit. "Think of it, mon," he said. "If there was only one monster in the Loch, she'd be bound to have a very deprived sex life, and nae Scottish lassie—monster or no—would put oop wi' that."

Despite the lack of conclusive evidence, however, Nessie is today being taken seriously by some in the scientific world, including the two dozen American, English, Scottish and Canadian scientists who were members of the 1976 New York *Times*/American Academy of Applied Science Expedition. As John Napier, British anthropologist, said about the Yeti, the mysterious man-beast of the Himalayas: "Yesterday's myths are today's scientific discoveries."

Of course, there still are those who continue to think of Nessie as a joke concocted by the newspapers. For a distinctive feature of her appearances has been the selectivity of her audience. Many of the gamekeepers, farmers and fishermen who have spent their lives along the Loch have never seen Nessie, and the explanation to some of those who have is that she is a deer, swimming from one end of the Loch to the other; leaping salmon; diving water birds; or unexplained optical phenomena caused by the wind on the water.

Nevertheless, even among the most case-hardened, native Nessie doubters, the question of her identity is never entirely closed. Jimmy McLennan, for example, has spent over 60 years on his farm in a glen overlooking the Loch, and he has never once glimpsed its most senior aquatic citizen. But when pressed, he admits, "Aye, there might be something in the Loch—but what it is, I canna say."

Nessie's stronghold, Loch Ness, is a 24-mile-long, mile-wide swath of sea trapped between hillsides of heather. Formed more than 25,000 years ago when glacial ice which covered northern Scotland melted and ran into the sea, the Loch is now 52 feet above sea level, fed by 8 rivers and 228 streams, and no longer salt but fresh. Deeper, at 970 feet, than the North Sea, it holds an immense quantity of water. Adding to the Loch's sense of mystery is the fact that the streams which run into it carry with them fragments of peat which remain suspended in the water, limiting visibility to four feet. In addition, the edge of land below the water surface juts out in a series of submarine cliffs. Bodies lost in the Loch get caught on these underwater ledges, and the natives say ominously, "The Loch never gives up its dead."

The fable, myth or reality of Nessie goes back more than

1400 years to A.D. 565, when St. Columba, a missionary from Ireland, reportedly spotted a dragon about to make a snack of a passing visitor standing on the shores of the River Ness, and chased the beast away with pious supplications. The years that followed have been filled with reports of its presence in the Loch. Sir Walter Scott had a word or two on the subject and, in 1880, a diver in the Loch reported that he spotted the Monster and got a very baleful look from its cold gray eye.

But it was not until 1933 that Nessie began to develop an international reputation. On April 10, some boys, hiking in the woods, reported to the Inverness *Courier* that they had spotted a strange, dragonlike creature the size of a horse, unlike anything they had ever seen. On May 2, the *Courier* carried another story entitled "Strange Spectacle on Loch Ness." It told of a prominent local businessman motoring along the Loch and suddenly being startled by a creature "with a body resembling that of a whale disporting itself in the water and sending up waves larger than those made by a steamer." From that time on, scarcely an issue of the *Courier* appeared without some mention of the Monster.

But the big news came on July 22, when a London couple named Spicer, motoring along the shores of the Loch, came practically face to face with the beast. The creature, reported Mr. Spicer in a letter to the *Courier,* was "between six and eight feet long, with a long neck that moved up and down like a scenic railway, a hump in its back, and was the nearest approach to a dragon or a prehistoric animal that I have ever seen in my life." The critter, Mr. Spicer reported, seemed to be carrying a small lamb in its jaws.

In London, the *Daily Mail,* sensing a story, sent a reporter to Loch Ness. He interviewed the sighters and wrote a story which made the front pages of papers throughout the world. Now Nessie—as she was christened by an inspired London editor—became a major tourist attraction. In April 1934, Robert Kenneth Wilson, a well-known London surgeon, pulled off a feat which had defied previous sighters by actually getting a photograph of the brute, with its neck above water and its humped back gleaming wetly. The photograph had a tumultuous effect. Throughout the summer virtually the entire 60-mile perimeter of the Loch was rimmed with visitors. Correspondents came from all over the world. Cottages metamorphosed into tea shops to feed the hungry hordes. Hotels were filled to the rafters and, for the first time, a road was built along the western shore. The Loch came alive with yachts, rowboats and any other craft that could carry paying passengers. Books offering explanations tumbled from the presses. The greatest question in Britain was not, "Will Adolf Hitler bring on World War II?" but "What is Nessie?"

During the war years, sightings of Nessie became fewer and, by the end of hostilities, she seemed to have been forgotten. Then, in the 1950s, just about the time that flying saucers became news, Nessie began bobbing up again. In 1957, she was sighted five times, and by the 1960s was back in full swing.

In 1965, Mrs. Constance Whyte, the wife of the superintendent of the Caledonian Canal, which carries the waters of the North Sea to Loch Ness and from there to the Atlantic Ocean, became interested in the subject. Where other investigators had depended on relatively few facts and large doses of imagination, Mrs. Whyte interviewed as many as possible of those who had sighted Nessie. She questioned them, compared their stories, then wrote a book, *More Than a Legend*, which had a profound effect on many skeptics.

One person particularly intrigued by Mrs. Whyte's book was Boston patent attorney Robert H. Rines. He had once visited the Loch, and now he returned to the scene and cross-examined some of Mrs. Whyte's witnesses. Rines was also interested in accounts that vessels had reported unexplained sonar contact with large moving bodies in the lake. A University of Birmingham expedition in 1968, for example, had set up a sonar station on the Loch and picked up echoes of "a large object, driving through the water at speeds up to seven knots and diving at a speed of 100 feet a minute."

The evidence led Rines to conceive of an entirely new approach to find Nessie. If sonar gear could be adapted to use the echo impulses bouncing off her body to trigger lights powerful enough to illuminate the peat-clogged waters of the Loch, he could get an underwater photograph and solve the mystery. Rines enlisted the aid of top scientists and set to work.

On the night of August 8, 1972, at 1 a.m., lightning struck. Rines and his crew, anchored offshore, saw on the sonar scanner what appeared to be two huge shapes, gliding underwater, out of range of the cameras and the strobe lights. Forty minutes passed. Then, suddenly, the waters of the Loch began to boil with salmon tumbling over each other in their terror to escape from an unseen pursuer. The lights flashed, the cameras clicked, and the members of the expedition, trembling with excitement, waited for the results.

Because of the peat-laden waters, not even the strobes were powerful enough for a perfect picture. The films snapped by Rines' cameras were sent to the California Institute of Technology and submitted to the same computer techniques as pictures sent to earth by space probes. Although fuzzy and indistinct, the results showed what appeared to be a diamond-shaped fin, a serpentine neck and a malevolent eye. All these could be taken for assorted anatomical portions of a 30-foot-long, water-dwelling brute with a family resemblance to the long-vanished plesiosaur, a marine dinosaur. If Rines and his crew were correct in believing the image was that of a plesiosaur or some close relative, they had photographed the greatest discovery of recorded time in the field of natural history—a gigantic living relic of the Earth's past.

However, some people remained skeptical. After carefully examining the photographs, a panel of senior British zoologists from the Natural History Museum in London publicly declared, "The pictures are too hazy to make identification possible."

If Rines and his crew were downhearted, they did not show it. They were back at Loch Ness in 1976 with improved picture-taking devices. This time the camera found what appeared to be skeletal remains—a carcass-like shape with a long neck—on the lake bed. Though they have so far failed to make contact with Nessie, Rines has said: "We're going to solve this thing. We're going to keep right at it. We're going to come back and back until we find out."

Meanwhile, it appears that the United States may have its own version of Nessie, residing in the depths of Lake Champlain, New York. There have been numerous sightings in recent years of a creature similar to Nessie. Most startling, a photo was taken in 1980 by Sandra Mansi and her husband which has recently been pronounced legitimate by the University of Arizona Optical Science Center—that is, the photo has not been tampered with or retouched. Whether or not the creature depicted is indeed a relative of the dinosaur has yet to be determined. Scientific investigation is currently underway, and there are plans to conduct sound wave experiments in Lake Champlain.

It may only be a matter of time until the towns surrounding Lake Champlain resemble Inverness, where the shops are crowded with replicas of Nessie in wood, cloth and pottery. Trash baskets bear the legend, "Look for Nessie but Don't Be Messie." Busloads of tourists swarm to the Loch, stopping at the Monsterburger stand by the side of the lake. And somewhere down in the waters, unwilling to show herself, is Nessie. Wherever she is, her mystery seems pretty safe for some time to come.

The Mysterious Snowy Owl

by Jean George

In December and January of 1979, when the winds blew down from the arctic, big white birds were seen on fields, beaches, highways, airstrips, steeples and stumps all across North America. Telephones jangled from the northern border states as far south as Texas, as excited people called newspapers and local museums. "There's a white owl walking around in my yard," they said. "He has strange eyes and looks lost. What is he?"

Photographs of the beautiful bird on dozens of rural front pages identified him as *Nyctea scandiaca*—the snowy owl—and perpetuated the story that he has come down from the north on his every-fourth-year foray for food. The true story is far more complex.

The astonishing migrations of the snowy owl are, in fact, part of an arctic picture puzzle so intricate that it has taken scientists years to put it together. I stumbled onto some of the pieces of this puzzle in the summer of 1969, when I visited the northernmost outpost of the United States—the Naval Arctic Research Laboratory in Barrow, Alaska. I had gone there to study the ecology of the tundra, that flat coastal plain that rims the Arctic Ocean near the top of the world.

Here, 1100 miles from the North Pole and on the edge of the turquoise-hued polar ice cap, is a major home of the world's snowy owls (they are also found around the pole on the tundras of Siberia, Norway, Labrador and Greenland).

My first encounter with a snowy on his native turf came

one morning as I walked the windy tundra near the lab. Suddenly, I found myself looking into two golden eyes peering at me from a mound. I yanked out my field glasses and focused them just in time to watch the comical little snowman walk to the top of the dome-like rise, blink several times, then turn his head around so far I thought it was going to twist off. About two feet in height, he was iceberg-white, flecked with clove brown, and snugly clad like an Eskimo from his round head to his feather-soled mukluk feet. He even had a ruff of dark feathers around his face, like the trim on a parka.

It was the sex life of the snowy owl that led the NARL scientists, who were studying the relationship of predators to their prey, to delve into the heart of the arctic ecological puzzle. In 1950, they began to realize that these owls practice a form of birth control. In June of that year, a male owl was observed to approach a female and court her. He bowed and lifted his wings and back feathers. The female was interested for a short time, then lowered her eyelids and turned away. The courtship stopped abruptly. She laid no eggs in her nest.

Snowy owls feed primarily on lemmings (a rodent about the size of a field mouse), which live on the tundra. The following year, when lemmings were more numerous, the same pair of snowy owls faced each other again. This time, however, the male held a dead lemming in his beak. Swinging it slowly like a pendulum, he danced with it, swaying from side to side while whistling like a tea kettle and croaking like a raven. The pair mated. The scientists surmised that, just as the singing of a male songbird may play a role in stimulating the journey of an egg down his mate's oviduct, so the sight of a lemming may trigger the hormones that begin new life in the female snowy owl.

The female laid one egg, then a second the next day, on a spot designated by the scientists as Hummock 2. With that, another owl safeguard against a dwindling food supply was revealed. Most other birds lay a full complement of eggs before they brood; consequently, all hatch on the same day, and each has a fair share of food brought to the nest. Owls, however, immediately sit on the first egg, and, when the first owlet on Hummock 2 broke out some 30 days later, the female stuffed him until he doubled his birth weight in one day. When the second egg hatched, the first owlet was so advanced and vigorous that he got most of the food—which, as it turned out, was getting scarce. Eventually, the second owlet died. Thus, instead of two weak owlets, the family raised one strong one. Moreover, they were numerically back in balance with the lemming supply.

This remarkable population plan was illustrated by a dramatic event in 1953, a year of peak lemming population. On June 26, scientists at NARL counted 83 dead lemmings banked in a half-circle on the north side of the nest on Hummock 2. The men also reported that the female had responded to this signal of abundance: there were eight owlets in the nest (the snowy owl record is 11). So, it seems that the more food the female snowy sees—and eats—the more eggs she lays.

The scientists weighed the owlets and found that, in accordance with the owl's instant incubation scheme, the first ones hatched were heavier than the last. But it was a good year. By the middle of July, all the owlets were healthy and testing their wings, while their father airlifted food to them around the clock. A growing owlet requires four or five lemmings a day. This means that the male must bring about three dozen rodents to the nest every 24 hours!

Six to seven weeks after birth, the eight owlets took to their wings. They joined hundreds of other snowy owls in hunting lemmings and ducks—and then headed south. Now the Eskimos shot scores of them, and froze them in their permafrost cellars. I asked Guy Okakok, an Eskimo, what they tasted like.

"Chicken," he replied. "But we don't get them often. About every four years, when they're abundant."

In September of that year, it was learned why the snowy owls go as far south as the southern United States. Lemmings had been multiplying at a prodigious rate. Therefore there was also a superabundance of owls—so many that they could not pass the winter in their regular hunting territories. Accordingly, many of them flew south searching for food.

Now another piece of the puzzle was ready to fall into place. It was discovered that during these peak years both the snowy owls and the lemmings suffer drastic reductions in their numbers. When lemming colonies become over-populated, the creatures run wildly, and masses of them die. (There is as yet no completely satisfactory explanation for this behavior.) The consequent drop in the lemming population drives the owls farther and farther south, where many of them are killed by collectors and sportsmen, or starve in the competition for food (an estimated 20 to 50 percent make it back to their summering grounds).

Miraculously, it usually works out that there are but one or two lemmings per acre when vastly reduced numbers of snowy owls come back to the arctic in May. The predator and its food supply are thus back in balance, ready to start the cycle over again.

During my Barrow visit, I asked Charles Edwardson, Jr., an Eskimo political leader, about the balance of nature in the arctic. Glancing at the elaborate lab equipment, he said, "You can't rush the arctic. We Eskimos are respectful of the tundra. We wait and watch. When the snowy owl behind the village hops and jumps, we'll know the lemmings are plentiful because he's catching them."

In June, if the females see dozens of lemmings in male beaks, it's a good bet that the owls from the north will fly down to California, Missouri and North Carolina. And as they are seen running and hopping on our "tundra," each one will tell part of the story I went to Alaska to find—the extraordinary relationship between bird and beast which is the ecology of the northland.

Where Did the Animals Go?

by James A. Michener

A MONSTROUS collection of dinosaurs once flourished in western North America. They must have formed a dazzling open-air zoo—gigantic beasts as tall as trees and bigger than any animals existing today. They became extinct about 65 million years ago.

Later a spectacular series of large mammals roamed this land, and these wonderful creatures also died out. They were huge animals, constructed in fascinating ways, and had they survived into the present, the United States would now have a collection of beasts that would make Africa envious.

There were elephant-like mastodons, mammoths with curved tusks, American camels, saber-toothed cats, giant beaver, huge bison, the rhinoceros-like titanothere, the dinohyus, or "terrible hog," with tusks so powerful he could root up trees, the horse-like moropus, ten feet tall, with claws, the huge uintathere, with six knobby projections dominating its head. There were more than 100 distinct species, and some were here as recently as 11,000 years ago.

What happened to these animals? Why did they vanish? This is one of the great mysteries of American natural history, and scientists are engaged in heated debate trying to sort out the explanations.

Before you blame man for this extinction, remember that, during the 50 million years before his appearance, hundreds of species developed, flourished for a while and then died out. It is likely that more than 90 percent of the animal types which have disappeared from the earth did so before the advent of man. Therefore, we should not be surprised that species continue to disappear. Some scientists argue today that the rhinoceros is an archaic animal whose course has been run and whose ultimate disappearance cannot be long delayed, whether man harries him or not.

Nevertheless, in the period coinciding with man's first appearance in North America, a fearful, speeded-up extinction occurred. Enormous herds of animals were wiped out; whole populations of birds were extinguished. And never was the carnage more concentrated than when men and women, probably from Asia, wandered across the land bridge that then joined Siberia and Alaska to sweep down upon a virgin continent.

To learn at firsthand what may have happened, I joined a field trip organized by America's foremost authority on animal extinctions: Paul S. Martin, a lanky, sharp-eyed professor of geoscience at the University of Arizona. Some time ago he started to explore a remarkable cave hidden on an almost inaccessible mountain face high above the waters of a western river. He now proposed to revisit this cave.*

To reach it we had to use a small airplane, a smaller launch, and rope ladders let down from a high cliff. Finally we clambered up a sheer wall and found ourselves at a rocky entrance 12 feet across and 7 feet high. "This is one of America's real treasures," Martin said, as we entered a spacious cave shaped like an H, 150 feet in length.

Reverently touching a five-foot-high wall of grayish, dried stuff through which trenches had been cut in search of fossil bones, he told me, "Sloth dung. Not fossilized, you understand, merely dried out. Look! You could pulverize this and use it for fertilizer right now." It smelled like dry cow chips.

"How old?" I asked.

"We can read the history of this cave like a book. The bottom dung was laid down over 40,000 years ago. Radiocarbon dating proves that. Sloths occupied the cave until 32,000 years ago. Then see this line? For some reason, probably climatic, the sloths left and pack rats moved in. The rats stayed

*Scientists consider the site so valuable and its contents so fragile that they request that it not be further identified.

13,000 years, as proved by this level. Then the sloths returned and lived here until their race died out, 11,000 years ago."

"What did the sloth look like?" I asked.

"Shaggy, awkward, moved about on his hind legs, used his front legs for pulling down branches of trees or grubbing. Not carnivorous. Ate much like a horse." At this point Martin picked up one of the precious "sloth apples" and demonstrated a remarkable fact: "By analyzing the seeds and twigs left in this dung we can say precisely what our sloth ate, and the exact dates at which his diet changed."

"Why did he disappear?"

We leaned against the trench walls as Martin explained the dramatic theory which has won him world-wide fame—and a lot of counter-argument. "I visualize," he said, "the arrival in North America about 11,500 years ago of a band of nomadic hunters from Asia. Let's say they reached Edmonton, Alberta, as a group of 100 individuals, reproduced normally and killed animals for their food, spreading out fan-like as they followed their prey."

Cranking these data into his computer program and making allowances for slow or fast reproduction and movement, Martin shows that his band of 100 would double every 30 years and move southward across an ever-widening, east-west arc at a rate of up to 20 miles a year. If only one person in four hunted actively, and if he killed only one large animal per week, the tribe would be able to kill off large numbers of their prey. Within ten years, large animals in any given area would become extinct. In 293 years the original human population would have increased to 288,000 people; the tribes would have reached southward into Mexico; and on their journey the hunters would have killed off the staggering total of 93 million large animals. Said Martin, "I believe that it was man, hunting and killing, who was the primary agent in exterminating the big animals."

C. Bertrand Schultz, paleontologist at the University of Nebraska and the foremost expert on the ancient animals of that state, does not accept the conclusions of the Martin computer: "In my opinion the sudden disappearance of our large mammals was due mainly to considerable changes in climate during the latter part of the Ice Age, 28,000 to 8,000 years ago. At times, in our region, temperatures plummeted from more than 100 degrees above zero to 70 degrees below. This affected pasture and foliage so drastically that whole herds of animals died from exposure and starvation. The worst of the great Ice Age droughts hit the region from time to time, changing the environment further. The invasion of bison from Asia, competing for grasslands, must also have threatened the mammoths, horses and camels. In this struggle for survival, only the bison was able to adjust to environmental changes."

Prof. James J. Hester, of the University of Colorado, proposed a theory that utilizes the views of both Martin and Schultz. He reasons that early man could not have eliminated so many large animals until natural forces—disease, predation, competition for available grass, and climatic upsets—had already weakened the species. At such a time, the addition of man the hunter could have accelerated the spectacular disappearances which we know did occur.

What we know for certain is that, even today, animals continue to disappear from the earth at an appalling rate. Since 1600 A.D., 36 species of mammals and 94 species of birds have vanished. This represents one percent of all mammal and bird species. Since 1900, the record has been one species per year and, in a world where an exploding human population fights for space, this rate will be accelerated.

Of course, some animals will die out from natural causes, whether man is present or not. On the other hand, we cannot afford to lose, willfully, even one more species. In ancient times any species that disappeared would probably be replaced by another just as interesting or even more so. But today, species are not being replaced. It is quite possible that in the future no conspicuous new species of large animals will generate.

Consequently, every animal that walks the earth, or swims, or flies is precious beyond description, something so rare and wonderful that it equals the stars or the ocean or the mind of man. Animals form an inalienable fragment of nature, and if we hasten the disappearance of even one species we diminish our world and our place in it.

Where to See Fossil Bones

Visitors have easy access to four sites at which they can study the early animals. The Dinosaur National Monument near Vernal, Utah, offers an exceptional display of dinosaur-fossil bones still imbedded in rock. Big Bone Lick State Park, Kentucky, not far from Cincinnati, is the site of the first excavation of ancient animals in this country. The Rancho La Brea Tar Pits, in the center of Los Angeles, are world-famous as a vast mausoleum encasing the skeletons of thousands of animals now vanished. And Agate Fossil Beds National Monument, in western Nebraska, contains skeletons of many such animals.

Four great museums display mounted skeletons of the mammoth, mastodon, sloth and other extinct mammals: in New York City, the American Museum of Natural History; in Washington, the Smithsonian Institution; in Lincoln, the University of Nebraska State Museum; and in Denver, the Museum of Natural History. In addition to the museums, the mammoth site of Hot Springs, South Dakota, also exhibits skeletons of extinct mammals.